101
WAYS TO
PROMOTE
YOURSELF

101

WAYS TO PROMOTE YOURSELF

Tricks of the Trade for Taking Charge of Your Own Success

RALEIGH PINSKEY

AVON BOOKS ◆ NEW YORK

AVON BOOKS, INC.
1350 Avenue of the Americas
New York, New York 10019

First Avon Books Trade Paperback Printing: December 1999
First Avon Books Mass Market Paperback Printing: July 1997

This book is dedicated with much love and gratitude
to my family, who taught me this basic yet
much underdeveloped principle of life:

"If you don't ask you don't get.
You don't always get for what you ask,
but if you don't ask,
you don't get."

ACKNOWLEDGMENTS

To my editor, Stephen S. Power, who had the brilliant foresight to see the need for this book, and edited through and into that brilliance.

To Wendy Keller, who adeptly agented me into and through this adventure.

To Jay Conrad Levinson, Terri Lonier, Tony Parinello, Paul and Sarah Edwards, Jay Abraham, Mark Victor Hansen, Jack Canfield, Dotty Walters, Dan Kennedy, Brad and Alan Antin, Ted Thomas, David Pennington, Gail Kingsbury, Mike Rounds, and all the meeting planners, agents, and speakers bureaus who believed in me and graciously requested my contribution to their platforms, thereby giving me my voice, and allowing the information to be heard.

To all my friends in the National Speakers Association.

To Dr. Lorraine Bonte, Deb Rentaria, and Denise Osso, who gently nurtured my body, mind, and spirit during this process.

To all those teachers who along the way, when this student was ready . . . unselfishly appeared.

CONTENTS

PART II: NAME RECOGNITION

CONTENTS

FOREWORD

P.T. Barnum is known as the "prince of promotions." Famous not only for his incredible creativity and imagination but how he applied them, he attracted people to his circus with such attractions as the sideshow and the midway. He used both as teasers to entice the public and focus their attention on the main attractions. Barnum's promotions were also infamous in those days. Tom Thumb, the bearded ladies, the two-headed animals, the tattooed lady, the giant, and many more lured you along the way into the Big Top.

But Barnum didn't just rely on the midway and the sideshow. He went one step further and took his message to the masses.

He held parades, showed off the attractions in the town square, put up posters, handed out fliers, got his name in the media.

Barnum is the father of a well-known marketing cry, "Without promotion something terrible happens— *nothing!*"

This book is all about stamping out that dreaded nothingness. Whether you want to improve your business, sell more of your product, bring your ideas to a wider audience, advance your career, or fulfill your needs. I believe these 101 ideas will help you achieve something wonderful.

INTRODUCTION

The room lights are dim. Just enough darkness to enhance the slides, just enough light to enhance the speaker and keep the audience alert and full of anticipation.

Projected on the slide screen is a picture of the upcoming speaker. She has a broad, inviting smile that implies competence and confidence, and provides the audience with a hint of what the next hour will bring.

A woman approaches the stage. She looks very much like the picture on the screen, right down to the red jacket and the pearls, but when she opens her mouth to speak, her words suggest something different.

"Ladies and gentlemen, it is my distinct pleasure to introduce our next speaker, Ms. Raleigh Pinskey, who is going to share with you myriad ways to promote yourself, ways that will allow you to take charge of your own success!

"Ms. Pinskey is the president of her own public relations and visibility marketing firm, and since 1979 she has guided the careers of entrepreneurs, service providers, and entertainers to successful heights, utilizing her unique spin on what it takes to get your name out there over and over again.

"She's here today to *show and tell* you how you too can take your place in the center of that limelight and make it shine for you. She's here to show you how to grab that brass ring that has your name on it, and how to take command of your birthright that reads success all over it.

"So let's put our hands together with a warm welcome for our guest speaker, who's going to show you how you can maximize your biz-ability through viz-ability . . . how to promote and prosper . . . Ms. Raleigh Pinskey."

The presenter exits the platform. As she approaches the halfway mark down the aisle, she turns, surveys the audience, and starts back to the front as if she forgot to tell them something.

The lady in red remounts the platform, and with a show business attitude exaggerates a strut to center stage, where she executes a large curtsy to the left, to the right, and to the center. By now a portion of the audience is clapping, chuckling, and whistling. More and more catch on.

As she rises from the center curtsy, she turns to the slide screen, then back to the audience, and begins with: "Hello, my name is Raleigh Pinskey, and why shouldn't you introduce yourself? Why shouldn't you tell the world who you are and what you're all about? After all, if you don't introduce yourself, if you don't tell them what you're all about, how are they going to know you exist?

"It's said that if you build a better mousetrap, the world will beat a path to your door. But ladies and gentlemen . . . they can't beat that path to your door if they don't know where to find your door! What you'll be left with is a garage filled with your better mousetrap, and a beautiful, path-free lawn for your neighbors to admire.

"In order to promote and prosper, I feel that you have to take responsibility for your own success, take charge of your destiny.

"I've taken my years as a publicist and visibility marketing expert and put those professional secrets down on paper so you too can have the success that I've had.

"What you'll learn are one hundred and one secrets that grow your business. One hundred and one ways for you to tell the world all about your business, talent, idea, or product so they can beat that path to your door. One hundred and one tools, strategies, and technologies to use in positioning yourself to your target market of existing and potential clients.

"You're going to learn the marketing secrets of how to make what you have to offer something that others will want to have. You're going to learn how to make what you have *sizzle*. You're going to learn interesting and provocative means to:

- Attract new customers, clients, or patients
- Keep the existing ones and recapture those who have gone elsewhere

- Generate leads
- Cultivate referrals
- Develop your image
- Promote name recognition
- Grow and expand your network and data base
- Increase your bottom line

"Every minute you're not engaging in visibility marketing you may be losing out to your competition, who may have already begun taking charge of their own success. Let's beat them to the punch . . . and to the customers who have your name written all over them."

Part I

BUSINESS BASICS

1

NAMING YOUR BUSINESS

Word-of-mouth marketing at its best

I've been told that naming your business is just as important as choosing a pension plan. Why is a name so important?

- It is your brand identity
- It announces who you are and what you stand for
- It acts as a directory of services
- It can cause your success or contribute to your failure
- It can lump you with the competition or raise you above them all

When is a name a good name?

- When it makes your business easy to market
- When it's easy to remember
- When it's simple to pronounce
- When it's simple to spell
- When it presents a clear understanding of what you do
- When it conveys your competitive edge, your niche
- When it stirs customer interest
- When it represents what you represent
- When it doesn't confuse you with a similar business
- When it sells itself with no explanation
- When it has a positive ring to it
- When it's optimistic
- When it doesn't limit you to your geographical location
- When it promotes the service if the owner is not a known name
- When it attracts the types of clients you want

3

How do you pick a winner?

Joan Delany, in her article "Naming Know-How, The Right Name Can Help Boost Your Company's Image and Bring in New Business. Here's How," in *Independent Business* magazine, offers these five sound suggestions:

1. Analyze your company
2. Evaluate your market
3. Start a list
4. Test your choices and make a final selection
5. Do your trademark homework

In *Getting Business to Come to You*, Paul and Sarah Edwards and Laura Clampitt Douglas suggest that you "generate a long list of words that describe what you want your business to reflect. Think of adjectives, time, place, uses, feelings, features, humorous aspects of what you do, images you have about the business, results you produce, and products you offer."

What are some examples of successful names?

Independent Business magazine and *Business 96* magazine (last year *Business 95*, next year *Business 97*) both hold business name contests.

These are the *Independent Business* winners for the first three contests (there were none in 1992 or 1993):

- 1991 #1: Juan in a Million (Mexican Restaurant)
  - #2: Twice Sold Tales (used book store)
  - #3: Loch Ness Lure Co. (fishing lure shop)
- 1994 #1: Curl Up and Dye (beauty salon)
  - #2: Johnny on the Spot (portable toilets)
  - #3: Brilliant Deductions (tax preparation services)
- 1995 #1: Rhythm & Brews (coffeehouse with music)
  - #2: Wreck-O-Mend (car collision repair)
  - #3: Engine Newity (car engine repair)

Business 95 held its first Great Names Contest in 1995. Here are the three winners:

- #1: Plain in the Glass (mobile windshield repairs)
  #2: Make Be-Leaves (artificial/silk plant shop)
  #3: Got It Maid (maid service)

NOTE: if you plan to do yellow pages advertising, pick a name that starts with an "A." Depending on your category, you might have to use several As.

RESOURCES

Trade Associations and Organizations
U.S. Patent and Trademark Office; Commissioner of Patents and Trademarks; Washington, D.C. 20231; (800) 786-9199. They have fax-on-demand (see the chapter, "Fax-on-Demand"). For a free booklet, *Basic Facts About Registering a Trademark*, select number forty-one.

Books
- *Naming for Power: Creating Successful Names for the Business World* by Naseem Javed; Linkbridge Publishing; (212) 876-5363; http://www.abcnamebank.com
- *How to Name a Business or Product* by Kate McGrath and Stephen Eias with attorney Sarah Shena; Nolo Press; (800) 992-6656

Software
- Decathlon Corporation; 41 Executive Park Dr.; Cincinnati, OH 45241; (800) 648-5646. Decathlon's software is called *NameMax*
- The Namestormers; 4347 W. Northwest Hwy., Ste. 1040; Dallas, TX 75220-3864. Namestormers' software is called *Namer, Headliner*, and *NamePro*

Contest
- *Business 96* magazine Great Names Contest Ballots; 125 Auburn Ct. #100; Thousand Oaks, CA 91362; fax (805)

496-5469. No contest membership required. Ballots available free from Wells Fargo banks or the above address.

Magazine
- *Independent Business* magazine is for members of the National Federation of Independent Business, a wonderful organization designed to assist small business in all their endeavors. Call (800) NFIB-NOW

2

YOUR MISSION OR VISION STATEMENT

This is a mission possible!

What is a mission statement?

A mission statement is a plan for companies and people to accomplish the goals they set. It shapes the company's identity, codifies a set of principles to act by, and supplies a foundation on which to build a future. It communicates the kind of business you are.

A mission statement can be based on a vision, goal, or ethics. It can be a slate of objectives, an environmental policy, an operating policy, or a basic business philosophy.

A mission statement creates a frame of reference, criteria, guidelines with which to govern.

Jeffrey Abrahams, in *The Mission Statement Book, 301 Corporate Mission Statements from America's Top Companies*, refers to a mission statement as "a part of the set of fundamental principles by which a business operates."

Patricia Jones and Larry Kahaner, in *Say It and Live It, 50*

Corporate Mission Statements That Hit the Mark, refer to a mission statement as "a map for the high road."

What are some familiar mission statements?

How about this one:

> "We the People of the United States, in Order to form a more perfect Union, establish Justice, insure domestic Tranquility, provide for the common defence, promote the general Welfare, and secure the blessings of Liberty to ourselves and our Posterity, do ordain and establish this Constitution for the United States of America.

Or this one:

> Neither snow, nor rain, nor heat, nor gloom of night stays these couriers from the swift completion of their appointed rounds.

Why do I need a mission statement?

Whether you're a big business or a mom-and-pop-store, whether you're global or on a street corner in a town with a population of 700, a mission statement:

- Presents a way to establish and understand goals
- Regulates the means and the time frame by which these goals will be accomplished
- Brings substance and meaning to why you are doing business

Why is this a good marketing tool?

Because it cements the relationship between you and whomever you're doing business with. They know exactly where you're coming from and where you're going. It grows your business from the inside out as well as on your spread sheet. Companies that have a mission statement have reported steady increases in business since they put that mission statement on paper.

It is also a good marketing tool for raising funds. I have some friends who were looking for money. They were turned down by banks and private investors because they didn't have a mission statement, but were considered once it was in place.

For those businesses going through great changes, such as acquiring, merging, or dissolving divisions, a mission statement can bring stability to the operation during times of growth and unrest.

What are some examples of business mission statements?

Kelly Paper Company (national)

The mission of Kelly Paper Company
is to operate the best chain of paper
stores in its marketplace by providing
its customers with an excellent
selection of quality products,
competitively priced with
excellent service.

I shop at Kelly Paper in Santa Monica, California, and Danny, the store manager, told me that he felt that the employees should know and feel the mission statement, so all of them—Danny, Irv, Mark, and Gary—sat down and created a mission statement that they could own.

Kelly Paper (Santa Monica)

Quality service and
teamwork in a clean
and friendly
atmosphere.

Hallmark

We Believe
That our *products and services* must enrich people's
lives and enhance their relationships.
That *creativity and quality*—in our concepts, products,

and services—are essential to our success.
That the *people* of Hallmark are our company's most valuable resource.
That distinguished *financial performance* is a must, not as an end in itself, but as a means to accomplish our broader mission.
That our *private ownership* must be preserved.

The values that guide us are:
Excellence in all we do.
Ethical and moral conduct at all times and in all our relationships
Innovation in all areas of our business as a means of attaining and sustaining leadership.
Corporate social responsibility to Kansas City and to each community in which we operate.

These beliefs and values guide our business strategies, our corporate behavior, and our relationships with suppliers, customers, communities, and each other.

Mrs. Gooch's

Mrs. Gooch's is committed to offering the highest quality natural foods, related products, service, and information which optimize and enrich the health and well-being of the individual as well as the planet.

Southwest Airlines

The Mission of Southwest Airlines
The mission of Southwest Airlines is dedication to the highest quality of Customer Service delivered with a sense of warmth, friendliness, individual pride, and Company Spirit.

To Our Employees
We are committed to provide our employees a stable work environment with equal opportunity for learning and personal growth. Creativity and innovation are

encouraged for improving the effectiveness of Southwest Airlines. Above all, employees will be provided the same concern, respect, and caring attitude within the organization that they are expected to share externally with every Southwest Customer.

Are mission statements always long?
No. For example:

General Electric

Boundaryless . . . Speed . . . Stretch

What's the difference between a mission statement and a vision statement?
Some consider them the same thing, but a mission statement is a reason for being. A vision statement is something you're aspiring to become. Simply vowing to be the best is too simplistic. A vision statement should raise people's minds and take them to a new place. The objective in a vision statement is to get into the heart, mind, and gut of where the company is going.

Odwalla, the juice company, has a vision poem.

> Odwalla
> A breath of fresh,
> Intoxicating rhythm,
> Living flavor.
> Soil to soul,
> People to planet,
> Nourishing the body whole.

And to insure that Odwalla practices what its vision poem preaches, the company hired a vice president of vision access.

This is the vision of Women Empowered,™ founded by visionary Nicole Rhodes:

Women Empowered inspires and engenders integrity, shared values, standards and ethics of excellence, innovation, and success in our personal and professional lives. We explore business-management techniques that contribute to and benefit our employees and our business's success.

We accomplish this by creating and maintaining an environment of mutual support and respect, with vulnerable sharing and sensitive feedback, in a confidential and trusting manner within a consistent format. We participate with a sense of joy and play.

We benefit by enhancing our own quality of life and well-being. We receive continuous learning, growth, and development, to achieve greater success, balance, and inspiration for ourselves and others.

How do people get to know my mission statement?
- Put it on your stationery
- Put it on your business cards
- Put it in your advertising
- Put it on your packaging
- Put it in your newsletter

NOTE: A mission statement is not only for a business; it can be for an individual as well.

RESOURCES

Books
- *Say It and Live It, 50 Corporate Mission Statements That Hit the Mark* by Patricia Jones and Larry Kahaner (Currency Doubleday)
- *The Mission Statement Book, 301 Corporate Mission Statements From America's Top Companies* by Jeffrey Abrahams (Ten Speed Press)
- *7 Habits of Highly Effective People* by Steven Covey (Simon & Schuster)

Organization
- Nicole Rhodes; Women Empowered™; 353 Puerta de Lomas; Fallbrook, CA 92028; (619) 732-0200

3

YOUR UNIQUE SELLING PROPOSITION (USP)

Tell them like it is

What exactly is a unique selling proposition?

Your unique selling proposition is your philosophy. Introduced in the 1950s by Rosser Reeves, then the chairman of Ted Bates Advertising Agency, it tells the business community three pieces of information:

1. What you have to offer (specifics)
2. What you do that makes you special (something they didn't know)
3. What you will do for them that would make them want to do business with you (the pitch in fifteen seconds or less)

A USP is an integral part of your personal or business headline. After the name, it is a phrase or slogan of your descriptive who, what, where, when, and why all wrapped up into a tidy package. A USP is the written equivalent of your essence, of what you stand for.

Why should I have one?

A USP is the advantage that makes you different from everyone else in your business arena. The reason you want to have one is because:

- A USP zeroes in on what you do best
- A USP tells your market what distinguishes you from your competition

- A USP tells your market exactly the service you are representing
- A USP defines your strengths
- A USP makes the claims you can deliver on

What does a USP appeal to?

The best USP appeals to emotional needs. It assures your customer that your company and your services or product will satisfy them the best.

What are some examples?

- Archer Daniels Midland: Supermarket to the world
- Outward Bound: Where born leaders are born
- IBM: Solutions for a small planet
- Xerox: A simpler way to do good work
- Federal Express: When it absolutely has to be there overnight
- CNN Headline News Sports Ticker: You'll always know the score
- Instashred Security Services: Better shred than read
- Liberty Mutual: Facing the issues that face our customers

Is it always one line?

No, but if it's more than one line and you can't say what you do or are in fifteen seconds or less, then you don't understand what you're all about, and neither will your audience.

Does it have to be on a product or service?

No. Teresita Pena Dabrieo, CEO of Success Partnership Network and author of *The Strategic Consultant*, newsletter, told me that Ross Perot designed his USP around his employees. "We will process your data with technically oriented businesspeople who will do whatever it takes to get the job done on time and to your satisfaction."

What are some other examples that are more than a few words?

When you read these, remember the question Dan Kennedy, in his *No B.S. Marketing Letter*, says a good USP should answer: "Why should I, your prospective client, do business with you, above any and all other options including doing nothing?''

Teresita Pena Dabrieo offers these USP examples from *The Strategic Consultant* newsletter:

- ''We're in the business of helping government departments or agencies to use their computing technology to avoid budget decreases''
- ''My company helps entrepreneurs who want to computerize but are orphaned by the big consulting firms because of their limited project scope or size''
- ''We work with aggressive lobbying firms who want to make sure that they are in front of advances in technology to help fund-raising and governmental access''

Here are others from *The Antin Marketing Letter: Secrets from the Lost Art of Common Sense Marketing:*

- ''Our House Cleaners will send a crew whenever you need one. We have twenty-five service people on call twenty-four hours, seven days a week, fifty-two weeks a year— yes, all holidays''
- ''When you use other plumbers you might get a limited year's guarantee. When you use our plumbers, you get a lifetime unlimited warranty with guaranteed twenty-four-hour service''

How do people get to know my USP?

As with a mission statement:

- Put it on your stationery
- Put it on your business cards
- Put it in your advertising
- Put it on your packaging
- Put it on your newsletter heading

Any parting words on a USP?

- Consider your USP as an extension of your yellow pages ad
- Consider your USP as your introduction in a networking situation

- Consider your USP as the words you need to make your prospective client, customer, or patient feel that you really understand what they are all about, and you're there to solve their problem, fill their need.

RESOURCES

- Dan Kennedy; *No B.S. Marketing Letter*; Empire Communications Corporation; 5818 N.7th St., #103; Phoenix, AZ 85014; (800) 223-7180
- Teresita Pena Dabrieo; *The Strategic Consultant* newsletter; Success Partnership Network, 1217 Broadway St., Pella, Iowa 50219; (800) 943-0012; *teresita-@dabrieo.com; http://www.dabrieo.com*
- Brad and Alan Antin, The Antin Marketing *Letter: Secrets from the Lost Art of Common Sense Marketing*; 11001 Delmar, Ste. 1200; Leawood, KS 66211; (913) 663-5552; fax (913) 663-5552; *antin@tyrell.net; 75706.2523@* CompuServe

4

YOUR LOGO

A fingerprint for your business

How important is it to have a logo?

Ask the Prudential Rock, the Jolly Green Giant, the Marlboro Man, the Park Service's Smokey Bear, or the U.S. Post Office eagle.

Is it necessary to have a logo?

I wouldn't say it was necessary to have a logo, but having a memorable one does add to your marketability.

Why is a logo a good marketing tool?
- It establishes brand or name recognition
- It adds to the image you're trying to build
- It reinforces advertising and marketing efforts
- It's an effortless way of reminding your audience what you do or who you are
- It helps to position you in and out of your marketplace
- It allows you to capture attention quickly

Besides my stationery and business cards, where would I use my logo?
- On every piece of marketing material
- On your videos
- On in-store signs and window displays
- On outdoor signs
- On promotional items
- On your car
- On your tie

What are my artistic choices?
- Graphic icons
- Pictures
- Symbols
- Abstract compositions
- Caricatures
- Animals, plants, minerals
- Special fonts for your business name
- Unique name design
- Your USP (unique selling proposition), which can be made into a logo design
- Slogans

What should I look out for?
- If you create an abstract, or use a picture or symbol that isn't the exact replica of your name, be sure to print your name somewhere in or around your logo. That way people can make the connection
- Don't pick the first one offered. Have your graphic artist create several to choose from. If you can afford it use more than one graphic artist
- You may be too close to the decision. Use your friends,

associates, and even focus groups to choose the winner
- Once you choose a logo, don't change it without a serious reason

NOTE: Software is available to design your own logos. Check with your local software store or magazine for the best of the bunch.

5

TRADITIONAL BUSINESS CARDS

How to put your future in the palm of someone's hand

What is the basic purpose of a business card?

The business card is designed to attract and set in motion the wheels of acquiring potential users of your product or service. A business card provides you with:

- A direct marketing vehicle
- A person-to-person sales call
- An advertisement
- A lead generator
- A networking tool
- A visual and kinesthetic representation of you

Why are business cards important?

Think of business cards as a mobile, one-dimensional version of yourself. A miniature you not waiting to happen but present and accounted for as long as the card is in circulation.

An effective card is arguably the most valuable marketing tool you can have in building a business. For those just beginning, sometimes it's the only tool.

Why is an effective business card considered the most valuable marketing tool I can have in building a business?

A business card creates and makes a statement about who you are and how you conduct your business. Among other things, a business card is:

- An image builder
- A first and powerful impression that can judge you positively or negatively
- A conveyer of your personality
- A unique insight into what you stand for
- A reflection of your soul in business
- A tangible vision of who you are and your purpose in doing business

How do I make my card stand out from the others in a pile?

- Use color stock
- Use mylar stock
- Use plastic
- Make it in the shape of your product or service
- Use oversize cards
- Create a fold over
- Make it subtly scented
- Present an origami (Japanese paper folding) figure with all the information printed on the small piece of paper, then do a follow-up mailing with a standard card
- Use a picture business card (see the chapter, "Picture Business Cards")
- Be unique

The two cards that impressed me the most aren't gathered from any of the hundreds of seminars or retreats I've spoken at. The first is from my Laundromat. It's see-through plastic, royal blue, with the picture of a front-loading washing machine surrounded by lots of suds and bubbles. The second is from my photographer. It too, is on plastic, designed to look like a piece of thirty-five-millimeter black and white film, including sprockets.

What should I put on my business card?

- Include all your contact information: name, company, address, phone, fax, e-mail. Also include your Web page, if you have one
- Use your USP (unique selling proposition), especially if your name doesn't describe the service you offer [see the chapter "Your Unique Selling Proposition (USP)"]
- Include your logo, and be consistent with your stationery and other printed materials
- Utilize a picture or a caricature drawing if you don't have a logo
- Use color stock or color ink. Gold or silver accents add an elegant touch
- Use the back for your mission statement or testimonials (see the chapters, "Your Mission or Vision Statement," "Get Testimonials," and "Give Testimonials")
- Use the back for a brief biography or product description
- Use the back for a marketing tool, such as a reusable discount coupon. You have to present the card each time to get the discount
- Use the back for emergency numbers, a calendar, tipping guidelines, sports activities (See the chapter, "Promotional Products")

What are some business card don'ts?

- If you have any contact changes, don't cross them out and write the new ones by hand. Print new cards and chalk it up as a business expense
- Don't even think about putting a sticker over the outdated information. Get new cards. It's your image we're talking about
- Don't use neon card stock. It's too hard to read the print
- Test the print size on friends who wear reading glasses. If their arms are too short to read your card, enlarge the print size
- Use thicker letters rather than fine, skinny letters
- DON'T USE ALL CAPITAL LETTERS. THEY'RE TOO DIFFICULT TO READ
- Don't use too many typefaces. The space is too small for variety

• Don't use script or such fancy fonts as **ALGERIAN** or *Brush Script MT*

NOTE: If you travel or do business overseas, have cards printed in both languages. **Be careful with the translation!** Hire a speaker to translate your text. Words in one culture don't always mean the same in another. Avoid socially unacceptable errors.

RESOURCES

Organization
The American Business Card Club (ABCC); Box 60297-B9; Aurora, CO 80010

Contest
Jane Applegate, author of *Strategies for Small Business Success* (Plume/Penguin) and a syndicated business columnist, holds a Best and Worst of Business Cards contest through her syndicated column. Write for details: Jane Applegate; Box 637; Sun Valley, CA 91353-0637.

Books
• *Print's Best Letterheads & Business Cards, Volumes Two and Three* by RC Publications Staff; (800) 222-2654
• *Make Your Business Cards INCREDIBLY EFFECTIVE!* The American Business Card Club (ABCC); Dept BK; Box 460297-B9; Aurora, CO 80010

6

PICTURE BUSINESS CARDS

A picture is worth a thousand words

Is the purpose of a picture card any different than a printed card?

In his *Secrets of Personal Marketing Power: Strategies for Achieving Greater Personal and Business Success*, Don L. Price says this about picture business cards: "If someone hands you a card with their picture printed on it, it becomes easier for you to associate that face with a previous conversation or encounter. The purpose of your business card is for others to make contact with you easily. It should also help them in connecting with you personally, and having your photo on it can help accomplish that goal."

How do I get one made? Will a candid picture do? Black and white or color?

Here are five options in order of effectiveness:

1. Cards that have your picture printed right onto the card stock. You can also use this picture on your stationery and envelopes. Ask your printer for photo specifications
2. A drawing or a caricature of you printed on the card stock. If you use a caricature on your cards, you can continue the theme on your stationery and envelopes
3. Made from a special process, and can take print on both sides. It is printed on sturdy stock and looks very professional
4. Made from picture stock, and can't be printed on the back. This process is available at most print and copy houses. For my taste it's flimsy in nature, bends easily,

and because you can't print on the back, doesn't allow for expanded coverage

5. Paste-on pictures the size of a postage stamp. They're great to add on to your existing cards and stationery. Acceptable colored stamps can only be made from excellent three-by-five or five-by-seven studio originals. Do not use Polaroids. Call for prices and quantity. This is an interesting gimmick that does get attention, but it isn't considered top of the line in the professional image department.

NOTE: Don L. Price has another great photo business card suggestion: Substitute your business card with a full-color photo bookmark.

RESOURCES

Photo Business Card Companies

• Superior Business Cards; 8025 N. Division St. Ste. F; Spokane, WA 99208; (800) 745-9565
• Daicolo Corporation; 21203A Hawthorne Blvd.; Torrance, CA 90503; (800) 772-9993 or (310) 543-2700
• U.S. Press; Box 640; Valdosta, GA 31603-0640; (800) 227-7377

Paste-on Photos

Blackie; Box 1418; Sarasota, FL 34230; (800) 237-6286. Tell them Tom Callister sent you

Caricatures

Joan Sotkin; 22692 Napoli St.; Laguna Hills, CA 92653

Book

Secrets of Personal Marketing Power, Strategies for Achieving Greater Personal & Business Success by Don L. Price; Box 7000-700; Redondo Beach, CA 90277; (310) 379-7797

7

AUDIO BUSINESS CARDS-BROCHURES

So they can hear you coming

Why would I want to go through the time, money, and effort when a written brochure can be made more easily?

As Janita Cooper of Master Duplicating Corporation tells it, "Don't look at an audio brochure as an expense; look at it as a revenue generator. You have great information to share. But as good as your product and services are, if the right people don't hear about it, your efforts are wasted. Written brochures serve a purpose; audio brochures create a purpose."

It's a well-known fact that in-person sales calls are the best way to do business. But if you can't be there in person, on video conferencing, or on a video brochure, then give them the next best thing. Give them who you are on an audio brochure.

Audio brochures, just like their video cousins, are a grabber, an attention getter, a keeper. Less expensive than most printed brochures and many direct-mail pieces, audio brochures have a life of their own.

Listen: Your mail arrives. The magazines are put in the take-to-the-bathroom pile. Junk mail with great teasers on the envelope are put in a maybe pile, bills in the ahuh pile, and all others get tossed in the circular file or kitchen trash.

But what's this different kind of envelope? Immediately you think, "Did I order something?" Not remembering, you tear it open and out comes a cassette with a professionally printed label announcing *Promote & Prosper, Raleigh Pinskey's Marketing Secrets of the Pros*. But you're in a hurry to pick up your son at Little League. Do you put it in the maybe pile?

Do you put it in the circular file? Do you put it in the bathroom file? No, you put in your purse to listen while you're on your way to the baseball game.

If the audio brochure arrived at the office, and you didn't have a cassette player there, surveys show that you wouldn't throw it away. You would save the cassette and play it on the way home from work. But printed brochures either get tossed in the circular file or buried under mounds of paperwork in a pile marked to be read.

What's the most important function of an audio brochure?

That question can be answered with one word: curiosity. People expect to receive the usual printed brochure, and with today's technology they even expect the video brochure. However, people don't expect an audio brochure, so it immediately piques their interest.

What does an audio business card–brochure tell people about me that a written card–brochure doesn't?

According to Janita Cooper of Master Duplicating Corporation, an audio card–brochure, tells the recipient:

- That by investing in your project you're investing in yourself
- That investing in yourself imparts the image that you're a winner
- That you're a risk taker, willing to be different
- That you see yourself as a cut above the norm
- That you're serious about your business

What else are they good for?

- They make for a great referral tool. People love to give them out for you. It's like passing out a treat
- They have a long shelf life. Because they're packaged in a vinyl album much like a videocassette, they sit well on a shelf
- They can take the place of your presentation materials. The covers allow for your picture, biography, testimonials, and partial client roster. All you need to do is provide an

updated one-sheet (a one-page information sheet) if and when requested. Inside is a generic letter to the recipient, the tape, and your business card

How can I create one?
You write the script, get a friend or a professional to ask the questions, contact any recording studio, record the tape, take it to a duplicating house, get a graphic designer to design the cover, have a printer print the cover, buy the vinyl albums, and put all the components together. Or call a professional for one-stop shopping.

RESOURCES

Specialists in Audio Business Cards–Brochures
Cold Call Cowboy Productions; Box 12488; Palm Desert, CA 92255-2488; (619) 568-5124. Send for a free sample audio brochure. Cold Call Cowboy's program provides you with a 190-page manual along with an eight-cassette manual that outline the process for making the investment in the tapes work. This gives a perspective on what to say to clients to make them comfortable but lead them to your objective: getting that appointment to get that business

Consulting, Recording, Packaging, and Duplicating
- Janita Cooper; Master Duplicating Corporation; 2907 West Fairmount Ave.; Phoenix, AZ 85017; (800) 228-8919 or (602) 279-6297
- Joe Beard; Audio Duplication Services; 2613 N. Andrews Ave.; Wilton Manors, FL 33311; (305) 568-5385

Duplication and Packaging
Steve Feldman; Tape Specialty; 13411 Saticoy St.; North Hollywood, CA 91605; (818) 909-5232

Packaging
Catherine Breckenridge; BCSP Group, Remington Stationery; 5413 Downey Rd.; Vernon, CA 90058; (213) 584-9435

Cover Art
Dunn + Associates; Box 870; Hayward, WI 54843; (800) 665-6728 or (715) 634-4857; fax (715) 634-5617

8

VIDEO BUSINESS CARDS-BROCHURES

So they can see you coming

What is a video business card–brochure?

It's a videotape that shows you talking about your product, service, talent, or idea. It can be sales-subtle in the form of pure information, or it can contain a direct sales pitch.

Why is it a good marketing tool?

As Don L. Price puts it in *Secrets of Personal Marketing Power*, "The video brochure is a real show-and-tell marketing tool that allows you to have customer testimonials or live-action demonstrations of your products or services, and literally appeal and play to the emotions of your viewers."

How long should the video be?

There are differing opinions on how long it should be. My experience puts a comfortable viewing length at no more than six to eight minutes. Jay Conrad Levinson and Seth Godin in the *The Guerrilla Marketing Handbook* like six minutes, and

Don L. Price in *Secrets of Personal Marketing Power: Strategies for Achieving Greater Personal and Business Success* goes as high up as fifteen.

What could I possibly say in six or eight minutes that is meaningful?

The purpose of the video is to give a taste of yourself, your product, or your service. It's an introduction, not a long discussion. Believe me, you can say a lot in six or eight minutes. Think about how long your sales pitch is, and act accordingly.

This six or eight minutes is all about attention span. Keep in mind that surveys show people change channels within four seconds.

How much does it cost to make a video?

The average cost comes out to be about $1,000 a minute when you use top-notch people and equipment. And I strongly recommend you use professionals for this task. It would be nothing short of disastrous to present yourself via a tape of home video quality. Don't be penny wise and pound foolish on this project.

Do video business cards–brochures really warrant the expense?

Absolutely. If you can't be there in person, the next best thing is a video representation of yourself.

As Jay Conrad Levinson and Seth Godin so aptly word it in *The Guerrilla Marketing Handbook*, "Video brochures combine the impact of a TV commercial with the targeting power of a mailed print brochure."

Where do I find a production company that can do this sort of thing?

Contact several public relations companies and ask who they use for their video marketing kits, also known as EMKs (electronic marketing kits). If one name comes up several times, then you have a winner. When you contact the company:

- View several product pieces
- Don't accept a sample reel; demand to see entire videos

- Call its clients and ask how the production company works
- Ask how well the videos work for them
- Ask if they would use them again
- Ask if they have other recommendations

Besides mailing it out to a data base of prospective clients, how will people know I have a video?
- Include it in your advertising
- Send it in your prospect mailings
- Use it as the basis of your classified ads
- Mention it on the back of your business cards
- Tell them about it in your brochures
- Offer it as a free gift on a business reply card
- Talk about it on radio talk shows
- Hand it out to interested prospects at your seminars
- Use it in your booth at trade shows and conventions
- Make it a direct-mail piece
- Use it in your office waiting room to educate your clients or patients
- Supply it for demonstration purposes for in-store play
- Leave it behind or send before a prospective client meeting

Do I charge people for my video?
Absolutely not. This is a promo piece. It's a business expense.

Why is a video such a great marketing tool?
Because it's unusual. People are expecting a printed brochure, not an in-your-face, hi, hey, hello there personal representation. And because it's so unusual, they keep them. Here's a very interesting side note: For some odd reason, people can't seem to throw them away.

Will people be so impressed that they will call me after watching my video?
Chances are some will call. But for the most part, you're the one who wants to sell them on you, your product, or your service. That means you need to follow up. I usually wait three to four days after they receive the package. That should give

them enough time to view it. Don't forget, many offices don't have VCRs as standard equipment, so people have to remember to take it home, then find the time to view it.

Your call is a gentle nudge and an announcement that says you mean business.

How will I know when they get it?
- Out of the area: Send second-day delivery
- Locally: Have it hand delivered

How do I get copies made?
That's the beauty of a video or audio card–brochure. You don't have to have zillions printed up all at once just to get a deal. You can duplicate them as you need them.

Ask the production company to suggest a duplication house. But also look in the yellow pages and compare prices. Call the companies' clients and ask about quality. Make sure you can get credit on faulty copies.

What if I'm doing a mass mailing? Are there companies that will do it for me and track the incoming calls?
Those companies are called fulfillment houses. The production people should know about them, or you can call your local mailing list house (see the chapter "Using Commercial Mailing Lists"), or look in the yellow pages under Mailing.

RESOURCES

Books
- *The Guerrilla Marketing Handbook* by Jay Conrad Levinson and Seth Godin (Houghton Mifflin)
- *Secrets of Personal Marketing Power, Strategies for Achieving Greater Personal & Business Success* by Don L. Price; Box 7000-700; Redondo Beach, CA 90277; (310) 379-7797

Video Gurus
- Robert B. Sommer; Best of the Masters; 6361 Yarrow Dr.; Carlsbad, CA 92009; (619) 929-1019; *somrob @aol.com*

9

WRITTEN BROCHURES

Your thoughts in print

What does a written brochure do?
- Positions your company
- Initiates a dialogue
- Gives your prospect a chance to know a little about you before you meet
- Helps breaks the ice
- Amplifies your letter of introduction
- Presents an immediate way to respond to inquiries
- Lends credibility when professionally executed
- Answers questions in a logical, meaningful way
- Provides an opportunity to tell your story in detail
- Shows off your merits
- Acts as a direct-mail piece when prospecting, anywhere, anytime, anyplace
- Offers the ability to present reference materials such as price lists in a subtle yet effective manner

Why is a brochure important?
Brochures are another part of the imprint arsenal. In other words, the more your name is seen and heard, the more people will come to know you. Remember, it takes an average of eight imprints for your name, product, or service to register in the section of the brain that gives the *AHAs!*

What are the key elements of a successful brochure?
- Create your brochure with the prospect in mind, not your ego
- Include a call to action. Ask for an order, an appointment,

a request for more information, or the intent to meet at a later date
* Include testimonials. They show and tell the prospect what benefits you provide your clients (see the chapters, "Get Testimonials," "Give Testimonials," "Endorsement Letters," and "Writing Direct Mail and Sales Letters")
* Include information that shows the prospects you know their market
* Create a relationship with your audience

What's the biggest mistake people make when designing a brochure?

People make the mistake of highlighting their features instead of showing their benefits. They toot their own horn instead of showing the prospects how they can help solve their problems, fill their needs, and make them look good in the eyes of their target audience.

What other mistakes should I watch out for?
* Not using a headline, graphic, element or photo on the cover to draw the reader in
* Using too much text and not enough bulleted information
* Not using testimonials
* Not listing a partial client list
* Using big words
* Using industry buzz words
* Using dated material
* Listing information instead of adding creativity
* Forgetting to put in the contact information
* Letting your ego run away with you in print

Is there any way for a small business to get around the huge printing bill?
* Print only a shell. In other words, design the graphics, the picture, the headlines, the headings, and anything else you know will stay the same. That way, when the text changes you take the shell to the printer and they print up the new information
* Use a design software program. Print out as many as needed. You can use a preprinted shell as discussed above, or you can buy preprinted brochure paper

Should I use folded brochures, and if so how many folds should I have?

If you have one page, a three-fold brochure is the most popular. If you have more than one page, you can make the brochure into a booklet. Either is fine.

What makes a businessperson keep my brochure?
- The hope that you can help
- The text that explains how you can help
- The graphics that show how you can help

RESOURCES

Newsletter and Consultant
Ilise Benun; *The Art of Self Promotion*; Box 23; Hoboken, NJ 07030-0023; (201) 653-0783; fax (201) 222-2494

Book
- *Better Brochures, Catalogs and Mailing Pieces* by Jane Maas (St. Martin's Press)
- *The Art & Business of Creative Self-Promotion* by Jerry Herring and Mark Fulton (Watson-Guptil)

Preprinted Paper
- Paper Direct; 205 Chubb Ave.; Lyndhurst, NJ 07071; (800) 272-7377. Call for a catalog
- Queblo Images; 1000 Florida Ave., Hagerstown, MD 21740; (800) 523-9080. Call for a catalog
- Check your local stationery stores

10

BANNERS AND SIGNS

Your silent sales staff

Are we talking indoor or outdoor banners and signs?
Both. If you have a product or service that you really want
to get in front of your audience, do it with signs.

Aren't signs boring?
There is an old saying: "Signs are not boring; it is the
people who make them who are boring." So hire someone
who makes a living at being creative. Sign makers abound in
the yellow pages. Graphic artists can design a sign for the sign
makers to craft.

What are some examples of signs that work?
• Have an electric sign. Don Kott Ford in Long Beach, California, has a huge electric sign fronting the 405 freeway.
It alternates prices, products, and services with motivational sayings chosen by Mrs. Kott. It draws customers
like bees to honey
• Have a sign that allows you to change the letters by hand.
There's a church in my neighborhood that changes its sign
every day. Today's message: *Prayer is God's 800 number*
• Paint your building with a mural. There's a flower shop
in a small town in Pennsylvania that covered the outside
of its building with a street scene dotted with flower carts,
shops with flower boxes, and flowering trees. Traffic always slowed down at that intersection. At peak traffic
hours, when the light was red, the store owners handed
out flowers attached to their business card. The card is
marked so they can track their efforts. So far it's paid off
more than their advertising.

- Have your sign imitate your business. I've seen haircutters with a sign in the shape of scissors. A pizza parlor sign in the shape of a pizza. An Italian restaurant sign in the shape of a dish painted with spaghetti and meatballs
- Challenge your neighbor with your own sign. Marketers Jeff and Marc Slutsky's full service hair salon client found himself with an inexpensive clone across the street. To upstage the competition, they advised their client to put a huge sign in front of the shop that said, We fix $5 haircuts.
- Cover all the bases. I heard Harvey MacKay, CEO of MacKay Envelopes and author of *Swim with the Sharks* and *Beware the Naked Man Who Offers You His Shirt*, offer this brilliant pearl of wisdom in a speech: "The easiest, least expensive, and most neglected form of advertising is painting on top of your truck. Then all those people who work in tall office buildings and look out from time to time will see only your advertising." He said he'd has been doing it for twenty-five years and swears by this technique
- Engage the earth's magnetic field. Put magnetic signs on your car or truck
- Be a moving target. Print up bumper stickers (see the chapter, "Bumper Stickers"). Pass them out, mail them out
- Walk your talk. Use sandwich boards
- Drive your point home, or anywhere for that matter. Use moving signs. Those are the flatbed trucks with sandwich boards that announce your product or service
- Look high and low. Rent billboards and bus benches

NOTE: Make sure you check city signage ordinances before you make your sign.

RESOURCES

Books

- *Street Smart Marketing* by Jeff and Marc Slutsky (John Wiley)
- *Swim with the Sharks* and *Beware the Naked Man Who*

Offers You His Shirt by Harvey MacKay (William Morrow)

Check your local yellow pages for sign makers and outdoor advertising companies

11

PRESENTATION VISUALS

The tools that can make or break self-promotion

Why use visuals to make a sale or get a project approved?
A picture speaks a thousand words, and if it's the right picture it can help you increase your business or get your project approved. In the 1980s, studies were done by 3M/The Wharton School, University of Pennsylvania, to determine the effect of visuals on a presentation. There were three major conclusions from these studies.

People who used visuals in their presentation were found to be:

1. More persuasive. When you use visual aids, people are 43% more likely to be persuaded by your presentation than when you don't use visuals. People tend to agree more with your presentation when you print it on overhead transparencies or slides. The kind of visual support you use can also make your presentation more persuasive
2. More professional. Visual support can make you and your presentation look more professional. People will listen more attentively to you and react better to you personally. If you're an average presenter, you can become a better presenter by using visual support
3. Better quality. The quality of your meeting may be in-

fluenced by the use of visuals. Visual support in your presentations can affect the audience's comprehension, retention, and consensus as well as the meeting length

In short, they'll understand you, remember what you said, decide in your favor if there's a decision to be made, and do it in a shorter amount of time.

How do I decide what kind of visuals to use?

When deciding whether to use visuals in your presentation and/or what kind to use, ask yourself:

1. What size is my audience?
2. What is the purpose of my presentation?
3. How will the audience be sitting?
4. Will they be trying to take notes?

What are the most commonly used visuals?

• Flipcharts: good for small audiences

PROS	CONS
flexible	not professional looking
interactive	

TIPS: Stapling two sheets together makes them easier to turn and also prevents your audience from reading ahead. Write notes to yourself on the edge in pencil.

• Overhead Transparencies (OHTs): good for small or medium audiences

PROS	CONS
flexible	tendency to put too much on them
lights up	

TIPS: Keeping your overhead transparencies in frames allows you to align them better, and you can write notes on the frame to remind yourself of key points. Don't use OHTs if they're going to be hand or type written.

- Thirty-five millimeter slides: good for medium or large audiences

PROS	CONS
number one choice among corporations	flexible
sharp, professional looking	lights dimmed
easy to carry, store, duplicate	

TIPS: If you have a complex slide, break it up into multiple "build" slides. Computer-generated slides look best.

- Prints: good for any size audience

PROS	CONS
supplements speech	audience reads ahead
reference for later	

TIP: Use speaker note capabilities; i.e., visual on the left, room for notes on the right.

- Video: good for any size audience

PROS	CONS
attention getting	inflexible
	expensive

- Multimedia/Electronic Presentations: good for any size audience

PROS	CONS
attention getting	possible equipment failure
	attention on media, not speaker

TIP: If you intend to use multimedia, either hire a pro to help you or practice with it a lot before attempting to use it in an actual presentation.

When should I use computer-generated visuals?

Use computer-generated visuals to increase attention, emphasize concepts on complex charts, and heighten the audience's perception of the presenter.

What should I avoid when using computer-generated visuals?

- Use animation with discretion to avoid sensory overload
- Use transitions selectively to avoid overpowering the message
- Use simple transitions to minimize audience distraction

What's the best way to create computer-generated visuals?

1. Hire a service bureau to do the creation and imaging of the visuals, and output in whatever format you require (i.e., thirty-five millimeter slides, OHTs, prints)
2. Buy a low-cost computer graphics software package, do the creation yourself, and send it to a service bureau for imaging. This will result in significant savings. Popular computer graphics packages are *Powerpoint, Persuasion,* and *Astound*

What are some visual do's?

When using visuals, you want to be:

- Credible. If you're making a point, it helps to have data to back you up (such as the 3M/Wharton School studies). Put these at the bottom of the visual for easy reference
- Organized. You want to move smoothly from point to point
- Clear. Use one point from the visual
- Impressive. You might want to have your logo in the corner, or use a textured background

What's the percentage breakdown of graphics and words?

Eighty-five percent of visuals are business graphics, and 70% are word charts (i.e., title, text).

What's the KISS method of visuals?
Keep it simple, sweetie! Don't use a zillion fonts, colors, or too much text.

What do I need to know about the text?
When you prepare your text:

- Make it legible. Those in the back of the room should be able to read the entire visual
- Follow the six-three-six rule: No more than six lines per visual, three to six words per line
- Use upper and lower case. Using capital letters actually slows down comprehension
- When projecting, use sans serif type (for example, Helvetica). For prints, serif (such as Times Roman)
- Follow the 10% rule: No more than 10% of your visual should be different (i.e., bold, underlined, et cetera)
- Use the same typeface within the visual and the presentation for consistency

What should I know about charts?
- Use line charts for trends
- Use bar charts for comparisons
- Use pie charts for percentages
- Use diagrams to show order and structure

What do I need to know about color?
- The 3M/Wharton School Study found that color is more effective in a presentation than black and white (20% more persuasive)
- Limit the amount of colors in a visual
- Be consistent with colors from visual to visual
- Make sure colors make sense
- Best combination: dark blue background, yellow title, white text

What do I need to know about using backgrounds?
- Dark backgrounds for slides and dark rooms
- Medium backgrounds for overheads and partially lit rooms
- Light backgrounds for fully lit rooms only

Grab them with glitz. A little is good, a lot is not. Remember the 10% rule.

Any words of wisdom that will put me over the top?

1. When using visuals, you need to allocate extra time for their creation (storyboard, implementation, imaging, costs). Allow extra time in case something goes wrong
2. Practice, practice, practice so that everything goes smoothly and you look professional
3. Arrive early to make sure the equipment you require is there and operational, the lights work the way you want them to, et cetera
4. Last, but not least . . . Remember, *you* are the presentation. Visuals will enhance you, but they are intended to support you, not replace you. When used effectively, visuals can help you in your quest for increased business

NOTE: A 3M/University of Arizona study found that audiences respond best to a presenter who uses technology as a presentation aid, but response declines rapidly when the presenter takes a backseat to complex on-screen visuals that appear "canned" to the audience.

RESOURCES

* This information is from Sharon Adcock, president of The Adcock Group, a public relations/marketing company that specializes in representing visuals and graphics companies. She is a professional speaker on the subject of technology of the 21st century. Adcock can be reached at 4108 Highland Ave., Ste. AA; Manhattan Beach, CA 90266; (310) 545-9731; fax (310) 545-5939; *Ski Adcock@aol. com*
* Keith Price; Synergistic Computer Solutions; 9219 Geyser Ave.; Northridge, CA 91324; (818) 727-7854; *kap@gnn. com.* Price will evaluate your visual presentation and help you add impact and clarity using Microsoft Power. He also specializes in simplifying standard office procedures in Microsoft Office

12

DEVELOPING YOUR OWN MAILING LISTS

Charity begins at home; develop your own

If you learn anything at all from this book, it should be that your current market is your best market to draw from. Or, as they say in the real estate market, it's the best place to farm.

Why is my current market the best place to farm?

Because your clients, customers, patients, or patrons already know you. If you've done your homework and provided them with great customer service, they'll want to continue knowing and buying from you.

Your own list is also the best place to farm because these loyal people will refer you to their friends and relatives (see the chapters, "Get Testimonials," "Give Testimonials," and "Endorsement Letters").

What kind of information do I need to gather?

Capturing the names of your clients, customers, patients or patrons, is the lifeblood of your business. If you do it right by getting all the demographic details you could possibly need, then the list is where you'll do most of your marketing.

Customize the questions to your business. Ask anything that helps put those dollars in your cash register and your pocket (see the chapter, "Tips, Trends, and Surveys").

- Where do they live? A house or an apartment?
- How many rooms?
- Is there a pool or exercise room?
- Do they belong to a gym? How often do they go?

41

- What do they like to do on vacation?
- How many cars do they have and what kind?
- What kinds of movies do they like?
- How many hours do they watch TV?
- What kinds of books do they read?
- What magazines do they subscribe to?
- Do they have pets? How many and what kind?
- When are their birthdays and anniversaries?

Why is a list such a great marketing tool?

Without this personal information there can be no up-front and personal marketing efforts, no I-care-about-you notes, and no look-what-else-we-have-that-you'll-like offers. You'll have no one to send your special report, your newsletter, promotional items, or those invitations to a VIP celebration day.

What's the best way to generate my own lists?

- Collect business cards at luncheons, civic meetings, and in waiting rooms
- Request a name and address from anyone who calls your business
- Capture the name of every person who enters your store. Put out a fishbowl for cards, a sign-in sheet, or hire a personal greeter to take the information
- Exhibit at trade shows. Get a very large see-through bowl to collect the cards. Offer a prize and have a drawing to encourage the foot traffic to contribute business cards
- Present mini-seminars to religious groups, civic and trade organizations
- Run sweepstakes or contests for people who use your services
- Send newsletters and ask subscribers for referrals. Give them a bonus for five names
- Offer to exchange collection bowls with a business that offers similar or compatible services
- Place suggestion boxes in your store
- Offer a free catalog
- Use mail-back inserts or coupons in a direct-mail piece or ad
- Offer warranties or guarantees. They'll have to fill out the

basics. Then mail or fax a comprehensive questionnaire to gather in-depth information.

How do I organize these names?
If you use a computer:

- Buy a business card scanner (less than $200) and scan the information right into your computer data base management program. No muss, no fuss, no time wasted
- Input the information by hand into your data base management system

What's a data base management system?
A data base management system is a computer software program with standard categories and boxes to customize information necessary to your needs:

- Name, address, phone, fax, and e-mail
- Where you met this person
- Who recommended the person
- The date when you met the person
- When you first called the person, when you should call again

Data base marketing programs allow you to keep track of conversations, write letters, and print out lists by numerous categories. Some even keep track of inventory, keep your schedules, and send faxes.

Two excellent data base marketing programs are *Telemagic* (high end, with many features) and *Act* (good for the basics). *Delrina's Communication Suite* does everything but walk your dog.

Every day there are more data base management packages coming out that interface with the Internet and have voice capabilities.

Is there a program that just has names, addresses, and phone numbers?
Yes. There are simple programs that just put in the basic contact information, perfect for mailing labels. In fact, Avery

labels has one. But this type of program doesn't allow you to keep track of the other valuable information. So if you do use this type of program, keep the other information somewhere on three-by-five cards.

Go to any computer store and ask questions. The salespeople there can help you find a data base management program to fit your business needs.

How do I make sure I don't waste money using out-of-date addresses?

- The best way to avoid this is to do a mailing at least once each quarter. If your mailing schedule doesn't allow this, offer your list to your colleague on the condition that he or she makes the necessary corrections from any incorrect address returns
- If your list is grossly out of date, the U.S. Post Office has a list of vendors that can clean up your list for a small per-name price. The post office is able to change addresses if the person has moved in the area within the last three years

How can I manage my lists if I don't use a computer?

There is an old saying: "Necessity is the mother of invention." Applied here it means that if you're not computerized, there are companies that will take the business cards, scribbled sign-in names, contest coupons, and other marketing means and input them into whatever system you want. Some places will keep your list, manage all changes, and even do the mailings for you. Since these places have computers, they can maintain an out-of-house data base for you, providing you with mailing labels when you need them.

Where do I find these companies?

They come in all shapes and sizes, and do different tasks, so you need to shop around for the best prices. You can find them in the yellow pages under various names, such as:

- Fulfillment houses
- Word-processing centers
- Mailing list houses
- Look in the yellow pages under Word and then Word

Processing, or under Mail and then Mailing Services
- Check the bulletin board at your supermarket or Laundromat
- Check the classified section or ads in your local weekly free newspaper
- Check an adult education course catalog and call the course teacher for a recommendation
- Ask for a recommendation at your local computer store

Can I use my mailing list for profit?

Absolutely. Renting mailing lists is a good way to earn extra money. But your list must be up-to-date, or word will spread and no one will want your list.

How much should I charge?

The industry average is ten to fifty cents a name. I know people who have a prime list of proven repeat buyers and charge a dollar a name. These kinds of lists are powerful sales tools, and command a good price.

Look in the yellow pages under Mail, then Mailing Services. Call them and find out their menu of prices, and apply that information to your needs.

How can I save money on my mailings?

Get a bulk mail permit for $85 a year. Postage is a lot less than regular mail.

I should use bulk and not first class?

Because of the media attention given to bulk mail discarded by carriers, many marketing experts argue this point. My opinion? If you can afford first class, use it. Not only are you assured it will get there, but it gets there faster than the three-week time frame required for bulk mail.

Bulk mail doesn't get returned if it's undeliverable. You won't be able to clean your lists with bulk mail.

Mailing costs are expensive. How can I get around this without using bulk mail?

If you're strapped you can always join forces with a non-competitor and split the mailing costs, or put your information in a larger mailing pool such as card decks, Val-Cards or coupon books (see the chapter, "Card Decks"). The point is, there are many ways to start a mailing list. There are no excuses not to market yourself or your business.

NOTE: I strongly recommend you subscribe to *Home Office Computing, Business Start-ups, and Entrepreneur* magazines. Each is a wonderful source for what's new and best for the entrepreneur and small business person. All three are available at newsstands.

RESOURCES

U.S. Postal Service Natural Customer Support Center; (800) 238-3150, or ask at your local post office. They will refer you to the nearest U.S. Post Office Business Center

Magazines
- *Entrepreneur and Business Start-ups* magazine; 2392 Morse Ave.; Irvine, CA 92714; (800) 864-6868
- *Home Office Computing*; 411 Lafayette St.; New York, NY 10003; (212) 505-4220

13

USING COMMERCIAL MAILING LISTS

Neither a borrower nor lender be . . .
except for mailing lists

Where can I get local, regional, or national mailing lists if I don't want to go through the time and effort of collecting my own names?

Believe it or not, if someone sells it and someone buys it, there is a list of names available. There is an entire industry that services the need for lists, and the good news is you don't have to look very far. The easiest place to find all the lists you could possibly want is in your local yellow pages. Go to Mail and then to the subtopic Mailing Lists. If your area is too small to support a local mailing house or a library, then check the resource list at the end of the chapter, "Writing Direct Mail and Sales Letters."

Why is the terminology *rent* a list and not *buy* a list?

The term *rent* is used because you are only allowed a one-time use. But once you receive any type of response from that list, i.e., a sale, a call, a return response card, et cetera, then that name belongs to you.

How does the broker know you've used it more than once?

- Brokers *seed* the list. That means they place names of friends on the list who report back when it is used
- Brokers rent Post Office boxes and have phony names buried in the list

How do I know what kinds of lists to rent?

Mailing lists come in three basic categories:

1. Response lists: These are compiled from people who buy services or products
2. Compiled lists: These include names from telephone books and other directories, magazine and newsletter subscriptions
3. Occupant lists: These include the names of every household in a demographic area

How much does a list cost?

Lists are sold two ways:

1. By total number of names. The average cost is $50 to $100 per 1,000
2. Per name: The average cost is from ten to fifty cents.

I've known premium guaranteed lists that go for a dollar a name. The sky is the limit. The better the list, the more the broker can charge.

What do I have to know about buying a list?
What you *want* to know is when was the list qualified?

1. Ask when the list was last used. This will give you an insight as to how many people are out there marketing in your specialty
2. Ask if and then when the list was *cleaned*. What this means is that the address corrections were made and the list is up-to-date. This is very important. Why waste your money on incorrect names?
3. Ask when any new names were last added

How can I be certain the addresses are still good?
In the chapter "Developing Your Own Mailing Lists," we talked about the services the local or regional U.S. Post Office Business Support Service of the National Customer Support Center offers. If you want to be absolutely certain the lists you rent are as clean as they can be, then pay the cost for a vendor search and correction. Fifteen to twenty percent of the people on the list move within a year. That is why you need to ask when the list was most recently cleaned and corrected. Then decide if it's worth the price per name to have it absolutely current as current can be.

How can I get the best mileage out of a list?
As Mike Rounds, co-author of *Mechanics of Mail Order* (see the chapter, "Mail Order") likes to tell it, "If you're selling collars and bones for small dogs, why mail to Great Dane owners? Don't buy the whole list just because it has to do with dogs."

Yes, there is a possibility that the Great Dane owner might also have a small dog. If you have the money to find that needle in the haystack, then go ahead and go wild. The rule of thumb is: better to pay for a 100 known users, and get a good return, than buy 1,000 maybes and only get a small percentage on the return. Depending on the purpose of the mailing, you need to look at the following:

1. Define and refine the market you are examining:

   • Organizations
   • Consumer or personal buyers
   • Business-to-business

2. Identify the particular needs of what you're selling:

   • Price range
   • Number of employees
   • Age
   • Occupation
   • Marital status
   • Number of children
   • Age of children
   • Et cetera

3. Rent the addresses that are within the reach of:

   • Your advertising
   • Publicity
   • Zip code

What are the chances of name duplications if I rent more than one list?

Good question. The chances of duplication are great. When you buy the lists ask the list broker to do a *merge and purge.*

Here's a very important tip. Make a special note of the duplications. This means that the name is an active buyer and should be at the top of your mailing list. This person is what is called a hot prospect and should get your attention.

Can I update the list with new names after I've rented it?

Yes. To update the lists you rented ask for the additions made after the date you rented the list.

What does "test the list" mean?

The key to any good list is, "Does it sell?" Another way to say this is, "Does it pull?" If a list doesn't match your purpose, wouldn't you want to know before you spent your money on all those names?

What you do is test the list by *sampling*, or buying a percentage of the names you've chosen. Mail to these names and compile the results. If it's a good list, then roll out the rest of it. If not, then redefine your needs and requalify the specifics as stated under the question, "How do I get the best mileage out of a list?" Ask the list broker for advice. Remember what I said before. At a good list house the broker is your friend. Yes, he's out to sell lists, but if he *sells* you wrong not only won't you come back, but you won't recommend the business to your community.

How do I ask for this test list?

Ask the broker for his hot line list. This comprises most recent buyers' names from the list you are purchasing, usually buyers within the last 90 to 120 days. If this list won't work for you, then the big list won't either.

If this portion of the list pulls well for you, then the rest of the list will not be as responsive. So don't expect miracles from the rest of the list. What this means is you should also do a percentage test from the remaining names before buying the whole list.

Remember that the best list is your own in-house list. Second is someone in the same or similar business who will share their list. Third is mail response lists of actual orders and inquiries. And last are those lists compiled from others, such as subscriptions, organizations, warranties, and general purchase lists.

NOTE: The list business is highly competitive, so list brokers want to keep your business. Make them your friend. Tap into their expertise. Ask them what you should know to do a successful mailing.

RESOURCES

List Brokers

The easiest way to find a list broker is to look in the yellow pages under Mail, then Mailing Lists

Mailing List Brokers Resources (available in libraries)

- Standard Rate and Data Service; 3004 Glenview Rd.; Wilmette, IL 60091; (847) 256-6067. It surveys 25 metro markets with populations of more than 150,000
- The Direct Marketing Market Place & Direct Mail List Rates and Data; 5201 Old Orchard Rd.; Skokie, IL 60077; (708) 256-6067
- Directory of Mailing List Companies; 18 N. Greenbush Rd.; West Nyack, NY 10994; (914) 358-6213

14

CREDIT CARD SALES

Accept credit cards . . . don't leave your business without them

What's the benefit of taking credit cards?

- The biggest and best benefit is the ability to turn "I have just enough cash on me to get out of the parking lot" into a resounding *"I'll take it!"*
- Accepting credit cards substantially increases sales by taking the cash availability factor out of the prospective buyer's decision-making process
- With credit card acceptance, the buyer only has two decisions:

    1. Is your product a benefit to the buyer's life?
    2. Is the price appropriate in relation to the perceived benefit?

I tried to get a merchant number so I could take credit cards, but because I work out of my house, I couldn't get one. Now what?

I had that problem, and so did many of my consultant friends. The banks say you must have what they refer to as a storefront. By that they mean a legitimate business doing business in a traditional place of business. Such home-based businesspeople as seminar givers, consultants, massage therapists, artisans, et cetera are without a storefront and are therefore ineligible for a merchant number in the eyes of many financial institutions.

Luckily there are independent companies who work with financial institutions in securing merchant numbers for those who are considered storefront-less. Jim Krause at Axin Financial Services saved my life. He went to bat for me and got me a merchant number so I could charge for my consulting, seminars, retreats, books, audio and video tapes.

How have credit cards helped your business?

My back-of-the-room services and resources include materials that build on and interact with one another. Purchases of $500, $750, and $1,000 are not unusual. Credit cards are more than very important to my sales; they are the lifeblood of my business.

The ability to accept credit cards is a necessity for selling your product or services on talk shows (see the chapter, "Be a Guest on Radio and TV Talk Shows").

NOTE: Credit cards not only grow and expand your business, they can be the why and how you do business. If you're in business, do business. Expand your mind; get a merchant number.

RESOURCES

Jim Krause; Axin Financial Services; (310) 694-0565

15

SAYING THANK YOU

Back-to-basics business

Why is saying thank you a good way to promote yourself?
Everyone likes to be appreciated. This is a given. But if you're appreciated when you least expect it, it makes an even bigger impression.

When you take time to notice people, they can't help but notice you back.

Are you talking about a thank you note, or something else?
- Krammer Motors, my Honda dealer, called to say thank you for choosing them to do my oil change. An $18.95 job was rewarded with a telephone call. They also wanted to know if I was satisfied with the service I received. I expect this from my dentist or my family physician. But my car dealership? I'll never change my oil anywhere else!
- I received a handwritten thank you note from the florist. A real thank you note, the kind your mother taught you to send after a dinner party. The inside wasn't fancy; the card just thanked me for choosing them. That would have been enough for me, but they also included a packet of seeds. Nice touch
- The dry cleaner sent me a handwritten postcard. It had a picture of him standing in front of the store, waving. I loved it
- The service station that dispatched the free AAA tow truck sent my car a get-well-soon card. The back of the card listed all the services the station offers
- My vet sent me a condolence card when my cat passed on. Even though I've since moved across town, I still go there with my new cat

I realize that large-volume stores might have more difficulty with the idea of a personalized note, but if at all possible try it. It's so much more effective than a form letter.

Where do you suggest the person power comes from?

If you're not able to tap your own resources, you might want to reach out to the community. Pocket change makes for a good incentive.

- Retired people are a wonderful resource
- Utilize interns from colleges and universities, and high school students
- Check the senior citizen centers

Who would you recommend I thank?

Those people who:

- Buy your product
- Come to your seminar
- Use your service
- Come into your store

Where do the names come from?

- From the business cards placed in the fishbowl by the register, or the sign-in sheets your greeter fills in
- From the bounce-back cards
- From the sales slips
- From the patient register
- From in-store promotions

Just a thank you note?

Putting in a generic discount coupon is a nice gesture. But I wouldn't use it to sell anything or to announce new merchandise.

Saying thank you is a great way to enhance your word-of-mouth marketing. People are so surprised when they get a thank you note, it's been my experience that they just have to tell their friends. Try it and see what happens! Let me know.

NOTE: And oh yes, thank you for buying this education resource tool.

Part II

NAME RECOGNITION

16

FLIERS

The paper trail that leads to success

What is the purpose of fliers?
- To educate and inform
- To promote ideas
- To present a call to action

How can I make my fliers most effective?
- Be clear. This is the most important key to effective fliers
- Present the intention in multiple ways to be sure you get the message across
- Know your intention and show your intention
- Use a typeface, headline, and visuals to support your message
- Color code the paper to enhance your message (red for urgency, green for money or success, royal blue for power, pastels for soft news)
- Question the role of each editorial and graphic decision as it pertains to the message you're trying to get across

What makes fliers good marketing tools?
- They can be read at a glance
- They establish curiosity
- They capture interest quickly
- They can lead to action
- They have the ability to generate results
- They're less time-consuming than a brochure
- They contain more information than a standard business card
- They don't require much time or attention

What are the classic mistakes I should avoid when making up fliers?

Sophia Tarila, author of *Flyers That Work: Promoting Products Events, Services and More*, teaches these key elements in her seminars.

1. Putting too much information on the flier. This is not a book, it's a flier—a quick take for immediate action
2. Using multiple typefaces. Use only one or two typefaces for the total content of the flier. One for 80%, another for 20%, probably in larger type. Three is possible if it includes your company's special typeface. Too many typefaces may defeat your purpose
3. Hiding pertinent information in small type or in the middle of a paragraph. The reader is likely to toss out the flier because you've made it too difficult to figure out. Shout out that important information by way of bold type, larger type, type set off from other information, boxed type or different type.
4. Putting too little contact detail or information on the flier—leaving off addresses, phone numbers, times, and dates, and making it more difficult for the reader to participate
5. Not proofreading before printing. When people see misspelled words, you've lost them. The trust level of a quality product, event, or service is diminished if you can't communicate to the reader in simple and proper English
6. Boring presentations with all the same type. Make your flier more interesting by varying the size, style, and placement of the type (centered, right flush, left flush). Use bullets. Where text is unavoidable, use serif type as opposed to sans serif type
7. Being visually deprived. A photo or graphic can say so much more than words. It's okay if your visual doesn't represent the person, place, or product but just acts as an attention getting element. It shows your effort to communicate
8. Carrying negative energy. If you create your flier under pressure or when you're in a bad mood, your flier holds that energy. Create your flier when you're feeling good, clear, excited about your project. Set your stage—with

nice music, a clean desk or whatever it takes you to put yourself in a creative space

RESOURCES

Book
Flyers That Work: Promoting Products, Events, Services & More by Sophia Tarila, PhD. Available from New Editions International, Inc., P.O. Box 2578, Sedona, AZ 86339; (520) 282-9574; fax (520) 282-9730; *newedit@sedona.net*; *http://infinite.org/newedit*. Sophia also offers an incredible resource directory: *New Marketing Opportunities: The Business & Trade Directory for the New Age/Metaphysical Marketplace*

17

BUMPER STICKERS

Declare yourself!

Why is a bumper sticker a good marketing tool?
Bumper stickers are moving business cards. They are a good marketing vehicle for free publicity and advertising because:

- You have a captive audience
- They don't take a lot of concentration to get the message
- They cater to curiosity
- They cater to emotions
- They can fill a need
- They can solve a problem
- If they're controversial they'll be memorable
- They can start conversation
- They entertain
- They can make people think

Can you give me a business marketing application?

In *Big Ideas for Small Service Businesses*, Marilyn and Tom Ross tell of a gas station operator who gives a bonus to anyone who'll stick on his bumper sticker. Everyone who agrees gets a free gallon of gas with each refill of ten gallons or more. The bumper stickers reads, *I buy my gas from Jim Breeson—5th and Marlowe.* This anecdote came from the 1994 edition of the book, and even then more than 1,000 people were driving around advertising for Jim. You can imagine how many he has now.

I've seen bumper stickers promoting local charity events, sports events, even a garage sale.

What makes a good bumper sticker?

I asked this question of Erin Rado, who creates customized bumper stickers as well as sells conventional messages. Her *What Makes a Good Bumper Sticker©* guidelines include:

- Clarity is rule number one
- A single line is best, more than two lines is crowded and doesn't read well
- Brevity is the soul of wit
- Don't use fancy fonts such as Old English or most cursive scripts. Make it easy to read
- The best type is Times New Roman in bold, or Bookman Old Style

Where's the best place to have them printed? Do I have to use a specialist?

No, you don't have to use a specialist. Any shop that does T-shirts, silk screening, or screen printing can make bumper stickers.

Can you give me some inside information so I can be prepared?

From Erin Rado's *What You Need to Know to Make a Bumper Sticker©* comes these useful tips:

- The price is based on the quantity ordered, the number of colors, the stock used

- Use vinyl, not paper; it won't disintegrate and it keeps the ink from fading
- One color should cost thirty to fifty cents for 500 to 2,000
- If you use more than one color, the cost goes up because you use more screens, therefore the labor is more
- If there is a screen charge, it should only be a onetime fee
- Artwork should cost an average of $10 to $20 an hour to create
- Creating a bumper sticker is a little like creating a campaign button; you have a small amount of space to say a large thought. Be succinct and you'll be successful
- To make a bumper sticker last, think timeless

Can you give me some examples of best-selling bumper stickers?
- NEVER trust a person who doesn't like CHOCOLATE!
- My other car is a broom
- Don't follow me, I'm following my bliss
- Minds are like parachutes: They must open to work
- Pro is the opposite of Con, therefore progress must be the opposite of Congress
- Guns don't kill, people do . . . HELLO! They kill with guns!
- Keep your laws out of my body
- Friends don't let friends vote Republican
- Ignorance, bigotry, and hatred should not be family values!
- And on the seventh day, God created chocolate
- Do not meddle in the affairs of dragons; you are crunchy and good with ketchup
- Ginger Rogers did everything Fred Astaire did, only backward and in high heels
- Those who laugh, last
- And the ever popular. . . . Practice random kindness and senseless acts of beauty!

What can really maximize this bumper sticker opportunity?
Turn your bumper stickers into T-shirts, mugs, caps, buttons, et cetera

RESOURCES

Expert
Erin Rado; The Goddess Shoppe; Box 6399; Fullerton, CA 92634-6399; (800) 777-1185. The Goddess Shoppe is a full-service distributor. Besides buttons and bumper stickers, the shop publishes metaphysical books and makes costumes for Renaissance fairs

Books
Big Ideas for Small Service Businesses by Marilyn and Tom Ross; Communication Creativity; Box 909; Buena Vista, CO 81211; (719) 395-8659

Turn your bumper sticker into Badges
Turn your bumper sticker into a badge using the Badge-A-Minit button-making system for your computer. The system comes with *Print Artist* graphic software and *Badges on Disk* layout disks. Dept. HOF296; Box 800; LaSalle, IL 61301; (800) 223-4103. Call for prices.

18

DESIGN YOUR OWN CALENDARS

Name recognition 365 days a year

Why is a calendar a good marketing tool?

The fall brings more than just leaves and sweaters out of mothballs. It is also the official arrival of calendar season. According to the Calendar Association of Libertyville, Illinois, the 1996 season brought 4,500 calendar choices . . . in many different shapes and sizes.

The Calendar Association statistics show that only 2% of U.S. households are now calendar-free, and that the average home has about five calendars.

How expensive would it be for me to make my own calendar?

You can go through the photo shoot and print it as a big four-color job, or you can buy existing calendar shells and attach your name to it.

Where do I get the calendar shell?

Ask any large printer or promotional items company. Associations and organizations will often supply their members with the opportunity to buy in bulk.

What if I don't want to use the conventional fall scenes or rainbows, but rather something more personal without the big expense of a photo shoot?

Depending on your need for professionalism, you could take your own pictures, then take them to a photo house to duplicate and mount. Then you buy calendars from a stationery store and attach them to the mounted photo(s).

Take pictures during the year of the people with whom you do business, and use their photos, with permission, for your calendar.

RESOURCES

Promotional Companies

- Jay Kristal; Crystal Kreations; 156 Fifth Ave.; New York, NY 10010; (212) 243-5489; fax (212) 243-6193: *http// www.crystalkreations.com*
- Shirley Palmer; Shirley's PR Works; PRomotional PRogram, PRoducts and PRemiums; 7947 Amestoy Ave., Van Nuys, CA 91406, (800) 892-2418

19

ESTABLISH A SEAL OF APPROVAL

Or disapproval, as the case may be

What is a seal of approval?
Usually it's recognition given to a product, place, or concept that meets certain standards created by an organization or person. But people can also be awarded a seal of approval.

What's the benefit to the giver and the receiver?
To name a few benefits, traditionally both get increased:

- Name recognition
- Sales or business where appropriate
- Renewed public interest and education
- Community goodwill

What's the history of the seal of approval in the business arena?
Good Housekeeping magazine was one of the first to use this promotion tool to its advantage. It's given within the family of *Good Housekeeping* advertisers, and carries great meaning in the marketplace.

The Good Housekeeping Institute has a select staff of more than seventy highly trained professional chemists, engineers, home economists, and other experts in science and technology. This dedicated group has two complementary responsibilities: evaluating products by rigorous, state-of-the-art scientific methods and, as editors of *Good Housekeeping*, communicating their findings impartially to the magazine's readers in the form of valuable buying information.

More and more associations and watchdog agencies are giving out a seal of approval. Its purpose is to inform and educate the consumer on the good, the bad, and then some.

J. D. Power & Associates conducts several studies each year and awards its seal of approval to winners in several categories. It was the company's announcement in the business section of the winner of their Frequent Flyer Satisfaction Study that most recently caught my eye.

How can I go about giving my own award?
- Contact the Consumer Product Safety Commission or the Department of Consumer Affairs for a free list of watchdog agencies. The list might help spark some ideas for your own business, product, or concept
- Contact an organization about giving a local award
- Develop your own award based on a hobby, interest, or community need

Can you give examples of how a business can become involved in awarding a seal of approval?
- Toy stores can give a toy safety list
- Baby furniture stores can piggyback with a product that a watchdog agency has already endorsed.
- Teachers can award children's films
- A retail store can approve of environmental products
- Parents can recognize good teachers
- Nonprofit organizations can honor people who make a difference

When I create this seal of approval, how do I tell the public it exists?
Notify the print and electronic media in your area (Part VII, "Using the Media to Word Out"). Be prepared to tell:

- How you came upon the idea of giving it
- How the honoree is chosen
- Why this person is getting the honor
- When the ceremony is taking place

How can I make the award into a media friendly event so I can maximize exposure?
- Present your seal of approval at a community organization meeting

- Hold a cocktail party at your office
- Hold a dinner at a local restaurant
- Plan a banquet and sell tickets
- Hold a fund-raiser
- Give the honoree a money award along with the seal of approval

Is it best to give an award in your own industry?

Not at all. You don't have to be involved in the industry to give a seal of approval. Survey your data base and ask them what toys, what household equipment, what environmental products, what movies would they want to receive a seal of approval.

Remember that people love a hero and like being associated with those on the side of truth, honesty, and justice. And if you are the sponsor, then you too get to bask in the same glory.

NOTE: Don't just give a seal of approval, give a seal of disapproval. Nothing creates attention like controversy!

RESOURCES

- Office of Information and Public Affairs; Washington D.C. 20207; *www.cpsc.gov*
- Department of Consumer Affairs; 750 17th St N.W., Suite 650; Washington, D.C. 20006; (202) 395-7900; fax (202) 395-7901
- Consumer Product Safety Commission; Silver Spring, MD; (301) 504-0580 fax (301) 504-0862

20

GIVE AN AWARD

And the winner is . . .

There you are, stepping up to the microphone, opening the envelope, and gleefully announcing to the crowded auditorium: "The winner of the Anne's Dairy Cream Student Scholarship Foundation Award, for a four-year paid scholarship to the University of Iowa, is . . . Thea Berlin!"

As you wrap the tearful recipient in an Anne's Dairy Cream Scholarship Award Winner sweatshirt, you present her with an oversize cardboard tuition check while the news cameras flash and roll. A reporter presses a tape recorder in your face, wanting to know, "How do you, the owner of Anne's Dairy Cream, and you, Thea, the recipient of the prize, feel at this moment?" The story appears on the front page, the ceremony is on the three daily news broadcasts, and the local radio station mentions it in all its news programs.

Within the next few weeks you and Thea are guests on local radio and community TV talk shows. You're invited to speak at the chamber of commerce and service clubs. You're besieged with offers to speak at high school assemblies on leadership and success.

How does this involvement benefit the sponsor?
- Quality name brand recognition, with more than just a "buy my product" attitude reaching hundreds of thousands of people
- Emotional tie-in that fosters name and product loyalty
- Customer delight
- Networking
- Free advertising

How do I evaluate the worth of this type of event?

- If you were to send a direct-mail piece to each newspaper subscriber and each member of the radio and TV audience, what would your hard costs be?
- If you bought time on radio and television to equal the event coverage, what would it have cost?
- If you had invested in the same size ad the picture and newspaper coverage provided, what would it have cost?

Besides media cover attention on the night of the award, is there any other coverage?

The award ceremony was part of a campaign that included:

1. Phase 1: the announcement that began the annual award search
2. Phase 2: the announcement of the semi-finalists
3. Phase 3: the winner presentation ceremony
4. Phase 4: the ongoing "Where is she now?" publicity

Do all awards have to be as big in scope as this?

Definitely not. An award can be as simple as choosing a category of excellence and awarding a plaque on behalf of your appreciation.

Jazz flutist Herbie Mann owns Kokopelli Records. Every year Herbie recognizes a nonmusician whose contribution of service and creativity enhances the jazz community. The award is a statue of Kokopelli, the Native American god/goddess of creativity and fertility, the same symbol Herbie has for his record label. A double name recognition whammy.

What are some examples of award categories?

- A service award to a tireless member of the community who has unselfishly contributed his or her time and effort
- A hero. Someone who has shown bravery above and beyond the call of duty
- The best teacher
- The best care-giver
- The best pediatrician, chiropractor, et cetera
- Small business achiever
- Patron of the arts

- Most honest politician
- Clergy who most promoted community interfaith relations
- Most environmentally conscious business

For example, Warren Olney, host of 89.9 KCRW-FM's "Which Way L.A.?" was the 1996 honoree of the Planned Parenthood Los Angeles' Distinguished Service Award. He was recognized for dealing with issues on his show that affect women and families.

How can I share the process with my employees?

Giving an award takes only time and effort on the part of the giver. Poll your employees for their suggestions on categories. The ceremony doesn't have to be a huge event; you or your employees can present the plaque, statue, unique gift, or certificate in your office.

NOTE: If you get involved in this form of visibility marketing, please let me know. I'd love to include you in my next book.

21

SPONSOR AN AWARD

The next best thing to giving one

What's the alternative to creating an award if I don't want to work all that hard?

If you want to contribute to the community, but don't want to get involved with the nuts-and-bolts grunt work, then sponsoring rather than creating an award could be the answer.

Sponsoring an award is basically the same as sponsoring an event or a contest. Find an existing award that, if you hook up with it, will give you name recognition, lead generation, and networking capabilities, and offer your support in the form of your name, money, services, or a prize.

The host organization does the work and you share the glory and goodwill, and garner self-esteem through your contribution.

How can I find out what awards are in existence?

Contact the social page of your local newspaper. Since these editors write about them, they would know about them. The newspaper research department would also be able to help.

The same applies to your local television news shows. Tell them what you're looking for, and they'll send you to the right department.

You could also check with the library, which would have the newspaper clippings on file, probably on microfilm. This is also a good way to see what you'll be getting yourself into, media wise.

You might also check with your chamber of commerce.

Can you offer some "hookup" suggestions?

- A landscaping business can join with a garden nursery to give the "Best Garden Award" or the "Best Landscaping Award" by an amateur
- A fitness club can join with a doctor to give the "Healthy Campaign Award"
- A personal security company can join with local law enforcement to give the "Hero Award"
- A real estate company can join with an activist group to give a "Community Watchdog Award" to any activist group or local community neighborhood watch group

NOTE: Sponsoring an award can be just as successful and meaningful as creating one, when you find the right match.

22

CREATE A CONTEST

And the winner is . . . you too!

Why are contests such a great marketing tool?
A contest provides you with:

- Name recognition
- A data base
- Publicity
- Goodwill
- Positioning in the marketplace
- Employee pride and delight
- Imaging in the community

Do you have an example or have to use a contest as a marketing campaign?
American Airlines and Citibank teamed up for their annual "What I Did for Miles" contest. Citibank AAdvantage cardholders were asked to describe their favorite purchase made with their card in one of five categories: romantic, shockingly ordinary, outrageous, celebratory, and humanitarian. The prize was 100,000 AAdvantage miles for the contestants and increased goodwill plus name recognition for the sponsors.

What needs to be considered in choosing to do a contest?
A contest fits the profile of all your marketing tools:

- You need to evaluate cost, time, and people involvement
- You must consider how well it penetrates your target market
- It must deliver what you are expecting to get from holding the contest

• It must fit your needs, or it is not a productive way of spending your time or money

Do contests have to be long and involved to be successful?
• If you're looking to expand your data base, then a simple coupon mail-in-and-win contest is sufficient. This can be done through direct mail, advertising, or a news release about the contest telling the public where to mail their names and addresses for the drawing
• If you're looking to attract people to your store or service, then an in-store, onetime coupon or multiple visit purchase card pickup for an in-person prize collection could be a more appropriate approach. Wild Oats Community Market in Santa Monica, California, held a make-your-own-ritual mandala contest. Since this contest was to encourage shoppers to use the store, the owners did two things:

1. The newsletter mentioned that the store's selection of beans, pastas, and candies made wonderful creative mandala-making items
2. To enter a mandala in the contest, customers had to bring it into the store
3. All participants received dried fruit rolls, and the winner took home a basket full of Wild Oats logo wear. That's good ongoing visibility marketing right there

• If you're looking to announce a new product, then a name search contest is a good hook. Actor Charlton Heston announced to the world he was too close to his life to pick a title for his autobiography, and invited the public to contribute title suggestions. The award was a personal appearance with Heston along with a media photo opportunity and a signed copy of the book, finally titled In the Arena
• If you're going for the educational aspect and name recognition, you could do what a biology teacher has done for the last twenty years. Wanting to pass along his appreciation of ornithology (the study of birds) to his students, he created a birdcall competition. For the past several years, the winners have won more than a cash

prize; they've appeared on "The Tonight Show" and now on "The Late Show with David Letterman"

Is there a book of contests I can study?

If you're looking for ridiculous, sublime, or somewhat memorable, *The Guinness Book of World Records* is filled with the biggest, the best, the brightest, the heaviest, the most, the longest, the tallest, the smallest, and so on. Undoubtedly it is the best place to find great ideas for, and examples of, contests.

What if I want a contest that will give me a long-term imprint in my target market?

If you're looking for long-term community outreach that establishes considerable name or product recognition, then I suggest a more meaningful type of contest that involves education and not just activity, such as the following examples:

- As publicity officer for a symphony orchestra in a midwestern region my client was always looking for ways to outreach into the community, drawing people closer to the wonders of music and keeping them there. She was looking for long-term devotion and contributions.

  Her contest needs were centered on making the next generation a part of the ticket-buying public, and that included enlisting the interest of the current generation for its support. She already sponsored a student education program of lectures, demonstrations, and "Meet the Visiting Conductors" through the school system. What she was looking for was something with pizzazz that would give more sizzle appeal to the passing of the generation baton.

  I took her "passing the baton" statement literally, suggesting a contest where the winner, drawn from the entire state's music classes, would win a chance to lead the symphony for one number.

  The contest would create great goodwill, not to mention the ongoing local and regional semifinals contests that would keep her in media sizzle all year round.

  The contest was a huge statewide success, and with her team of volunteers and interns, she did just fine.
- An advertising agency opened a division targeting new

businesses, figuring it could help them grow into mature, sizable accounts. My company suggested a contest that would put the agency in contact with virtually the entire business community, allowing them a perfect opportunity to show its wares while contributing something meaningful.

In order to involve the adult business population, we targeted their children. The campaign vehicle we created was an art contest titled "My Favorite Place in Town Is . . ." The art contest was a coventure with the schools, and we chose elementary grade six. The schools facilitated the contest, getting the children to draw their favorite place as best they could, whether a park, a building, a tree, or their mother's lap.

We listed every business category that could be useful to the project, sending our client out to engage participation in this coventure adventure. We needed display space for the drawings, so our client met with malls, banks, and corporate buildings with large ground-floor lobby space. To secure client introductions to the downtown retail businesses we created an art walk that would utilize store windows to display the entries.

We asked graphic artists to make signs, paper companies to donate the drawing paper and stationery, art supply houses for the brushes, paints, et cetera. Video companies were approached to make a documentary of the project. We needed secretarial help, copy places, answering services, business machines. If it did business, it was on the list.

The art walk was a favorite of the media. They gave us massive coverage in the weekend section the whole month of the contest.

Judges were recruited from the media and government. Members from every service club—from the Boy Scouts, Girl Scouts, Lions, Rotary, Kiwanis, and the Police Athletic League—were enlisted as official Art Walk Volunteers. We signed up the retired, the unemployed, anyone who wanted to be a part of the event.

The contest was planned to raise funds for participating schools, and the business community came out in force, donating the paper, layout designs, and distribution so drawings could be converted to a 365-day wall calendar, a 365-day tear-off calendar, a fifty-two-week and a twelve-month meeting planner. Drawings were made into posters, bumper stickers, greeting cards, postcards, and bookmarks. There were T-shirts, mugs, place mats, and anything else that could display the designs. A fabric company created bed and bath accessories.

Since proceeds were going back into the schools, catalog costs were donated and businesses were encouraged to buy the products as holiday and year-round gifts. Stores were solicited to sell the products and the catalog. Credit card companies inserted the catalog announcement in their billings, and restaurants included a marketing insert with their meal checks.

The campaign was hugely successful. Massive amounts of media attention were logged all through the year-long campaign. There was a picnic honoring all the artists and the entire community of participating companies. Of course the food and entertainment were donated.

The newspaper dedicated a page listing all the participants, and the TV stations aired the documentary several times.

And yes, the advertising agency received a host of new business.

What are some suggestions for a smaller scale contest?

- If you're a bookstore, conduct an essay contest for college-bound students and provide books for the year
- If you're an association, service, or business, ask your clients, customers, or patients to choose their best teacher, doctor, supermarket bagger, or bus driver, and give away a year of products or services to the winner and the company that suggested them
- If you're an art gallery, hold an art-graffiti contest and auction the winning paintings for sale
- If you're a garden nursery, hold a "name that tree" contest, then donate trees to the local park or parkway in both your names
- If you're a consultant, offer your present and prospective client list a chance to win your services if they can provide the best example of the strangest business story, largest growth figures

Is there a way I can participate if I'm not able to organize a contest?

By all means. If you can't create a contest, then read the next chapter on how you could sponsor a contest.

NOTE: Everyone loves a winner, and contests provide just that. They also provide you with a winning marketing strategy. Try one. The joy of presenting the winner is outmatched only by the joy of the business you get from name recognition, lead generation, and referrals.

23

SPONSOR A CONTEST

A prize is not concerned with the person who gives it

How involved do I have to be if I only want to sponsor a contest?

Your involvement can mean money, time, people support, facilities, media buys, prizes, et cetera. You could even be the type of partner whose name alone would add great credibility to the contest, and you wouldn't have to do anything except show up to help announce the winner and have your picture taken.

What kinds of contests work best?

All contests work best, if what they do is what you need. And just as importantly, it's how much attention the contest gets before, during, and after that contributes to the success you need to make it worthwhile to be involved.

What are some examples of contests that don't require too much money to sponsor?

• If you're a diaper service or baby food distributor, hook

up with a baby furniture or a children's clothing store. Then align yourself with a battered women's shelter or a family homeless shelter. The store has the contest drawing for your goods and services that you'll donate to the winner, and to the shelter. Because there is no purchase required, this encourages foot traffic in the store, giving the public an opportunity to be introduced to your merchandise and the store's as well

- If you're a retail provider, you can hook up with a school to sponsor an essay contest. Ask for an essay on a topic such as most favorite, least favorite, biggest, best, most memorable, why we should . . . et cetera
- If you're a camera store, you can hook up with a civics class or a community club and sponsor a "Meet the Candidates Day Treasure Hunt." Working with the schools or organizations, you provide disposable cameras, and the entrants must take their pictures with the candidates. In order to get the parents out to vote, have the rules include the statement, "Must be accompanied by one or more parent." Give them lists, and the one with the most candidates' pictures and signatures wins cameras, classes, film developing certificates, et cetera. Have the candidates situated in all the government buildings or offices so everyone also gets an education
- If you're a printer, hook up with a messenger service and sponsor a recruiting contest for new messengers or a competition among current ones
- If you're a hotel, hook up with a linen or mattress company and hold a recruiting contest for chamber people, or have the "Fastest Bed Making Contest" involving your current employees
- I represented the original singing telegram company, and when we needed new singing delivery people we held an "Open to the Public" contest. The media loved it! We got a florist, a cookie company, and a messenger service to sponsor it

Anyone with a business, talent, product or concept can sponsor any type of a contest. It's a great vehicle to get your name out there, year after year.

If I sponsor the contest, how can I protect my investment and make certain there will be media coverage?

Although there are never any guarantees that the media will show up, if you don't alert them to the contest they can't possibly know about it.

There are three ways to handle this:

1. Hire your own publicity consultant, PR company, or event specialist to help you with the media process
2. Use the contest benefactor's media relations or event specialists. You can stipulate that the contest benefactor must have a publicity company or consultant in order for you to be involved
3. Read books on the subject and do it yourself (see Part VII, "Using the Media to Get the Word Out")

Where do I find a good publicity company, PR consultant, or event specialist?

The best way to retain an expert in this field is to call your local newspaper and ask the feature section editor for the name of several companies or individuals with whom they work well. Also ask who to steer clear of, and the reasons behind both referrals.

Or, when you hear or read about a local contest, call the organization holding or sponsoring the contest and ask for the name of the publicity person.

NOTE: When you sponsor a contest you offer others a chance to benefit from exposure they might never get. Sponsoring a contest is a good thing.

24

CREATE AN EVENT

Everyone loves a happening

What is an event?

No matter how large or small, or whether you wear jeans or a tux, events are definitely a great way to get your name out there in front of your public or prospective public, over and over again. The term *event* can be used to represent:

- A conference
- A gathering
- A parade
- A seminar
- An award presentation
- A book signing
- A Thanksgiving dinner for struggling comedians and actors
- An animal show at a retirement home
- A fashion show at a mall
- A store opening
- An in-store contest
- A hayride

But for promotion purposes I want you to think of an event not as a specific promotional effort but as an overview of all that goes into that effort. There is more to an event than a dinner dance, a ball, a gala affair, first night at the theater, symphony, or opera, or a museum exhibition.

Can you give examples of doable or manageable events for small businesses and service providers?

- PROGRAM USES BLOCK PARTIES TO PROMOTE SAFETY IN CITY

City officials encourage neighborhoods to sponsor block parties by loaning them a block party kit which includes road barricades, a barbecue, volleyball nets, folding tables, and a helium tank with balloons . . . all free

- STREET SENSE: WEEKLY FAIR HELPS MERCHANTS

After a large warehouse chain opened in his town, the president of the merchants' association organized several like-minded small business people and started a festival on Friday nights. The event was named Family Nights. It brings 8,000 to 10,000 potential customers past the retail store's front doors every week, and it costs the merchants nothing

- NOON MUSIC

Harpist gives a lunchtime concert at a downtown mall. Free

- MALL TO DISPLAY WORKS OF ART BY STUDENTS

A shopping center may not be most people's idea of an art gallery, but for eight art students it'll do just fine. Through the end of the month, ten banners created by these students will be exhibited in Center Court

- AURA FIXATION

Photographer of people's magnetic fields (called auras) gives lectures on auras, takes your aura picture, and then interprets the colors. Held at the library. Lecture free; picture $20

- BABY FURNITURE STORE TO SPONSOR VIDEO-YOUR-CHILD DAY

In case of emergency, parents are encouraged to have fingerprints, a videotape, an audio recording, and a still photograph of their children. Area businesses are donating the tape and film, and local photography studios will take the photos. The police will be there to do the fingerprinting honors. Channel 4 news anchors will act as spokespersons for the event

- **A PERMANENT FOR THEIR HAIR TO HELP EASE THE BURDEN OF NOT HAVING A PERMANENT HOME**

A hair salon owner sets up a director's chair outside his shop every Sunday, offering a spruce up or makeover to the residents of a different shelter each week

- **CHILDREN'S HAIR SALON OFFERS FREE HAIRCUT TO A HOMELESS CHILD WHEN YOU GET YOUR CHILD'S HAIR CUT**

A children's hair specialist beckons families to participate in a hair exchange. Certificates are given to both sides, and the families can meet and share the experience if they so choose

- **CHILDREN'S SHOE STORE TO SPONSOR ANIMAL ADOPTION DAYS**

A local merchant and animal lover is helping the ASPCA with its adoption program. Try on a Pet takes place every Sunday from eleven to three. When a pet is adopted, children also receive a discount coupon on a pair of shoes for any member of their family, but not for the pet

- **DUCK REGATTA TO BENEFIT CHILDREN'S LEUKEMIA**

All bets are on for the fifth annual Duck Regatta on the Lackawanna River. Ducks will enter the water at the north end of the avenue to the side of the railway station at 3 P.M. Sunday. Proceeds of all bets will go to Mercy Hospital's Children's Leukemia Wing. A cocktail party follows in the Radisson Hotels' Train Station restaurant. The adoptive family of the winning duck receives a ride in the retired but still proud *Phoebe Snow* engine cab.

- CHIROPRACTORS TO GIVE FREE SCREENINGS TO INFANTS AND CHILDREN

Infants who cry constantly might be suffering head and neck discomfort from the birth process. The Montana Health Clinic offers free screenings to all infants and children under thirteen every Saturday morning from nine to noon. Don't be afraid to come, as "no bones will be cracked." There are other methods to help heal the pain. Come learn and see for yourself how the healing art of chiropractic works. Screenings are free. Call Dr. Loraine Bonte at (310) 453-6127 for more information

How can I learn more about events?

The best source is your daily newspaper. Every day there are announcements of meetings and events going on around town. Sometimes these listings are on a page of their own, and in other newspapers each section displays its own category.

On Thursday or Friday, newspapers usually run a section such as "Weekend Happenings," "What's Going On," "54 Hours," "72 Hours," "The Weekend Parade," "Free and Not So Free." Study these sections. Use them to come up with events you can adapt for your needs.

TV and radio community bulletin boards also list events, as do local magazines.

NOTE: With these helpers, creativity can be a joy.

RESOURCES

- *You Can Hype Anything, Creative Tactics and Advice for Anyone with a Product, Business or Talent to Promote* by Raleigh Pinskey (Citadel Press)
- *The Zen of Hype, An Insider's Guide to the Publicity Game*, an eight-audiocassette home study publicity course by Raleigh Pinskey (310) 209-0990. *Raleighbk@aol*

25

SPONSOR AN EVENT

Giving comes in many shapes and sizes

How can a small business help sponsor such large events as marathons, sports tournaments, and the big televised Fourth of July fireworks displays?

You can be a participating sponsor for all those events. Each and every one of you can do something for almost every event imaginable that will cost you practically nothing but time and/or services with no significant cash outlay, and you can still be considered a bona fide sponsor.

What's a participating sponsor?

Let's take your local ten-, five-, or even two-kilometer run. The organizers have long lists of service and product needs, but they are usually short on money.

- They need entry forms and all kinds of correspondence printed. Printers and graphics people, are you listening?
- How about data entry? Computer people . . . heads up!
- Maybe they need someone to handle the entry fees, or a bank, CPAs, bookkeepers, or legal counsel
- Even the clergy can be involved
- Restaurants can donate their chefs
- Businesses can volunteer for beverage pouring or serving the pre-event dinner
- How about you massage and body balance professionals?
- What about volunteering your services in the runners' tent? Several of us were studying the Japanese healing technique jin shin jyutsu in Hawaii at the time of the triathlon. We offered our services to jumper cable the run-

ners' energy and care for their body health. It was a great
experience, and we were thanked in the postrace publicity

How can I sponsor something more in the arts field?

You can sponsor the opera, ballet, symphony, or any number of arts-related organizations.

How is sponsoring an event a good marketing tool?

- Many events take out ads in newspapers and trade journals
  listing sponsors and volunteers. It's surprising the number
  of people who read that seemingly never ending list of
  thank yous
- You get to network
- Your name appears in the program in big print

Is sponsoring only for events and galas?

Not at all. Sponsoring something, anything, no matter how
large or small, is still sponsoring something. And most of all,
remember that you don't have to sponsor an event in your
own industry or field of expertise. See the sections, "Relationship Marketing" and "Networking." There are many
more examples of sponsorship in the chapters "Sponsor an
Award" and "Sponsor a Contest."

Here are several examples of getting to your target market
or potential markets by using other hosts for what you have
to offer:

- A children's shoe store can sponsor a pet adoption, either
  at a pet store or on premises
- A clothing store can sponsor a nonprofit organizational
  effort to plant trees on Arbor Day
- A baby furniture store can sponsor law enforcement efforts to implement a child safety day

Any more words of wisdom?

So what can you do for a ten-kilometer run, AIDS walk,
charity gala, telethon, or even the local PBS membership
drive?

Can you offer the services of your company? Can you offer
your company's people power during the workday? Your de-

livery trucks during off-peak hours? Your printing presses during downtime?

I belong to the nonprofit group Earth Communication Office (ECO). Among many other great environmental efforts, ECO volunteers its time and expertise in producing those great earth awareness movie shorts for which the studios so graciously donate screen time. All the people who contribute services that go into making those shorts are sponsors of ECO, and appear on the group's literature as such.

One of the great side effects of sponsorship, of being personally involved as well as having your employees or fellow workers participate, is increased pride in belonging to a company that shares and cares. Self-esteem in the workplace is a nice side benefit for some time and services, don't you think?

So find your niche. Find an organization and offer to sponsor or be a partial sponsor.

NOTE: Be a sponsor. Be involved. It's good for giving and getting business. Sharing and caring and just plain feeling good about yourself are also good. Remember, what goes around comes around.

26

DONATE PRODUCTS OR SERVICES TO CHARITY AUCTIONS

Giving to get, a win-win situation

What's in it for me if I donate goods or services that cost me money?

This goes along with the ''how much does it cost to get a client, customer, or patient'' theory.

Figure out the cost to you of your product or service. For products it's the hard cost of the product added on to the hard cost of doing business. For services it's a little different: how much your time is worth plus the hard cost of doing business.

Put that up against what you'll save in advertising and marketing costs. I bet you get more than you give!

How is this a good marketing tool?
Just to mention a few things, you get:

- Name recognition
- Goodwill
- Visibility
- Networking
- List acquisition
- Market expansion
- Publicity

How do I find out about a charity auction?
Constantly check the social section or calendar listings of your newspaper for announcements of lunches, dinners, dances, lectures, theater parties, outings, meetings, for:

- Charity events
- Association events
- Service organization events
- Businessmen/businesswomen's events
- Children's events

How do I get my product or services into the auction?
Call the RSVP number and offer your product or service. It's that simple.

Do I have to wait for a specific notice of an event, or can I just call?
You don't have to wait for a specific auction to donate your products and services. I've never been to an event yet that didn't have a raffle. It's been my experience that it's safe to assume every meeting and every event has a raffle, a table gift, a sample or goody bag, or some sort of gold fishbowl giveaway that you can take advantage of.

NOTE: I was at a meeting once where the gift was so popular the donor was swamped afterward. Instead of giving out her business card, a gesture sure to lose many of the ready-to-buy impulse shoppers, she pulled out a bunch of discount coupons for the same item. She told me she gave out twenty-seven coupons, and twenty-one came back into the store. Trust me. Donating your product or service is good business.

27

PROCLAMATIONS AND CELEBRATIONS

What a difference a day makes

Did you know that for every one of the 365 days, fifty-two weeks, and twelve months in the entire year, more than 10,000 people, places, things, and organizations have a day, week, or month dedicated to their cause?

Chase's Calendar of Events, The Day-by-Day Directory to Special Days, Weeks and Months, and *Celebrate Today* by John Kremer, are two books that list celebrations, events, and observances of all kinds from all over the world.

What are some of the categories I can hook up with or designate as my own?
  • Proclamations
  • National days and state days
  • Sponsored events
  • Astronomical phenomena
  • Historic anniversaries, folkloric events, and birthdays
  • Religious observances
  • Festivals
  • Culinary celebrations
  • Entertainment awards

How is this a good marketing tool?

Proclaiming your own day, or capitalizing on someone else's birthday or anniversary, is a wonderful opportunity to do some visibility marketing.

Take Valla Dana Fotiades, an author, speaker, and consultant on the topic of self-esteem. If you turn to page eighty-two in *Chase's*, sandwiched in between Humpback Whale Awareness Month and International Embroidery Month is Valla's own *International Boost Your Self-Esteem Month*, February.

Valla proclaimed it and then submitted it to *Chase's* for a listing. She's even built an organization around the month (see the chapter, "Start an Organization, Club, or a Salon").

What happens after I proclaim it?

Chase's and *Celebrate Today* are used by the media for filler items. During the month of February, Valla is often called on for an interview to discuss International Boost Your Self-Esteem Month.

But she doesn't sit and wait for the calls. Each year, with ample time to spare before deadlines, she sends out news releases to schools, associations, and organizations, encouraging them to adopt the program and celebrate it their own way. Then she sends releases to the media, reminding them it's that time again.

She assists the organizations with information on how to petition local government to proclaim their very own role in the monthlong celebration, and how to get the media's attention.

Everywhere Valla speaks she encourages people to celebrate the month with events. She has suggestions, but she encourages participants to be creative and to add their contribution to the mix. Then she shares this information in a newsletter, which she also sends to the media.

How can those in retail or the health field use existing historical dates or events for marketing?

These are existing dates in *Chase's* that you can join forces with, or think up your own:

- Pet stores: Responsible Pet Owner Month, sponsored by the ASPCA
- Women's organizations: Women's Heart Health Day
- Mattress and bed linen stores: Sleep Safety Month
- Pizza parlors: Great American Pizza Bake
- Sporting goods: Babe Ruth Day
- Bookstores or libraries: Edgar Allan Poe Day

What are some ways to celebrate the date?
- Honor it with a sale
- Hold a contest
- Have an in-store promotion (see Part IX, "In-Store Promotions")

Be creative with your hookup. The more creative and the more bizarre, the more involved, the more visibility, the more notoriety.

How do I go about getting a mayoral proclamation for my day, week, month, or year?
- For local proclamations: Contact the mayor or city council's office and ask for guidelines and an application
- For state proclamations: Contact the governor's office
- For senatorial or congressional proclamations: Call the appropriate office in your state capital, district, or the main number in Washington, D.C.
- For presidential proclamations: Call the White House

How far in advance should I contact the proper political office?
Deadlines being what they are and bureaucracy being what it is, I recommend you check at least a year in advance. But if you're reading this book now and either don't have a year or want to plan something immediate, give it your best shot now. I requested and received a mayoral proclamation in New York City within one week of an event.

Always ask. What's the worst that could happen?

What are some ways I can stretch the marketing beyond the proclamation itself?
- Use it as part of a direct-mail piece or a broadcast fax

- Make it into an invitation
- Put it on T-shirts
- Develop an advertising campaign around it
- Make it into plaques and give them as presents
- Offer a proclamation as a door prize at your event
- Don't forget to tell the media about it

NOTE: Submit your custom-created day, week, month, or year to *Chase's* and *Celebrate Today* by calling and requesting an application. Good luck. Let me know what you've created. I'd love to add you to my next book.

RESOURCES

Books
- *Chase's Calendar of Events*, Contemporary Books, Dept. C; 2 Prudential Plaza, Ste. 1200; Chicago, IL 60601-6790, (312) 540-4500
- *Celebrate Today*, by John Kremer, Prima Publishing; Box 1260BK, Rocklin, CA 95677; (916) 632-4400

28

PRESENT SEMINARS

Share and prosper

Why is presenting a seminar a good marketing tool?
- It is a highly effective means of positioning yourself or your business in the marketplace
- It is a promotional vehicle that increases awareness of what services you offer
- It shows your expertise on the subject matter

- It establishes you as a spokesperson in your field
- It provides you with name recognition
- It sets you up as a consultant on the subject matter

Take the case of Suzie Pruden. In New York, she was a household name. But when she moved to Los Angeles, she was just another expert in the personal growth industry. Advertising was expensive, so to rev her engines in a new community she set about giving seminars, and in no time at all her name was once again in the forefront of decision makers. She has made a name and a lucrative consulting business for herself, not to mention she's a sought-after speaker for conventions.

Mary Samuels, a corporate downsizing casualty, became a nutritional products distributor. Pressed for time and financial resources, she chose to showcase her product not by joining organizations but by giving seminars on "How to Create a Successful Home-Based Business With $39 Down." With that hook she attracted audiences like flies, advancing up the quota ladder in no time.

I go to seminars, but I never thought about giving one. How do I go about doing so?
There are two basic types of seminars:

1. Self-promoted
2. Those hosted by someone else

What is the best route if you're just starting out with limited funds but boundless energy?
If you're just starting out, depending on your finances and level of seminar savvy, your needs might be better suited if you try number two: those hosted by someone else. This way you're bankrolled while you're getting your name out there.

Who are these people and how do I find them?
- Check events listings in the newspaper. Call the RSVP phone number and ask for the program chairperson. Tell that person you're interested in presenting a program that will benefit the organization's members
- Contact the chamber of commerce. It maintains a list of

local organizations and associations such as Rotary; Kiwanis; Lions; Women in Business; sales and marketing executives; the Marketing Club; et cetera. The chamber also books speakers for its own meetings

- The chamber of commerce or your local government offices maintain lists of area businesses and corporations. Suggest to the sales or marketing manager that your area of expertise can contribute to the staff's productivity, attitude, teamwork, skills, techniques, et cetera
- Check with your local library. It often presents community programs. Being an author is not always a prerequisite
- Call bookstores. Many rent meeting rooms for seminars. Here, too, being an author is not necessary
- Contact your local college, university, or adult education facility. I did this and ended up on the faculty at UCLA Extension (see the chapter, "Teach a Class")
- Contact church and synagogue men's and women's clubs

Do clubs and businesses pay speaking fees?

As a general rule, nonprofits and service clubs don't pay. Many national associations and organizations don't either. Sometimes they will pay your expenses, and many times they won't. But as in life there are always exceptions, and so I have learned that "all speeches are paid until proven unpaid."

I've been told by some organizations that they don't have the money in the budget to pay. Do they always mean it, or do they have a budget but try to get you for nothing?

Sometimes the phrase "we don't have a budget" really means that if they can get away with having you speak for free, then they can apply the money elsewhere. Politely suggest your desire for an honorarium (a fancy way of asking for a speaking fee), and negotiate until you have a win-win compromise. Sometimes even gas money or lunch is considered a good win-win compromise.

If you're going to be treated like a professional, you need to present yourself like a professional. You need to establish a fee and sell yourself with that fee. Setting fees is a whole topic by itself, and can be found in depth in Dottie and Lilly Walters' *Speak and Grow Rich.*

What if there is no fee. Should I turn it down?

Remember that speaking for free affords you the opportunity to:

- Build a reputation
- Acquire a data base
- Get exposure
- Attract media attention
- Get referrals
- Collect testimonials and endorsements

But in the long run your mantra, your cause, and your object should not be "I want to be a speaker" but "I want to be a paid speaker!"

What are the pros and cons of doing self-promoted seminars?

- The pro side is that you're in complete control of everything from soup to nuts. You choose the location, food, setup, and time frame
- This can also be the con, because you're the only one to blame if the seminar doesn't come off the way you've represented it in the brochure. Even if the hotel is to blame for any snafu, it ultimately reflects on you because you are the sponsor.
- The biggest pro of a self-promoted seminar? If the seminar makes money you get to keep it. The biggest con? If you don't bring in the bucks, you get to pay all the bills.

What's the scoop on speakers bureaus?

Speakers bureaus are in business. If you command fees of $2,000 to $2,500 and more a speech, then they'll consider representing you as part of a roster of many speakers.

Dottie Walters of Walters Speakers Services has produced a two-tape series called *Being Booked by Speakers Bureaus: Everything You Always Wanted to Know About But Didn't Know Who to Ask.* It's very helpful.

How do I make my talk exceptional?

- Provide your audience with a success opportunity
- Provide high content and lots of information

- Teach skills
- Nurture attitudes
- Solve problems
- Give answers
- Add value to people's lives
- Offer benefits that improve current status

Can you give me some examples of topics that will bring them through the doors?

Topics are like flavors of the month: popular today, gone tomorrow. But these few seem to display staying power, often attracting the many:

- How to make money
- How to invest money
- How to get a better job
- How to get a date
- How to have better relationships
- How to feel better
- How to move forward
- How to be successful
- Any timely topic

Can you give me some suggestions on how to develop topic ideas?

- Watch news broadcasts and talk shows to see what's currently on the minds of audiences
- Attend meetings in your own or related fields and listen for topic ideas
- Study the calendar section in the daily and Sunday sections of your local newspaper for topics and issues already in the seminar loop
- Browse the bookstores. Study current and best-seller nonfiction release titles
- Check out the school of continuing education catalog for nonacademic course topics
- Ask your librarian about the most requested nonfiction topics for research and pleasure
- Check the bookshelves at airports
- Look through magazines

How do I capture potential participants beyond my personal data base?

- Renting lists from a broker is one way to approach new markets (see the chapter, "Using Commercial Mailing Lists")
- Depending on your marketing budget, invest in a small ad or a classified in a local alternative paper or business journal (see the chapter, "Classified Ads")
- Advertising on a popular and complementary radio talk show is also appropriate marketing behavior
- Publicity! Send the who, what, where, when, and why, in other words the topic, place, address, time, admission charge, and your name to the calendar section of all the local newspapers, plus the commercial TV, public access TV, and radio community bulletin boards. Call and check on their deadlines. The media usually require your information, or copy, two to three weeks before the event (see the chapter, "Calendar Listings.")
- Call the talk radio stations and ask the programming department for the shows that best suit your topic. They'll give you the producer's name, and you take it from there (see the chapter, "Be a Guest on TV and Radio Talk Shows")

Where can I obtain a local media list?

You can compile your own, because all media are listed in the yellow pages under Radio, Television, and Newspapers.

But if you're the instant gratification type, check with the chamber of commerce or the mayor's office. Call and ask if they have a media directory, and could they send you a copy. Sometimes there is a small fee; often it's free.

Don't forget your local library. It has everything and is happy to share.

RESOURCES

Speakers and Trainers Organizations

- Toastmasters International, Box 9052; Mission Viejo, CA 92690; (714) 858-8255; fax (714) 858-1207

- National Speakers Association (NSA); 1500 South Priest Dr.; Tempe, AZ 8528; (602) 968-2552
- American Society for Training and Development (ASTD); 1630 Duke St.; Box 1443; Alexandria, VA 22313; (703) 683-8100
- The International Society of Speakers, Authors, and Consultants; Box 6399; Kingwood, TX 77325-6399; (713) 354-4440; fax (713) 354-4615
- Walters Speakers Services; Box 1120, Glendora, CA 91740; (818) 335-8069: *Call4Spkr@aol.com*

Associations and Organizations

- *Encyclopedia of Associations*; Gale Research; 835 Penobscot Blvd.; Detroit, MI 48226; (800) 877-4253
- Directory, Meeting Professionals International; 1950 Stemmons Freeway, Ste. 5018; Dallas, TX 75207; (214) 712-7744
- *National Trade and Professional Associations of the United States;* Columbia Books; 1350 New York Ave., N.W., Ste. 207; Washington, D.C. 20005; (202) 737-3777
- *Nationwide Directory of Association Meeting Planners*; 1140 Broadway; New York, NY 10001; (800) 223-1797

Books

- *Everything You Wanted to Know About Being Booked by Speakers Bureaus But Didn't Know Who to Ask* by Dottie Walters; Walters Speakers Services; Box 1120; Glendora, CA 91740; (818) 335-8069; fax (818) 335-6127; *Call4 Spkr@aol.com*
- *Fearless and Flawless Public Speaking With Power, Polish and Pizazz* by Mary-Ellen Drummond (Pfeiffer & Co.)
- *Flip Charts: How to Draw Them and How to Use Them* by Richard Brandt (Brandt Management Group)
- *How to Develop and Promote Successful Seminars* by Howard Shenson (John Wiley)
- *How to Talk Your Way Onto Talk Shows* by Raleigh Pinskey; (310) 209-0990
- *How to Run Seminars and Workshops* by Robert Jolles (John Wiley)

- *How to Put on a Great Conference* by Dorian Dodson, (Adolfo St. Publishing)
- *I Can See You Naked* by Ron Hoff (Andrews and McNeel)
- *Money Talks: The Complete Guide to Creating a Profitable Workshop or Seminar in Any Field* by Dr. Jeffery Lant; (617) 547-6372
- *Power Presentations* by Marjorie Brody (John Wiley)
- *Sharing Ideas Magazine;* Walters Speakers Services; (818) 335-8069; *Call4Spkr@aol.com*
- *Speak and Grow Rich* by Dottie and Lilly Walters (Prentice Hall)
- *The Quick and Easy Way to Effective Speaking* by Dale Carnegie (Pocket Books)
- *You Can Hype Anything: Creative Tactics and Advice for Anyone With a Product, Business or Talent to Promote* by Raleigh Pinskey; (310) 209-0990; *Raleighbk@aol.com*

Audio

- *Mega-Success System for Speakers: How to Build a Maximum Income Speaking Business* by Dan Kennedy; Empire Communications Corporation; 5818 N. 7th St., #103; Phoenix, AZ 85014; (602) 997-7707; fax (602) 269-3113. Marketing expert Dan Kennedy offers six audio cassettes and six sets of notes and printed information in one notebook on the business of speaking
- *Present With Success* by Marjorie Brody; (215) 886-1688; *BC886S@aol.com; http//:www.Brody.comm.com*
- *Best of the Masters*, 6361 Yarrow Dr.; Carlsbad, CA 92009; (619) 929-1019; fax (619) 929-1073; *somrob@aol.com*. This includes audio and video programs of some of the best speakers on the speaking and training circuit

Video

- *Present Like a Pro* by Marjorie Brody (215) 886-1688; *BC886S@aol.com; http//:www.Brody.comm.com*
- *Life Is Like a Presentation* by Marjorie Brody

NOTE: I strongly suggest you peruse your bookstores and library shelves. *Books in Print* lists more than 325 books under the categories of seminars, speaking, and public speaking.

29

TEACH A CLASS

A classy way to market yourself

Why should I teach an adult education class?

Continuing or adult education programs in colleges and universities are a good way to promote yourself and get business. The great thing about this avenue is that you get your name marketed in the community, you get attention and credibility for free, and you get paid for your efforts, too. Now that's what I call a bargain and a half!

How do I get my name marketed in the community when I only have fifteen students in my class?

It's the catalog mailing we're talking about. I taught a nine-week course in public relations for UCLA Extension, School of Journalism and Public Relations, and the catalog was mailed to more than 250,000 names. That means that my name, the name of my first book, *You Can Hype Anything: Creative Tactics and Advice for Anyone With a Product, Business or Talent to Promote*, and the name of my business, The Raleigh Group Public Relations, was promoted by direct mail to more than 250,000 people "× 3."

What does the "× 3" added to the 250,000 mean?

The law of direct mail averages says that the catalog recipient will probably pass it on to three friends. To use the term from the direct marketing industry, this is called the pass-along rate. So multiply the original 250,000 by 3, and now you have my name, my book, and my business probably seen by more than 750,000 people. And I got paid $100 for each of the nine sessions.

I also taught a three-hour course at the Learning Annex in

San Francisco, which has a catalog circulation of 45,000, and
the same course for the Learning Annex in San Diego, where
150,000 people saw my name. Multiply those figures by three
and you have about 600,000 people who saw my name and
credentials.

How do you know that it works?

Years later people who come to hear me speak remember
seeing my course description in the UCLA and Learning Annex catalogs. Good viz-ability, wouldn't you say? And remember I got paid too!

Beside viz-ability, are there any other benefits?

It was an opportunity to:

- Try out my material
- Sell my products
- Build my confidence
- Build my speaking business
- Add to my bank account
- Have my name marketed and paid for
- Do a good deed and teach others how to succeed

When I started doing public seminars, I thanked my lucky
stars for the opportunity to learn from those adult education
students.

Here's another testimonial for "learning and earning," as
Edmund J. Pankau, a National Speakers Association (NSA)
member, calls it in an article he wrote for the speakers' magazine *Sharing Ideas*. He teaches adult education programs in
the same town where he's speaking to earn extra money in
addition to the professional engagement.

Pankau writes, "I spoke at a seminar program on Friday
morning in Washington, D.C. Took the train to New England
and taught a Saturday morning class in Hartford, Connecticut,
and an afternoon one in Providence, Rhode Island. Between
the two programs we brought in 100 students at $39 each, sold
books, tapes, and my new infomercial kit as well. A stream
of mail orders for our products continued from the attendees
for the next two weeks. Each student goes into our ACT data
base and becomes a candidate for both future programs and

products as well as a referral source for outside speaking engagements and business.''

When do I have to contact the schools to set up my dates?

I was in Santa Monica, California, and was going to New York City to give a presentation at the Women Incorporated conference. I wanted to teach at the Learning Annex in New York City and called two months before the conference to ask about availability. I learned that although their course catalog comes out every two months, they schedule classes for listing in the issues that come out three to four months ahead. This is for advance sign-ups and publicity to make the date successful.

Are the fee structures the same in all the programs?

Payment schedules are set up in several ways:

- Straight salary, no matter how many students
- Flat rate to a certain number, and flat rate per student, or head, above that
- Per capita or set dollar amount for each head
- Percentages for each head. This is popular with adult or continuing education courses. When I taught at the Learning Annex, the administrators offered 15% and up, depending on how long you had taught for them, how many students your name brought in, or how big your name value was in general

Can I sell materials at the course?

Course materials are popular money-makers. At seminars they are called handouts or work sheets.

- They consist of anywhere from one to three pages of notes on what you're teaching
- They contain ''take-home information,'' so the audience has a tangible reminder of you and what you have to offer

What's so great about this one- to three page handout is you can charge the students a fee for it. It falls under the category of ''class materials'' in the catalog. But please remember the following anecdote when you set up the class.

I take a lot of courses at the Learning Annex in Los Angeles, as I did when I lived in New York City. Next to the course fee was printed: course materials, $3. It was like another arm or leg to the fee schedule. I never questioned it or asked how it got there or what would make it go away. It was always there, like taxes. When it was my time to teach, I filled out the course description, prepared my handouts, and waited to collect my "extra" $3. As the class filled up I counted the enrollment against the sheet and smiled my way into $3 heaven. "Let's see," I silently told myself, "three dollars times twenty-one is sixty-three dollars."

I brought my handouts in a manila envelope and, as I had seen countless instructors do, I took my handouts out and used that very envelope to collect my $3 course materials fee.

Only something went wrong. The students were up in arms. I had neglected to fill in what I learned was standard operating procedure, and the $3 course material fee didn't appear in the class description, so the students weren't going to pay—no, they refused to pay. Needless to say, I was crushed, and out $63.

Moral of the story, make sure you establish your course material fee with the person who hires you, and make sure you put it in the course description.

Can you describe a handout or work sheet in more detail?

Handout styles largely depend on content and how extensive the information you want your audience to take away. Examples include:

- An outline of the material covered
- Pages from your teaching manual
- Fill-in-the-blank question and answers taken from the outline
- Quiz questions students fill in as you speak
- Article reprints, either self-written or by others, on the topic

When preparing a handout, always:

- Include a brief paragraph on the benefits of what you do
- Mention that you are available for consultations

- Mention that you speak at luncheons, conferences, and retreats
- Prominently display your name, address, and phone number
- Get the school to use your picture or a caricature with the copy

What are some examples of other selling materials?

This is a list of resource materials I sell BOR, back of the room, during intermission and at the end of the class:

- *101 Ways to Promote Yourself: Tricks of the Trade for Taking Charge of Your Own Success.*
- *You Can Hype Anything: Creative Tactics and Advice for Anyone With a Product, Business or Talent to Promote*
- *How to Talk Your Way onto Talk Shows*
- *The Zen of Hype: An Insider's Guide to the Publicity Game: an eight-audio cassette PR home study course*
- *The Media Release Survival Kit*, a 150-plus-page binder of media releases
- 101 *Promotions That Worked and Those That Didn't*
- *Soul Candy, Nourishment for the Body, Mind and Spirit*
- My newsletters, and of course you get a discount on a subscription
- A collection of special reports, concentrated information on various subjects of visibility marketing and public relations that are not in my books
- *Flyers That Work: Promoting Products, Events, Services and More*, by Sophia Tarila
- *Word of Mouth Marketing*, by Gene Call (four audio-cassettes)
- *How to Get 100 Bookings a Year—The First Year: The Rubber Band Circuit, Colleges, Universities and Adult Schools*, a video by Mike Rounds, a speaker who made his living in this niche when he first started out

What if I don't have materials to sell?

Develop some! Many times I have made much more in BORs than I did in fees. Here's another suggestion. If you don't have materials of your own, you can sell other people's. Instead of reinventing the wheel and spending a year writing my own book on the subject, I sell a book called *Flyers That Work, Promoting Products, Events, Services & More* by the very knowledgeable Sophia Tarila of New Editions International, Inc., Sedona, Arizona. I sell other books on marketing, presentations, seminars, et cetera. If it fits what I talk about and I believe in the book, I'll sell it.

Find out who publishes the book, the company, call and order it at its multiple book discount. That way you can make a few dollars on the sale. Don't try to mark it up past the printed price. It makes people very uncomfortable, and stains you as a price gouger. Not a good image to have. Besides, they'll pass up your book and go get it in the store just to save the extra dollars, and to spite you.

How do I get a list of the places where I can teach?

You can check the yellow pages under Schools, the local free magazine stacks for catalogs, as well as the newspaper display boxes on the street.

As for a national list, contact Mike Rounds or the Clearing House of the Association of Adult Education Centers.

RESOURCES

- *How to Get 100 Bookings a Year—The First Year: The Rubber Band Circuit, Colleges, Universities and Adult Schools,* a video by Mike Rounds; Rounds Miller Associates; 6318 W. Ridgepath Ct., Palos Verdes, CA 90275; (310) 544-9502
- Clearing House of the Association of Adult Education Centers, 1554 Hayes Dr.; Manhattan, KS 66502; (913) 539-LERN

30

BE A TOASTMASTER

Smiles and profundities are your calling card

What does a toastmaster do?

A toastmaster is the person at a banquet who proposes toasts, introduces after-dinner speakers, and keeps the program moving. But as all things evolve, it has also come to mean the person who delivers the keynote speech for the breakfast, lunch, or dinner at organizational meetings.

Do toastmasters get paid?

It all depends on the organization's budget.

Why do I want to be a toastmaster?

Speaking for local service, business, and nonprofit organizations is a great way to promote yourself and your business. The main reason is these organizations are in a business-to-business environment. Appearing in front of them in such a high-profile position is great for collecting imprinting points.

It's a great networking opportunity, and you can collect business cards or add the attendance list to your data base.

Do I have to be a professionally trained speaker?

No, you don't have to be professionally trained with lessons and coaching.

What are some of the traits of a good toastmaster?
- A love of communicating
- A flair for performing
- A knack for interacting
- A sense of humor

- An enjoyment of being in front of a crowd
- A passion to want to motivate

What are some tips on how to be a good Toastmaster?

Marjorie Brody, author of *Power Presentations*, speaker, and CEO of Brody Communications, teaches presentation skills to corporations all over the world. She offers these "10 Tips to Becoming a Good Speaker."

1. Plan with the audience in mind
2. Be polished and practice before your presentation
3. Arrive early—get to know the audience
4. Have a strong opening that connects logically and emotionally with the audience
5. Keep the presentation interesting by using examples, stories, and humor that relates to the subject and audience
6. When appropriate, make your talk interactive and include questions throughout
7. Visually look the part—pay attention to dress, eye contact, gestures, body language, movement
8. Have vocal variety to hold interest
9. Work the room
10. End with strength—have a strong close

How do I find these organizations?

Your chamber of commerce has a list of organizations and associations that welcome speakers. In fact, you can use the chambers in any city to acquaint yourself with organizations and associations.

What if I want some formal training?

Check out these avenues to further your career:

- Toastmasters International
- National Speakers Association
- Local continuing education classes

RESOURCES

Book
Power Presentations by Marjorie Brody (John Wiley)

Video
How to Speak for Free and Still Make Money on the "Rubber Chicken" Circuit by Mike Rounds, Rounds Miller Associates; 6318 W. Ridgepath Ct.; Palos Verdes, CA 90275; (310) 544-9502

Organizations
- Toastmasters International, Box 9052, Mission Viejo, CA 92690; (714) 858-8255. Call the national office for the chapter nearest you. The organization also sells videos and audiotapes
- National Speakers Association (NSA); 1500 South Priest Dr.; Tempe, AZ 85281; (602) 968-2552. NSA has an extensive video and audiotape library and a speakers' magazine. Call for a chapter nearest you
- The International Society of Speakers, Authors, and Consultants; Box 6399; Kingwood, TX 77325-6399; (713) 354-4440

NOTE: Check recommended reading resources in the chapter, "Present Seminars."

31

DEVELOP A BOARD GAME

A roll of the dice, moving pieces, and thou

How is this a marketing tool?
Here are some examples:

- Joline Godfrey, the author and well-known women's business advocate, founded An Income of Her Own (AIOHO), an organization that aims to expose minority and at-risk young women to the possibility of owning their own businesses. The tool used to teach group decision making and partnering skills, as well as to stimulate entrepreneurial creativity, is a board game.

  As a marketing tool the game, sold to schools, organizations, and private individuals, acts as a catalyst to spread the word as well as creating a revenue stream for AIOHO.
- Barbara Geraghty, sales trainer, speaker, and consultant, developed a 100% interactive sales training game to develop strategically brilliant salespeople. Teams of salespeople work to creatively achieve objectives and strategically overcome obstacles presented in case studies and clues, and is industry-specific to products, customers, and challenges.

  As a marketing tool it put Geraghty ahead of the pack during hiring decisions. This hiring hook was responsible for 100% of her income during a three-year period. Initially, you couldn't buy this game without buying Geraghty's speaking and consulting services. She and the game became so popular that she attracted the attention of a company that convinced her to let it market and distribute the game through its trainers and consultants, who in turn sell it to their clients. Now Geraghty gets a commission on all sales, setting up a steady stream of passive income.

- When video producer Michael Wiese moved to Los Angeles, he needed to make big noise in a hurry. He accomplished this by developing Goin' Hollywood, a board game about getting a movie produced.

  As a marketing tool it became his calling card. It also brought him a revenue source. *Premiere* magazine gave out 500 as Christmas presents to movie studios, and *Video* magazine gifted video production companies. To add to this exposure, the game generated international media coverage.

What should I include in my game plan?

- Make certain you have a clear objective of the outcome
- Establish player benefits before you begin
- Consider what players should do differently after they play the game
- Make sure the game is fun as well as challenging and motivational
- Make sure the game board is colorful and energizing
- Have a master plan before you begin, and alter it as you test the game
- Make the game so that it gets the players involved with themselves as well as the other players
- Make it knowledge driven as well as chance driven

What are some important do's?

Marion Their is the CEO of Expanding Thought, a company that teaches people and companies how to expand the way they think about change. She developed her Think Tank board game to enhance the training programs she sells to corporations. She gave me these very important do's:

1. Test market until there are no more suggestions from the focus groups
2. Trademark at the beginning stages; don't wait until you're finished
3. Trademark in the categories of Board Game and Computer Game, and include print and electronic rights

4. If you can afford experts, don't do everything on your own
5. Consider certifying and licensing for passive income

After I have the game and design ready to go, how do I get it into a finished format without mortgaging my house and firstborn?
- Heidi Wilson of Operations Resources took her Business Process board game series to a blueprint service. The service printed it out on its color plotters. Then she took the finished product and had it laminated. This way she could make different sizes for different applications
- Ask a design or graphic artist for suggestions on creative printing sources

Who besides trainers and teachers can take advantage of this as a marketing tool?
Anyone who needs to educate their client, customer, or patient is fertile ground for a board game:

- Financial institutions
- Health care providers
- Relationship builders
- Entrepreneurs
- Money managers

What are some other applications?
- It's a great trade show booth attention grabber
- It's excellent for employee team-building skills
- It's excellent for problem solving
- It's a great way to break the ice and introduce employees to one another

NOTE: As you can see, board games are not just child's play.

RESOURCES

- Joline Godfrey; An Income of Her Own; Box 987; Santa Barbara, CA 93102; (800) 350-2978 (board game: An Income of Her Own)

- Barbara Geraghty; Idea Quest; (714) 240-8788; *Idea-Quest@aol.com* (board game: Klue)
- Marion Their; Expanding Thought; 3180 Westwood Ct.; Boulder, CO 80304; (303) 440-1278 (board game: Think Tank)
- Heidi Wilson; Operations Resources; 150 W. Iowa Ave., Ste. 202; Sunnyvale, CA 94086; (408) 733-5243 (board game: Business Process)

32

AUDIO PRODUCTS

Credibility in stereo

Why is making audiotapes a good marketing tool?
1. You can sell them to create multiple sources of income
2. You might want to give them to your clients, customers, or patients, creating value added for:

- Customer service
- Holiday gifts
- Networking
- Name recognition
- Free offers
- Contest prizes
- New client welcome
- "Twenty-fifth purchase" by that person

What is an example of a value-added usage?
I came home from the plant store with six new plants, each a different variety. By the time I tried to remember which got what fertilizer and how often to water them, I had already sealed their fate.

I called the nursery and recommended that they provide their salespeople with cassette players to record the care and feeding of nature's children at the same time they're advising the customer.

Avery Labels has computer labels for audiocassettes. Print your business name, logo, and contact information, and you have a dynamite customer service vehicle that would stand up with the most elaborate plans.

This application goes for anyone explaining anything to someone.

What if I want to do a whole line of product care or service explanations?

There are two ways to do this. The first is a simpler version of the two, involving less bells and whistles, but more personal elbow grease:

1. You could produce and record audiocassettes at a studio, or you can do it yourself at home with high-quality equipment. Then place the recorded cassettes in those plastic cases (known as jewel boxes). Add on the computer printed labels. This version has no cover art or information jacket (called a J card)

2. You could produce audiocassettes that have music, another voice for introductions and transitions, vinyl album packaging, professional artwork, and printed or dye-stamped labeling

How does the first one work, the one without all the bells and whistles?

- Write the script
- Find a studio to record the material
- Hire a producer familiar with spoken word recording (or don't hire a producer and wing it)
- Find a duplication facility
- Find an audio album cover supplier

See the chapter, "Audio Business Cards–Brochures" for resources.

You mentioned that I have to write a script. How do I do that?

Ask yourself:

- Who is my audience?
- What do I want them to know?
- What do they want to know?
- What is the easiest way to tell them?

Can I outline it?

Outline it only to see what you want to cover. You must script the whole thing. Every word.

What if I'm not capable of doing this?

Hire a writer. Look in the yellow pages or call the journalism department of your local educational facility.

Or make it a group effort. Ask your employees to contribute questions most asked and questions most answered.

How much more difficult is it if I want to go the second route and create a more professional image?

Difficulty, as with beauty, is in the eye of the beholder. Just because there are more bells and whistles doesn't mean it's more difficult. To me, it's difficult when you do all the components yourself.

If you want the production to be first-class through and through, my advice is to hire the professionals whose business it is to walk you through the process. Give it up to them instead of trying to do some or all of it yourself. Piecework, until you know the industry and what you should be looking for, can produce a shoddy product. A shoddy product doesn't serve the purpose you set out to accomplish.

How do I find these people?

Go to the source. Many of you have bought tapes at seminars. Call the seminar presenters and ask these questions:

- Who produced their tapes?
- Would they use them again?
- If not, who would they recommend?

What's the most important thing to look for when hiring a "soup to nuts company"?

Janita Cooper works at Master Duplicating Corporation, "a soup to nuts company." She feels that "most professional companies will do a good job for you." What you really need to look for, along with the usual contractual questions, is:

- How do you get along with the people you would be working with?
- What kind of impression do you have about them?
- Are they concerned about customer service and customer satisfaction?
- Are they patient and considerate of nonexperienced people?
- Are they too busy for small orders?
- Do they return your phone calls promptly?
- Do they ask you if you have questions, and do they answer those questions to your satisfaction?

Can you give me some overall production tips and product enhancements?

These come from *What You Really Need to Look For In a Production Company* by Janita Cooper of Master Duplicating Corporation:

- Hire a professional voice to introduce you on your program. You may even have to hire a professional to do the entire tape. There are voice-over companies that specialize in this. (See the chapter, "Hold Buttons" for a profile on Berkley Productions.) You can also hire a local radio personality
- Add music to the beginning, end, and transitions. It's a minimal expense and adds professional quality. (See the chapter, "Hold Buttons")
- Have three copies of your script: for yourself, your producer, and your engineer
- Do twenty to thirty minutes per side for optimal listening and value perception. The mind tunes out between twenty-five and thirty minutes
- Less than twenty minutes feels like a rip-off to the buyer;

in many cases, more than thirty minutes per side requires thinner tape, resulting in breakage

NOTE: Even if you use a professional company, you still have to come up with the script. No one but you knows the ins and outs of your material, and just what it is you want to communicate.

RESOURCES

- Janita Cooper; Master Duplicating Corporation; 2907 West Fairmount Ave.; Phoenix, AZ 85017 (800) 228-8919 or (602) 279-6297
- Berkley Productions, Inc.; Susan Berkley, president; 780 Piermont Ave.; Piermont, NY 10968; (800) 333-8108
- More resources available in the chapter, "Audio Business Cards–Brochures"

33

VIDEO PRODUCTS

Credibility right in front of your very eyes

Are these the same things as a video business card–brochure?

No. This is what the industry refers to as a long-form video. It's used as a product presentation or promotional tool rather than as a brochure.

What is the video about?

It could be a complete marketing or a sales demonstration, or perhaps a seminar presentation.

How long is a long-form video?

The video business card–brochure averages eight minutes, while the long-form video may average twenty to thirty minutes, an hour, or longer.

This is used for more in-depth coverage of the subject matter, such as a course or an all-you-wanted-to-know-but-were-afraid-to-ask instructional piece.

How do I go about making this type of presentation video?

The same production companies that make the video business card–brochure also make this type of product.

Check the chapter "Video Business Cards–Brochures" for how to do it and resources.

What else can I do with the video?

- Separate the audio portion of the video project and use them both for promotional materials
- Transcribe the video or audio portion and use it for a manual or workbook
- Take some of the important points, and transcribe them for special reports or a newsletter in audio, video, print, or CD-ROM form
- Break up the video presentation, editing it into smaller segments for a video postcard marketing campaign

34

GIFTING PEOPLE RESOURCES

Good things come in breathing packages

What in the world does gifting mean?

Gifting means to sponsor a speaker, a consultant, or any kind of an expert to a person or an organization in need. This is a very simple yet very powerful marketing tool.

What is an example of gifting?

I received a call from a local businessperson who offered to pay my speaking fee. Nothing unusual about that. But here's the catch. The keynote address wasn't for him; it was for a seminar he had gifted to the local boy's club. He put up the money and gave me to them as a gift.

The program read: *keynote speaker Ms. Raleigh Pinskey, a gift from the Foundation for World Peace.*

Isn't that the same as sponsoring you?

Yes it is, but the word gifting has a much deeper meaning. Not only is it similar to sponsoring, but it could be said that it is an extension of a testimonial or endorsement. After all, the person *gifting* me is affirming my credibility, sanctioning my expertise, and supporting my outlook on the subject matter.

How is it a marketing tool?

Because the person who is gifting me gets to have his or her name mentioned right up front, another contribution to the marketing imprint.

What's the best way to go about gifting someone?

As with all marketing:

116

- Determine your market
- Determine your need
- Determine your outcome

What's in it for the both of us?
- Publicity
- Name recognition
- Networking
- List acquisition
- Image enhancement
- Notoriety
- Community acknowledgment
- Goodwill
- A good feeling
- Visibility

NOTE: Be aware that once you are known as a gifter, you may be besieged by every organization in town and then some. But isn't that part of the marketing, too?

35

GIFTING INTELLECTUAL PROPERTIES

*A gift is like flattery—it makes
both parties feel good*

What is the value in gifting someone else's materials?

If all you mail are bills, promotional fliers, and sales letters, your letterhead could lose its charm to your data base.

Put the romance back in your letterhead with other people's materials that charm, educate, and entertain, especially if you don't have a newsletter or if you don't write articles for other newsletters, journals, or magazines and thus can't regularly send these to your loyal followers.

Can I just lift someone's article and send it out under my name?

No. Instead, when you read a particularly interesting article that you feel might also be interesting to others, think about sending a "thinking of you" gift. Of course you'll give the author and publication credits.

Do I need permission?

There is a law that says you can't reproduce copyrighted material without permission. When you take the material to any printer that knows the law, before they accept your order they just might ask you for that permission. I've seen people turned away because they didn't have written permission.

How do I get permission?

The industry term for what you want is a reprint. Getting reprint rights is a very easy process. All you do is call the newspaper or magazine and tell whoever answers, "I'm interested in getting reprint rights." Every newspaper and magazine I've ever dealt with has a reprint rights department.

Is there a charge?

This depends on the newspaper or magazine. They'll ask you why you want reprint rights, in other words what you are going to do with the article. When they know that they'll determine if there is a charge, and just how much it will be.

I've paid $10, I've paid $100, and I've paid nothing. Besides payment, they ask that you put "Reprinted with permission from _____" somewhere on the page.

Because of copyright laws, ask the newspaper or magazine for a letter of permission. It's easier than trying to convince the clerk at a print shop that you really did get permission by phone.

How often should I send articles?

Depending on your budget, I would send an article as often as possible. Once a month, bimonthly, quarterly. It can serve the same marketing purpose as a newsletter. If you have a newsletter you might alternate it with an article.

Can I put fliers and promotional items in with the article?
That's your personal decision. You need to establish why you are sending the article. Is it a gift or an ad for your business? When you answer that you'll know what to do.

What do you mean by gifting information?
Information makes a wonderful present, especially how to books. Each year I would dread the end-of-the-year gift giving. No more. Now I send books, tapes, newsletter subscriptions, et cetera.

How does that help as a marketing tool?
Information is knowledge, and knowledge is power. When you give information, knowledge and power automatically come in the envelope. People who receive such a gift know this. This knowledge is then transferred back to you, the giver.
Write a brief message, sign your name, then sit back and wait for the calls to come in.

Isn't that expensive?
Not really. Not any more than any quality gift you would choose to give.

If I want to give books, can I buy them in bulk somewhere?
Yes, you can buy them in bulk from the publisher. The contact information is usually on the copyright page that immediately follows the title page. When you call, if the number is not for customer service, ask for the special order or sales department. The publisher has special prices depending on how many copies you order.

How do I know which book to choose?
Pick a book that can be useful to everyone. Books on health, basic business (such as *101 Ways to Promote Yourself: Tricks of The Trade for Taking Charge of Your Own Success*), saving money, quotation books (such as my *Soul Candy, Nourishment for the Body, Mind and Spirit*), et cetera.

Is the same idea behind giving gifts as giving videos and newsletters?
How many times have you gone to a seminar and com-

mented to yourself about how your friend would be perfect for that video? Or how many times have you copied someone's newsletter to send to a colleague?

Here's your opportunity to put your money where your mouth is. Call the speakers with the video or with the newsletter and make a bulk price deal. It's in their best interest also.

Videos and newsletter subscriptions cost much more than books. How can I keep the cost down?

You're right. So maybe you don't buy them in bulk like the books. Maybe you select an A list for these gifts.

Or maybe you ask the video and newsletter people if you have anything you could exchange in goods and services to equal the cost of those videos and newsletter subscriptions.

NOTE: Don't forget magazine subscriptions. Bulk subscription prices are available from most publishing houses. When you send gift subscriptions the publishing house sends a notice, or you can send your own along with a personal note. Gifting makes for good business!

36

POSTERS

There you are, larger than life

How can posters be a great marketing tool?

I have posters of myself. When I speak I put a ticket in one of my books. When someone buys the ticketed book, they get the poster that was on the stage with me.

Sometimes I have the audience sign my poster, and I give

it to the meeting planner with all the nice things people say on it.

But how can it be a marketing tool for the small business person?

- Take pictures of your product and have them made into posters for your store window, inside the store, in other people's windows, in other people's stores
- Take your newspaper publicity story and have it blown up to poster size. Take a picture of you and your TV or radio guest and blow it up. Put it in your window, on the wall behind the cash register, your office waiting room, or in the rest rooms
- Make a poster cutout of yourself and put it around your store or in your office waiting room. It's a great conversation piece, and gives people a mental picture of you that they will take home with them
- Speaking of pictures, have your customers take pictures with the cutout
- Posters make great giveaway items
- Use them as a direct-mail piece
- Use them for a contest mailer. Hide a design in the picture. Put numbers in them and have a drawing. The winner must come into the store to pick up the prize
- Hang them from the ceiling like banners
- If they're artful, give them away
- Be creative with the artwork to announce special events. Use the theme in your advertising
- Put your products or service on a poster and print emergency numbers or the schedules for the local theater or sports arena
- Use them for trade shows
- Use them for court displays
- Use them to show off your services
- Use them as giveaways when you give a presentation
- Insert them in trade journals, local papers, association newsletters

Where do I get posters made?
- Any graphics house can help you
- Any photography lab can do it

- Computer imaging places can do it. This place is great for short runs. Just bring them your disk
- Most large print and copy shops have enlarging capabilities off the printed page

If I'm mailing my posters, do I fold them or send them in a mailing tube?

Which would you rather have on your wall, a folded picture or a nice smooth one with no folds or creases? Buy the tubes in bulk. Ask your graphics house for resources.

RESOURCES

Poster Makers

- U.S. Press; Box 640; Valdosta, GA 31603-0640, (800) 227-7377
- National Posters, Box 1448; Chattanooga, TN 37406; (800) 624-0408
- Blow Up Picture Poster Company; 6733 Hollywood Blvd.; Hollywood, CA 90028; (213) 462-8243
- Look in the yellow pages under Posters. I found the Blow Up Picture Poster Company under Photo Finishing–Retail

37

MID-AIR MARKETING

*Is it a bird, is it a plane, no,
it's your name in mid-air*

WHAT IS AIR RECOGNITION?

Promotions using everything from skywriting to hot air balloons, and all that flies in between.

WHAT MAKES AIR RECOGNITION GREAT FOR MARKETING?

It's great for name recognition. I'm told that beach communities are big on skywriting and banners for all kinds of beverages and marriage proposals.

WHAT ARE SOME EXAMPLES?

- Marketing experts Brad and Alan Antin suggest you "wait until your competitor is having a big sale or event. On that day, hire a skywriter to perform right above his store." Those Antins know their stuff
- I heard about a writer who hired a banner plane to fly over the Oscar ceremonies trailing a banner that advertised "the world's funniest script" and, of course, a phone number
- 20th Century Fox promoted the movie *Independence Day* with four flying banners, one behind the other: "No Warning," ... "No Negotiation," ... "No Los Angeles," ... "Independence Day, July 3"

What other kinds of air recognition can I use?

Hot air balloons are also a great way to fly. You can even have them made in all kinds of shapes. But even the conventional ones with your logo and company name are great name recognition.

- Albuquerque, New Mexico, has the largest hot air balloon event in the world. If you have a national or international product, there are hundreds of festivals, fairs, sporting and entertainment events where you could exhibit the balloon
- If you're local but want the charisma a balloon creates, then rent a balloon for a product or service promotion
- To announce a new product, I suggested to a client that we hold a two-for-one contest. The prize was a ride in a hot air balloon for the winner, and we added a make-a-dream-come-true gift for a terminally ill child or adult. We had an abundance of media attention!
- How about the event I orchestrated for a wedding photography studio? We held a drawing for a hot air balloon wedding. My idea was to do a one-step wedding. We called churches, temples, catering facilities, wedding gown stores, photographers, florists, stationery stores, limousine companies, jewelry stores, travel agents, and beauty salons to ask if they wanted to join in the promotion. We got one of each, and it was a huge success. What a promotion that was! Everyone benefited greatly and prospered from the name recognition. The media pickup turned out to be more national than local, generating requests across the country for people who wanted to take advantage of the *One Stop-Balloon Shop-Air Hop*

Can you recommend any smaller flying objects for a smaller budget?

These are referred to as *spotlights,* because they attract a great deal of attention. They can be helium filled, cold or hot air filled, and they come in all shapes, sizes, and prices.

Why are these such a great marketing tool?

I had three months to buy my godchild a present. But while driving down an interstate highway, I saw this huge Godzilla floating in the sky over a toy store . . . I pulled right in.

NOTE: The Goodyear Blimp is available to nonprofit organizations, but only for public service announcements (PSAs)—no more free rides for charity. There are three home bases. Contact the blimp base in your section of the country and ask the public relations manager for the PSA guidelines.

Pompano, Florida: (954) 946-4629

Akron, Ohio: (330) 796-5272

Carson, California: (213) 770-0456

RESOURCES

- Aerostar International: Box 5057; Sioux Falls, SD 57117; (605) 331-3500. Aerostar makes the Macy's Day Parade balloons
- Giant Advertising; 15221 Transistor Ln.; Huntington Beach, CA 92649; (800) 648-7907. Giant makes standard fifteen- to thirty-foot customized baseballs, the Unocal 76 ball, from Snapple to Pepsi
- Look in your yellow pages under Advertising—Outdoor, and Advertising—Aerial for skywriters, hot air balloons, and inflatables. If your phone book doesn't have that listing, go to the library and check the yellow pages of a large city. Companies that advertise usually have 800 numbers and do business anywhere, anytime, anyplace

Newsletter

- *The Antin Marketing Letter: Secrets from the Lost Art of Common Sense Marketing*; 11001 Delmar, Ste. 1200; Leawood, KS 66211; (913) 663-5775; fax (913) 663-5552; *Antin@tyrell.net; 75706.2523@CompuServe*

38

TRADE SHOWS

Booths are us . . .

Do I have to take a booth in those big national shows that come to town?
This is one possibility, but you can also participate in the local trade shows put on by the chamber of commerce or any association or service organization. No matter what the size, the same marketing opportunities apply.

How do I know if the show is the right place for me to exhibit?
There are two basic levels of shows;

- A vertical exhibitor show is one in which the majority of the exhibitors manufacture products for a single market, function, or industry
- A horizontal exhibitor show contains a broad mix of companies that exhibit products from many different industries

Talk to the show manager about your participation if you're uncertain. Ask for a list of exhibitors; see if you fit. That's how you decide if the show is right for you.

What is the primary benefit of this expense and effort?
Trade shows give you a unique marketing opportunity. It's the only place people pay to get in to see products and services. This means there is a certain level of qualified lookers.
Trade shows are the best way to see a great number of people in a very short period of time. Think of it as making more sales calls in an hour than you can make in a day, and

more in a day than you can in several months.

In *Big Ideas for Small Service Businesses,* Tom and Marilyn Ross estimate that using trade shows will cost you just $107 per lead instead of the $230 you'd spend when making a sales call. If you pull in 200 leads, your total savings is $24,600.

What are some other reasons for exhibiting?
- To sell your product(s) to the people attending the show
- To sell your product(s) to the people exhibiting at the show
- To have your product(s) seen by distributors, reps, catalog houses, et cetera
- To test your marketing materials
- To test your promotional talk
- To introduce or test new ideas and concepts
- To test future ideas
- To create an industry or community presence
- To collect leads
- To meet and great your current customers
- To hold meetings with people otherwise unavailable to you
- To get media attention

What about giveaways?
Mark S. A. Smith, the leading consultant on trade show marketing, suggests this strategy in his *49 Ways to Be Your Best at Trade Show Selling:*

"You've been to shows, swiped goodies from the candy jars, collected a bag of trash and treasures, and taken them home to either throw them away or give them to the kids. What impact did these giveaways have on your buying decision?

"If you choose to use a giveaway, make sure you're trading the prize for your visitor's name, address, and phone number, and not just giving things away.

"If you want to attract visitors into the exhibit to qualify them, use a controlled giveaway. Some of the most attractive giveaways are T-shirts, hats, sunglasses, and other apparel. Ask the visitor to complete a questionnaire or have them listen to a presentation to qualify for the prize."

What are some trade show do's?

- A sign with big readable letters is a good people grabber. It makes a better impression if it's color coordinated with your materials. My sign, materials, and products are red, black, and white . . . and so is my suit
- Are your graphics and words easily viewed from all sight lines?
- Friends are great to staff the booth, but make sure they know the product inside and out. They are useless to you if they have to defer the majority of questions to you, especially while you're talking with someone
- M&M's, hard candy in lots of colors, or a mixed bowl offering are good grabbers, because while people are picking out their favorites, you have a window of conversation time
- Offer a show price. People love a bargain. One third to a half off is a good deal
- To collect cards you want to think of giving something away. If you do, make sure it's something someone would want. Do some relationship marketing here. Ask an electronics store if it wants to give away a piece of equipment. For this piece of equipment you'll display a sign with the store's name, contact information, and even dispense its cards
- Have the biggest bowl you can find. That alone will draw them to you
- I always bring blank business cards (you can buy them in a stationery store) for those people who conveniently ran out or didn't bring them. A sign-in sheet will work just as well, though it's often difficult to read the names even when they print them
- Make sure you bring enough media kits and fliers for the *media* room. Ask the show manager what company is running the media room, and talk to them about media kit needs
- Before the show, ask for the media list. Call or write the media and invite them to stop by your booth. Set up an appointment. After the show, for those media who didn't come to your booth, follow up with releases and product information
- Ask if you can give a media conference

- Send invitations to your current client data base. Many shows will give you a number of free passes. Don't forget to put your booth number on the invitation, as well as a map of the hall. Mark your booth with an X
- Since you'll be giving away a TV or a VCR or some type of electronic equipment in conjunction with another store, include this information in your invitation. It gives people who know you a better incentive to come see you at the show
- Make sure you talk to show management, even if you've done shows before and know what to expect. It's always good to check in and let them know who you are in case you need anything
- Especially talk to show management a day before the show to find out what exhibitors are having parties and seminars
- Ask the show manager if there's a show raffle to which you could contribute your product or service. Don't you agree that having your name announced over the loud-speaker is a good thing?
- Either bring lots of business cards and brochures, or do what I've learned to do: I take several laptop computers to my booth. On one computer I have the prospects type their names and addresses into my data base. On the second computer I have a fax-on-demand system (see the chapter, "Fax-on-demand"). Here they can select any document that interests them, and I have it faxed to their office. Don't forget to have a card bowl for those who might not want to stop long enough to do the computer entry

How can I maximize my trade show experience?

Know why you're taking a booth, then you won't be out of line if your goals aren't met

- Are you there to get leads?
- Are you there to get noticed?
- Are you there to sell your product?
- Or all of the above?

What's the biggest mistake made in trade show participation?

Every expert and every successful participant has talked about follow-up as the key to trade show success.

What's the key to follow-up?

Mark S. A. Smith told me that more than 80% of all sales leads are not followed up effectively. Mark says that when you follow up immediately after the show, you will be way ahead of most companies. If you have a small exhibit, get those leads off to the main office today, by overnight mail, or enter them into a computer and modem them to the office. If you're expecting lots of visitors, consider hiring local help to enter the lead data into a portable computer on the spot. This will eliminate the time lag when you return to the office, plow through your in tray, and go to meetings, and then get to the leads a week later. This happens more often than most companies wish to admit.

NOTE: If you are interested in exhibiting locally, request a convention calendar from your chamber of commerce or the convention center to find out who's coming to town.

RESOURCES

Mark S. A. Smith consults, writes, and speaks on how to make tons of money with trade shows. His company, Valence Press Publishers, has a library of resources I highly recommend.

- *49 Ways to Be Your Best at Trade Show Selling* (book)
- *How to Get the Most Leads for Your Trade Show* (video)
- *The 10 Things Most Companies Do at Trade Shows That Don't Work and How You Can Fix Them* (video)
- *7 Steps to Trade Show Success* (audiotape)
- *Trade Show Secrets* (audiotape)

Contact Mark at The Valence Group; 3530 Cranswood Way; Colorado Springs, CO 80918; (800) 488-0780; *MSASmith@aol.com*

Books
- *Guerrilla Trade Show Selling: Meet More People, Get More Leads, and Close More Sales* by Mark S. A. Smith, Orvel Ray Wilson (coauthor of *Guerrilla Selling*), and Jay Conrad Levinson (coauthor of *The Guerrilla Marketing Handbook*), Houghton Mifflin
- *Big Ideas for Small Service Businesses* by Marilyn and Tom Ross; Communication Creativity; Box 909; Buena Vista, CO 81211; (719) 395-8659
- *Guide to Profitable Trade Show Marketing and Exhibit Selling;* Skyline Displays, Inc.; 12345 Portland Ave., Burnsville, MN 55337-1585; (800) 328-2725

39

WRITE ARTICLES

Be a feature in a featured article

Why is writing an article so important?
- Writing an article automatically puts you at the top of the experts' list
- It's very good visibility, reaching thousands of prospects in one effort
- It affords great name recognition
- It reaches thousands of people for *free*
- It shows that a prestigious media outlet thinks enough of you and what you have to say to put it in print, thereby endorsing your expertise
- Articles are a better representation than most any brochure you could put together
- Having a mailing piece from the reprint enables you to reach thousands more people

Do article writers really benefit from sending out the articles to their data base?

Peter Meyer of The Meyer Group specializes in helping executives and managers get more results with less time, fewer people, and less money. This is what he told me:

"When I started my practice, I decided that I wanted to have an article published every six months or so. I knew that no one would read them, but I wanted the reprints to use as mail pieces. I had no idea how thirsty the media are for content. I now have a backlog of requests, am a contributing editor to a prestigious journal, and publish about as often as I care to. I have been in *The Wall Street Journal, The Business & Economic Review, Entrepreneur*, and *The Canadian Business Review*. They have so much more value. The articles are responsible for a steady stream of business that brings six figures to the bottom line every year. Now, instead of sending brochures, we send copies of the articles."

But I can't write!

It's interesting what happens to people who talk their knowledge all day, and when you ask them to put what they know and say to clients, customers, and patients on paper, this is what I usually hear. Are you one of these?

- "Write an article? Me write an article?"
- "I wouldn't know where to begin"
- "My English teacher told me never to write in public"
- "I can't spell"
- "I don't trust my knowledge of grammar"
- "I dangle more participles than all the bungee jumpers in the world"
- "I didn't know you could contribute an article. I thought they had people on staff who did the writing"

I'm still not convinced I should take the plunge. Tell me about more success stories.

- I'd like you to meet my friend Michael Laskow, president of TAXI, the Independent A&R [artist and repertoire] Vehicle for the Music Industry. When I explained how he could get the equivalent of a whole page of advertising by writing an article, it was if a gigantic cartoon light bulb went off in his head with the words "Wow, I can do that." Since that AHA moment he's had at least one article published in a national trade publication every month for the last eighteen months. One drew as many inquiries as placement in four $1,200 ads. That one paragraph generated 756 responses, resulting in $15,000 worth of business at $350 apiece.

An article for a recording studio magazine grew into a monthly column, expanded into a newsletter now sponsored by two prestigious audio equipment manufacturers, inserted in the very same recording studio magazine for which he wrote the column. This newsletter-insert accounts for a third of new clients

- Another success story is Susan Berkley, president, Berkley Productions, Inc., specializing in voice and presentation skills training. She was ready, not once but twice, to plunk down $3,000 for an ad in an industry trade journal. She was in my seminar audience when I stressed how many editors welcome articles on topics that benefit their audience, for free. It took her two weeks to process this information and get up her courage and overcome her fear of selling herself
- Look for the masthead, the list of magazine editors and employers, usually found in the first five pages. Look for the editor's name, then the telephone number; then take a deep breath and take the plunge. Also, it is a good idea to write down two or three topic ideas and be ready to defend or sell them. The editor Susan called picked not one but three topics, requesting a 1,500-word article on each. This ten-minute phone call yielded articles two pages in length, worth the equivalent of $3,000 each page in advertising costs
- Results? In the first week of publication Susan netted two consulting positions worth $50,000 each. Now do you have your pen ready?

How do readers contact me to hire me or buy my product?

The usual agreement between author and editor is the editor gets an article for free, and you get your name, address, phone number, and the possibility of a picture in lieu of payment. This small but significant contact paragraph placed at the beginning or end of the article does three things:

1. Presents you as an expert, provides credibility, and allows for a certain positioning in your appointed field
2. Provides your contact information
3. Shows your parents you are a contributing member of society and really do work for a living, even though it's not a nine-to-five job

If publication doesn't provide that information, should I do it anyway?

Contact information can be a deciding factor whether or not I'll submit my article to that publication. If publication doesn't provide it, then I look at circulation, target readership, and how I will be positioned, and then I make my decision. Sometimes the magazine will print your picture and your byline, but no phone number or address. But all is not lost if there is no contact box. If people really want to get to you, they'll call the magazine; they will either be given your information or will be told to write you in care of the editor and your mail will be forwarded.

Do I get paid for my articles?

Payment. Now there's an interesting word and subject. At many publications money is neither the payment nor the reward. Here is how the hierarchy of the school of payment thought goes:

- Editors feel they are providing you with an avenue (some feel they are doing you a favor) by giving you the opportunity to expose you and your work to their readership (this is okay with me)
- Editors who are grateful to have you, the expert, perk up their pages have been known to sometimes offer ad space (I always try for this negotiation anyway)
- Editors who do pay money. Monetary remuneration can be a flat fee or by the word. I've been offered anywhere from ten to fifty cents a word. One of the highest fees I've

heard of is *Parade* magazine paying $4,000 for 1,500 words, but then again it is not a trade journal

But remember this. If you accept money then by rights the publication owns the article.

Does the publication own it forever?
You need to establish your policy up front and make your decision accordingly. These are your options:

• Some publishers retain what is called first run rights. They decide on how many months before the article reverts back to you for you to use as you wish
• Others will claim ownership forever as work for hire
• Others don't care, giving you carte blanche to use it wherever and whenever you please right from the start

What kinds of publications take articles?
There are three readership categories:

1. Trade journals (magazines, newspapers, such newsletters as *Motorcycle Industry Magazine, Los Angeles Business Journal, Communications Briefings*)
2. Consumer publications (magazines and newspapers such as *Working Woman, Parenting, Cosmopolitan, GQ, People*)
3. Like-minded publications, a cross between consumer and trade (semitechnical, genre specific, such as *Stereo Review* or *Harley Women*)

Trade publications are industry- or topic-specific. The word "trade" reference takes its meaning from the ancient trade unions, and now today's retail market, which deals "to the trade only."

This type of publication, sometimes called a vehicle or house organ, usually has a controlled subscription, but there are those that do accommodate outsiders.

But what I know isn't applicable outside my field of interest.
Now, don't turn the page just because you don't think you

know anything about semiconductors, house painting, or international banking. Before you go, take this short quiz:
True or false?

- The office staff of a semiconductor company can benefit from time management techniques
- The telephone operators at the house painting scheduling office benefit from pointers in presentation skills
- The office managers in the international banking division can benefit from customer relation skills
- IBM managers can learn about sitting and standing properly from a chiropractor

Obviously, the answers are all true. And that's the joy of writing articles. You can impart information and play ball even though you aren't part of that playing field. Now here's the tough question. True or false?

- Everyone can benefit from learning about skills, training techniques, interpersonal relationships, client management, visibility marketing, smile training, stress management, lead generation technology, and a list of hundreds of other topics

Right again. The answer is true. See what I mean? Now do you have your computer warmed up?

What if I suffer from writer's block?
- Pretend you are writing a letter to your best friend telling her all about what you do and how it can help others. Right away you'll have the makings of an article
- If you give a speech at the Kiwanis or Rotary or the chamber of commerce, tape it and then transcribe it
- Take a tape recorder in your car, and when you're driving to work put your thoughts into it, then have it transcribed
- Any journalism school has someone to edit for you. Look in the yellow pages under Writers
- Take a writing class from your local adult education facility
- Check your yellow pages and the journalism department for local writers' organizations

Where do I find the names of trade publications?

The best way to familiarize yourself with magazines or newsletters is:

1. Focus on the associations and organizations that interest you
2. Then call or write, requesting a copy of their newsletter, magazine, newspaper, or journal. Ask the associations or organizations which publications they subscribe to
3. Look up the industry in any one of the media directories listed below in Resources

How do I approach general-interest magazines?

Each magazine has a specific agenda for submissions. Call the magazine that interests you. You can find its number on the masthead, situated in the first five pages. Make sure you're completely familiar with the magazine before you go ahead and send in your query letter. Go to the newsstand and look the publication over carefully. It's senseless to waste the editors' and your time if the magazine isn't appropriate to your subject matter.

Is it possible to get published in general-interest magazines?

I was attracted to the new *International Business Woman* magazine. I went through all the steps, and the editors accepted my article on visibility marketing. They liked it so much they made me the visibility marketing columnist. Be persistent; your efforts can pay off.

Then what?

- If you want to submit an article, you have to send in a query letter. This letter tells the editors the who, what, where, and why of your article content and how you intend to develop the topic or premise
- Each magazine has its own query agenda, so pay attention. It is important that you follow its individual instructions to the letter. The editors don't have the time, energy, or humor to fool around and decipher your codes or your need for control
- They will either give you the agenda over the phone, or

tell you to send them a self-addressed stamped envelope, commonly called a SASE, and they will mail it to you

How about writing articles for newspapers?

Most newspapers, dailies, weeklies, and monthlies have staff writers or get their copy from wire and syndicated services. Newspapers as a general rule don't usually accept outside articles. But if there is an exception, it's easy to find out. Just call up, ask for editorial, and ask if the newspaper accept contributions from outside writers. It can happen especially in local or regional papers.

All papers are open to letters to the editor, commentary and op-ed articles. This is a good way to get name recognition on an on-going basis (see the chapters, "Write Letters to the Editor" and "Op-Ed Pages and Commentaries")

What kind of submissions are newspapers open to?

The weekly and monthly papers are usually open to contributing or syndicated experts' columns, and tips, trends, and surveys. You need to be aware that in many cases smaller papers might charge you for the column inch, because they view your article as an advertisement. Sometimes it's worth the price. I would at least give it some thought.

Any words of wisdom here?

- If you think you have information to give, and people can benefit from it, no matter who they are or what they do or what size the physical plant, then give it to them. Write that article
- Always remember this. People interested in success and being successful are always open to tips and trends, hints and help
- Instead of limiting yourself only to your sphere of influence . . . go out and influence other spheres

RESOURCES

For publishers of directories of trade and consumer publications see the "Million-Dollar Media Rolodex" in the back of the book.

Magazine Resources
Writer's Digest Books, (513) 531-2222. This is the most comprehensive book of its kind. It not only gives you addresses of all the magazines, but query letter specifics and article fees. Your local bookstore carries this as a staple resource item. So does the library. The price is around $20 and is a must own if you're at all serious about writing articles

Books
- *You Can Be a Columnist* by Charlotte Digregorio; Civetta Press; Box 1043; Portland, OR 97207-1043; (503) 228-6649. If you want to remain anonymous, don't order this book
- *Beginners' Guide to Writing & Selling Quality Features: A Simple Course in Freelancing for Newspapers/Magazines* by Charlotte Digregorio; Civetta Press; Box 1043; Portland, OR 97207-1043; (503) 228-6649
- *National Directory of Newspaper Op-Ed Pages* by Marilyn Ross; Communication Creativity; Box 909; Buena Vista, CO 81211; (719) 395-8659; (800) 331-8355
- *The Complete Guide to Magazine Article Writing* by John M. Wilson; Writer's Digest Books; (513) 531-2222
- *The 30 Minute Writer; How to Write and Sell Short Pieces* by Connie Emerson; Writer's Digest Books; (513) 531-2222
- *The Handbook of Magazine Article Writing* by Jane Fredette; Writer's Digest Books; (513) 531-2222
- *Magazine Writing That Sells*, by Don McKinney; Writer's Digest Books; (513) 531-2222
- *How to Sell More Than 75% of Your Free-Lance Writing*; (Prima Publishing)
- Ask the journalism department at your local university, college, or adult education facility what books they use

40

WRITE A COLUMN

A simultaneous symphony of words and ideas

What is the significance of writing a column?

As Charlotte Digregorio, author of *You Can Be a Columnist*, says, "Prestige and professional enhancement are easy to attain. You could gain local, regional, and even national exposure by writing a column. Being a columnist on any topic will open opportunities for you that you never dreamed possible, personally and/or professionally. Your photo and name, regularly seen in one or many publications, can bring you great exposure, credibility, and financial enrichment. Becoming a columnist can bring you a larger practice and can unlock rewarding avenues, such as lucrative speaking engagements and consultations." And she ought to know. Her book is the authority on the subject. If this chapter convinces you to go for a syndicated column, don't make a move without it.

Who could I interest in my column?

It may be tough to get into the *Los Angeles Times*, but there are 7,000 newspapers across the United States that may be interested in you. They come in many shapes and sizes:

- Daily
- Weekly
- Monthly
- Bimonthly
- Quarterly
- Free community newspapers

Many papers don't have the money for a full staff. In fact, many of these papers are not only run and managed by the owner but staffed by that very same person. It's not unusual to follow up a news release and have the person who answers the phone be the owner's husband or wife, or the owner. This in no way means the paper is too small for you to deal with. It just means ad budgets aren't what they used to be.

How can going to an understaffed newspaper help me write me a column?

Because the paper is understaffed it has to rely on outside sources for material to fill the pages. And that's where you come in.

Do I have to contact every one of those 7,000 papers to see if they want me to write a column?

Not necessarily. There are several ways to reach them:

1. The hard way: contact every newspaper
2. Use an outside feature placement service
3. Try to get your column picked up by a syndicate
4. Syndicate your own column

But I've never written a column before. I don't have a writing track record. Won't they want to see something? How should I do that so I'll have a column to show them?

Yes, they will want to see something. Lots of something so they know you're just not a onetime writer. Unless you have a friend who has a newspaper, or someone at a local paper who believes in you, the only other way to get a column is to buy one, either locally or nationally.

How do I go about getting a local column?

Go around town collecting those wonderful free newspapers. Notice how they're filled with smiling faces writing about legal issues, real estate, health, et cetera. Those smiling faces buy that space, much like buying an ad.

Call the paper—the number is listed in the masthead—and tell the editor you want to write a column, and you'll be given the ad rates. You decide how big you want your column, depending on the rate.

Can I use the same column in papers in surrounding areas?

Yes, you can. That's known as self-syndication. You pay for placement, which means you own the column and are free to place it anywhere.

Will the big syndicates pick up my column?

I've learned to never say never. The syndicate's name is listed under the headline, the writer's name, or on the first line of the story. Ask the paper for the address of the syndicate, call them, and ask for their guidelines. *Writer's Digest* is a wonderful resource. It has a list of the syndicates, plus individual magazines and newspapers with their guidelines and fees.

What if I want to be published nationally, and no syndicate wants me?

There are services that feed or send filler to those 7,000 newspapers. They take the column you write, or take your notes and write the column for you.

What is filler?

Filler is the soft news that fills the pages. You've seen it every day you open a newspaper, only what you don't know is it isn't generated by the newspaper itself, but instead, comes packaged from an outside source. In the industry these are called theme packages. What I'm describing are feature sections on food, back-to-school issues, cars, fashion, brides, Father's Day, Valentine's Day, recipes, et cetera. These services also provide columns to newspapers.

Is my column guaranteed to get into the 7,000 papers?

No, not even one paper is guaranteed.

What does pickup depend on?

It depends on the needs of the paper. If you take this particular column route, I advise you to test it for several months before signing a lengthy contract.

How much does it cost?

The fee is based on half-inch rates. Call for current rates.

RESOURCES

Book
- *You Can Be a Columnist* by Charlotte Digregorio; Civetta Press; Box 1043; Portland, OR 97207-1043; (503) 228-6649. If you want to remain anonymous, don't order this book

Feature Services (they have a unique way to "syndicate" your column)
- Metro Publicity Service; 33 West 34th Street New York, NY 10001; (212) 947-5100. Talk to Nancy Stroop
- News USA, Inc., 8300 Boone Blvd., Ste. 810; Vienna, VA 22182; (703) 827-5800, (800) 355-9500. News USA produces broadcast, faxes, radio news, and home pages
- Derus Media, 500 N. Dearborn, #516, Chicago, IL 60610; (312) 644-4360. Derus will write your column in Spanish
- North American Precis Syndicate; 201 E. 42nd St., New York, NY 10017; (212) 867-9000; (310) 552-8000

41

NEWSLETTERS

The modern-day town crier

What is the purpose of a newsletter?
- Newsletters are a powerful way of developing name and brand recognition
- Newsletters are a way of telling people who you are and what services or products you have to offer. They build awareness

- Newsletters are a good way of showing that you are a credible expert in your field
- Newsletters inform your prospects on why they should want to shop with you
- Newsletters encourage repeat business
- Newsletters expand your client base
- Newsletters build trust and confidence
- Newsletters promote goodwill
- Newsletters continue customer service

How many different kinds of newsletters are there?

Basically there are two kinds of newsletters: hard and soft sell, or as I call them, selfish and selfless.

1. The hard sell. You can see this as strictly a marketing tool, with the same purpose as an advertisement, brochure, sales letter, catalog, or long-form media release
2. The soft sell. You can see this as a wonderful vehicle for self-promotion, interacting on a level of education with your existing or potential clients, customers, or patients, and including the community at large

What is the difference?

1. The hard sell: Traditional marketing tools are designed to close a sale. The purpose is to persuade you to pick up the phone and order or rush right down and buy, buy, buy. The motivational design behind these tools is to take your money. This kind of newsletter is geared to price lists and availability
2. The soft sell: A promotional newsletter is used as an alternative marketing tool. Its motivational design is nonthreatening. It means to inform through entertaining and education. It's designed to grow credibility and give customer service rather than sell outright. It's more a giver than a taker.

What would I write about in a soft-sell newsletter?

- Information in the community as well as your business
- Institute a dialogue with your readership about its needs
- Educate your audience about you and your product or services

- Help people enjoy better lives
- Show people how to do their jobs or live their lives more effectively
- Show off your talents and those of your products or services
- Offer a behind-the-scenes view of your business
- Use it as a forum to show you're an expert in your field
- Expand on audience views
- Make a statement
- Solve a problem
- Fill a need
- Gather and share information about your readership
- Report on community happenings
- Raise donations through coupons or special offers
- Share articles from businesses or services that would benefit your audience

Do people really read newsletters?

Ilise Benun is a self-promotion specialist who publishes her own quarterly newsletter, *The Art of Self Promotion*. She told me that newsletters have a 400% higher readership than such standard sales and promotional materials as brochures and letters.

How difficult is it to publish a newsletter?

More than difficult, it is time-consuming.

What makes it time-consuming?

- The set-up time
- Article coordination
- The articles themselves
- Writing your letter from the editor
- Inputting the text and art (if any)
- Editing
- Proofreading

Is there a way to cut my time commitment?

- Involve your employees
- Hire journalism students
- Use interns
- Source it to a newsletter company

What if I don't have the ability to do any of those right now, but would love to have a newsletter?

Engage in relationship marketing. In other words join forces, or joint venture, with another noncompetitive service provider or retailer and combine the effort and the cost (see the chapter, "Joint Venturing")

For example:

- A podiatrist can co-venture with any health professional. Even a shoe store
- A juvenile furniture store with a juvenile clothing or toy store
- Car dealers with automotive parts and accessories
- Painters, carpenters, plumbers, and electricians
- Architects and landscapers
- Bakeries, cheese stores, fish and meat markets, coffee-houses, and wine shops

What if I can't afford to co-venture?

No matter what you do or what you have to offer, you can contribute articles to any newsletter (see the chapter, "Tips, Trends, and Surveys"). Everyone could use tips on stress, health, relationships, business, insurance, cars, buying furniture, et cetera.

How many pages should a newsletter be?

There is no minimum or no limit. However, a reader's average attention span is between four and eight pages.

Remember, the purpose of a newsletter is for name and brand recognition. If all you can put together is a one-page, back-and-front issue filled with joy, humor, and information, that's a newsletter, and I recommend that you go for it.

What are some ways to cut my costs?

- Newsletter employees don't have to be full-time or in-house. Use contributors. Find design and input people with whom you can communicate by phone, fax, or mail
- Shop for services. Prices for design and printing can vary by 100% among suppliers
- Design your newsletter as a self-mailer. Don't even think of using an envelope

- Many industries have prewritten newsletters you can subscribe to. All you have to do is apply the text to your own design. There's no fuss or muss. Ask your association if it provides one
- Create your shell and have it printed in quantity. Each issue can be printed onto the existing shell at a fraction of the cost
- A large computer monitor will help you see page and design details clearly. This could save you time and money in production costs
- If you use color for your name, masthead, and other information that remains the same, you can save money by printing up a large quantity. Each time you do an issue add the text separately
- When staffing your newsletter enterprise, hire someone with more than just typesetting skills to prepare the layout. That way you get more for your money
- Hire a freelance designer to produce the first edition. Then train a staff member to follow the design

What are some newsletter do's?
- Set a clear editorial purpose. Create a mission statement that identifies your goals and the needs of your audience. Frequently query your audience to determine whether you are on target.

    Communications briefings newsletter prints its purpose under the mailing label.

    Purpose: To provide you with down-to-earth communication ideas and techniques you can put into action to persuade clients, influence peers, and motivate employees; to help you earn approval, command respect, spur productivity, gain recognition, and win public support

- Determine the audience you want to reach and why
- Remember that readers average only seven seconds a page
- Write about your readership. People love to see their names in print
- Proofread, proofread, proofread. Mistakes in your newsletter will be viewed as mistakes in your business. Mixing

up numbers is a more common error than mixing letters.
If you wrote it have someone else proofread it
- Watch out for tone and style. Don't let your words or
  writing style sound as if they've come from an institution.
  Write conversationally. Be real
- Print with black ink. People respond best to black and will
  retain the information longer. Highlight or frame with a
  second color
- Using color type on color background makes it difficult
  to distinguish figure from ground. This includes reverse
  type (white type on a black background)
- Fancy typography is read less than traditional and more
  acceptable typefaces

How soon will I see payoffs from my newsletter endeavor?

I asked this of Nicole Millman-Falk, a very talented publisher of newsletters who specializes in but is not limited to
trade and professional membership associations and other not-
for-profit organizations. Her longstanding expertise in the
newsletter publishing field brought her to tell you this:

"It is unlikely that you will see immediate positive payoffs
from your newsletter. However, you will feel the negative re-
percussions right away if you fail to be timely, accurate, and
informative. If you've failed in clearly identifying your purpose, your audience, and your message, that too will reap immediate negative results.

"And perhaps the worst mistake is publishing information
that interests only you rather than what interests your clients
and prospects.

"Great newsletters combine quality editorial material and
exciting graphics and layout. A newsletter is a marketing tool
that reinforces the personality of your company. It offers you
a chance to shine several times a year. It helps you define your
marketing goals and helps you crystallize your marketing messages for your customers."

RESOURCES

Associations
- Newsletter Publishers Association: 1401 Wilson Blvd.,

Ste. 207, Arlington, VA 22209; (800) 356-9302
- National Association of Desktop Publishers: Box 508, Kenmore Station; Boston, MA 02215-9998; (617) 437-6472

Directories

- *Hudson's Subscription Newsletter Directory*; Newsletter Clearinghouse; Box 311; Rhinebeck, NY 12572; (800) 572-3451
- *Newsletter Directory*; Gale Research; 835 Penobscot Blvd.; Detroit, MI 48226; (800) 877-4253; *http.// www.Gale.com/Gale.html*
- *Internal Publications Directory*; National Research Bureau; 225 W. Wacker Dr., Ste. 2275; Chicago, IL 60606; (800) 678-2724
- *Oxbridge Directory of Newsletters:* Oxbridge Communications; 150 Fifth Ave. New York, NY 10011; (800) 955-0231; *http://www.media finders.com*

Newsletters

- *The Newsletter on Newsletters*; Newsletter Clearinghouse, Box 311; Rhinebeck, NY 12572; (800) 572-3451
- Nicole Millman-Falk; *MFC Messenger, Communication and Marketing Tips*; Millman-Falk Communications, Inc.; 32 Franklin Pl.; Glen Rock, NJ 07452; (201) 652-1687
- Ilise Benun's *The Art of Self Promotion*; Box 23; Hoboken, NJ 07030; (800) 737-0783
- *Communication briefings:* 1101 King St., Ste 110, Alexandria, VA 22314; (703) 548-3800

Tapes

How to Make a Fortune in Newsletters: The Newsletter Clearinghouse; Box 311, Rhinebeck, NY 12572; (800) 572-3451

Books

- *Publishing Newsletters* by Howard Penn Hudson; Newsletter Clearinghouse; Box 311; Rhinebeck, NY 12572; (800) 572-3451
- *How to Buy, Sell and Price Newsletter Properties*; Newsletter Clearinghouse; Box 311; Rhinebeck, NY 12572; (800) 572-3451

- *Winning in Newsletters*; Newsletter Clearinghouse; Box 311; Rhinebeck, NY 12572; (800) 572-3451. This book presents thirty-six case histories of newsletters after their launch
- *Marketing With Newsletters* by Elaine Floyd; EF Communications; 6614 Pernod Ave.; St. Louis, MO 63139-2149; (800) 264-6305 or (314) 647-6788

Seminars on Newsletters
- Newsletter Clearinghouse; 44 West Market St., Rhinebeck, NY 12572; (800) 572-3451
- Marketing With Newsletters; Elaine Floyd; EF Communications; 6614 Pernod Ave.; St. Louis, MO 63139-2149; (800) 264-6305 or (314) 647-6788
- The Newsletter Factory; 1640 Powers Ferry Rd., Bldg. 8, #110; Marietta, GA 30067; (404) 955-2002
- Pattison Workshops; 5092 Kingscross Rd.; Westminster, CA 92683; (714) 894-8143
- Padgett-Thompson; 11221 Roe Ave.; Leawood, KS 66211; (913) 451-2900
- Ragan Communications; 212 W. Superior St., Ste. 200; Chicago, IL 60610; (312) 335-0037; (800) 878-5331; fax (312) 335-9583; *service@ragan.com; www .ragan.com*
- Check for newsletter classes at your local adult education facility and posted on the bulletin board of your print shops

Filler Articles, Clip Art
Ideas Unlimited for Editors; % Newsletter Services, Inc.; 9700 Philadelphia Ct.; Lanham, MD 20797-0614; (800) 345-2611

42

SEND SPECIAL REPORTS

Sweets for the sweet, a special for the special

What is a special report?

It's an in-depth article on a particular topic of interest to your market.

What's the purpose of a special report?

Everyone likes to think they are special, so why not use this to your marketing and promotional advantage? Sending a special report not only shows people they count, but tells them that right up front.

Why is it called a special report?

It's all in the packaging. Like when someone calls themselves "King of the Jingle Jungle," "The Best of the Best," or "The Fastest Gun in the West."

What makes it special is, you've packaged it to be a special report.

Who benefits from a special report?

Anyone. Entrepreneurs, service providers, nonprofits, retailers, home-based businesses, wholesalers, professionals, homemakers, students. As long as it's your market, as long as they can use what you have to offer, then they will benefit.

What makes it such an important marketing tool?

What makes it such an important tool is two things:

1. The information
2. The thought. Everyone likes being considered, thought

about, remembered. By sending a special report you're doing just that

People have this quality that when someone gives them something for free, they remember. The most appropriate way they thank you is to give you their business.

What do you put in a special report?
- Helpful information
- Useful information
- Necessary information
- Trivia
- Your information
- Another person's pearls of wisdom
- Surveys
- Trends
- Reports
- Findings

What's the best kind of information a special report can provide?
To succeed, the information should:
- Provide solutions to a problem
- Fill a need
- Tell people something they didn't know

People are a natural for emotional appeals. These three principles should be the mainstay of your promotional arsenal. Follow them and you will have your audience eating out of your copy.

How do you address emotional needs in words?
How to's. Write about how to do anything, and you'll see undivided attention.

What are some examples of good how to's?
- How to make money from . . .
- How to improve your health by . . .
- How to court success in . . .
- How to improve your relationship with . . .
- How to invest in . . .

- How to buy a . . .
- How to choose the right . . .
- How to save money
- How to use your time wisely
- How to care for your aging parents

What are some special reports for specific professions?
- Dentists: innovations in tooth whitening, nutrition for healthy teeth, et cetera
- Doctors: findings on prostate or breast cancer or whatever is their specialty
- Banks: credit repair, mortgages, getting loans
- Garden centers: office plant selection and care, window box herbs
- Funeral directors: buying caskets; handling grief, buying a headstone, et cetera
- Dry cleaners: best and worst spots, best and worst fabrics

I offer special reports on self-promotion: "How to Get Yourself on Radio Talk Shows"; "How Tips, Trends and Surveys Help Promote Yourself"; and "How To Get Your Word Out Fast!"

How do you determine what the audience wants to know?
There are two basic ways to do this:

1. Sample your data base by asking them what keeps them up at night, or what the latest topics are at happy hour. Faxing, mailing, calling, or on-site questionnaires will tell you what you need to know
2. Think about what questions your audience asks most frequently. What do they want you to solve? What makes them come to you in the first place?

What if I'm not good at this, or if I don't have time to do it?
- Call your local education facility and ask for the journalism department. Someone there—a student, an assistant, a professor—might want the experience or the work for hire
- Your local yellow pages lists writers and researchers for hire

- Utilize the talents of retired businesspeople. Senior citizen centers are a good place to start, as well as government organizations

You mentioned that the information doesn't have to be mine, but could belong to someone else. Could you please explain what you mean?

What if you are not a writer or a compiler? Rather than be stranded out in the cold, you can provide information from another source.

Here's the beauty of sending another expert's special reports: They can be on any subject, even topics outside your industry. If the subject matter fills a need, solves a problem, tells them something they didn't know, or entertains them, the people who do business with you will appreciate the information. Look at it this way. If you would appreciate getting it, wouldn't they?

How can I get special reports written by others?

Many business magazines or newsletters advertise their own special reports. *USA Today* articles overflow with free or low-cost pamphlets you can offer to your audience. Start checking your own paper more thoroughly. Feature stories on people or businesses appearing in the lifestyle, health, and business sections often tell of special reports or pamphlets available for the asking. Call and ask if you can buy these in bulk and distribute them to your current or potential audience. It's a promotional win-win for both parties.

What is an example of how to apply another person's information to my clientele?

Everyone does business with people who travel. I saw this in *USA Today:* Go Ahead Vacations offers "144 Travel Tips," a twenty-four page, pocket-size guide aimed at travelers preparing for their first trip abroad. It covers twenty topics ranging from preparing to go, to health, insurance, and shipping purchases home.

Call up Go Ahead Vacations, order a quantity of guides, and add a personal letter to your clients, customers, or patients who are about to go on a trip or are thinking about traveling abroad. Think of a way you can be included:

- Doctors can write about shots and medication
- Nutritionists can write about what foods to eat and what to avoid
- Tax professionals can write about deductible applications
- Luggage shops can write about packing
- Clothing stores can write about wrinkle-free garments to pack

What is the best marketing advantage for a special report?
- It wears many hats. It is a great lead generator, a client pleaser, and a way to keep in touch with those who haven't been around for a while
- To those who don't know you, they will now
- To those who do know you and are acquainted with your product or services, you are giving something value added
- To those who are with your competitors, they are reminded that you still care and will welcome them back with open arms

Who else should be on my special report mailing list?
- The business editor of your newspaper
- Business- or industry-related TV and radio talk shows
- Your industry newsletters and journals
- Your banker
- Your lawyer
- Your tax people
- Your vendors
- Anyone who supports your business
- For the pièce de resistance, send it to your competitor's list. You never know what could happen

Are special reports always free?
No, you can sell them. Often marketers will sell a special report as a prelude to a book or set of books on a particular subject. Many newsletters combine specific information compiled over several issues and offer them for sale as a special report. There are no rules. Be creative. Promote and prosper!

NOTE: Add a special report to your promotional repertoire and, please, let me know what you did and how it worked for you.

RESOURCES

- Go Ahead Vacations; (800) 242-4686

43

WRITE A BOOK

Books are the words of angels come to earth

Why would anyone want to write a book? Is it that great a marketing tool?

Being published can open many doors not readily available. Doors such as:

- Career and personal recognition
- Career and personal credibility
- Authority status in your field
- Enhanced job status
- Monetary compensation
- Promotions
- The start of a new career
- The opportunity to become a spokesperson or a consultant in your field of expertise
- The opportunity to go out on the lecture circuit
- The opportunity to appear on radio and TV talk shows
- The opportunity to help others through the information you know

I've always thought there was a book in me, but how do I get it out?

Actually, writing a book is like falling off a log, especially if it's a how-to log. If you're an expert in your field, you can write a book. And most people are experts at something. For example, a secretary can be an expert in phone etiquette. A high-wire electrician can be an expert in courage and fear. A belly dancer can be an expert in the art of persuasion or flirting.

What's the first thing I have to do to write a book?

If you've written articles, special reports, columns, and newsletters, you may already have your book. Just put them all together and have them printed.

What if I don't have any of these written gems?

Then do what I did when I wrote my first book:
- Make an outline of the tasks or points of interest you want to cover
- Place them in a meaningful order as if you were doing an actual presentation exercise
- Construct a brief subject matter outline for each chapter

What if I don't have the time to write the book?

- Put the outline on index cards. Take a tape recorder in the car. When you're driving to work, to school, to the gym, or shopping, put your thoughts into the tape recorder
- Look in the yellow pages under Secretarial Services. Find a transcription service and have it do the typing. The service can print out your outline or put it on disk
- Then you edit it. Add, subtract, move things around, and return it to the transcription service. Do this until you feel it's to your satisfaction

What if I want someone to edit it? Where do I find them?

- Look in the yellow pages under Writers
- Call your local university's school of journalism

Now that I have the content done, what do I do about a cover design?

Covers are easy. Any graphics house can design and execute your book cover.

Are there people who specialize in book covers? Where would I find them?

- Go into a bookstore and find a cover you like
- Call the publishing house and ask for the contact information on the person who designed the book cover
- Call, ask for the fees, and strike a deal

How do I get my book published?

There are two ways to publish a book:

1. Have it published by a publishing house, such as this book. The publisher takes care of everything from editing to printing to distribution and collecting the money
2. Self-publish. This means you take care of everything from editing to printing to distribution and keeping track of the money

How can I get published by a publishing house?

You can take one of these routes:

1. Get a literary agent to represent you
2. Contact the publishing houses yourself
3. Put your manuscript up on the Internet through such companies as Carl Galletti's Writer's Web

Let's discuss the first two. To get a literary agent or publishing house to read your material, you have to write a proposal with specific information they need to sell or buy your property.

Here's where you can find an agent, publishing house, and the kind of material they specialize in:

- *Literary Marketplace* (bookstores)
- *The Insider's Guide to Book Editors and Publishers* (bookstores)
- *Writer's Digest* (newsstand)
- *Publishers Weekly* (newsstand)

Can I send my book to an agent or publisher without their requesting it?

This is called unsolicited material. There are some agents and companies that don't accept unsolicited material, so it's best to call first and ask if they take it.

Even if they do accept unsolicited material, they probably will want a proposal or some sort of outline and marketing plan first. So it's best to know how to write a proposal, even if you decide not to go through an agent.

Always send a self-addressed stamped envelope (SASE) with sufficient postage for a response and large enough for the return of your materials if they are rejected. Without an SASE, many agents and publishers will not respond.

Where do I learn how to write a proposal?

- Check your local adult education classes
- Check around town to see if there's a writers' club
- Contact book agent Wendy Keller for her workbook and seminar on how to write a book proposal
- Contact book agent Jeff Herman for an outline on how to write a book proposal

Why would I want to self-publish?

- If you try to have your book published, and no agent will represent you or no publishing house will buy your book
- If you want or need total creative control
- If you want to reap the monetary benefits of selling the book yourself at your lectures, classes, and events

What's the best way to learn about self-publishing?

- Take a seminar from self-publishing expert Dan Poynter at his home base in Santa Barbara, California
- Call Dan Poynter's fax-on-demand program, filled with great resources (see the chapter, "Fax-on Demand" for explanation of fax-on-demand)
- Read books on self-publishing
- Attend the university sessions put on by the Publishers Marketing Association (PMA), prior to the American Book Sellers Association convention
- Attend the Small Publishers Conference run by Jerrold Jenkins

- Contact the Small Publishers Association of North America (SPAN), formed by self-publishing experts Marilyn and Tom Ross

If I do self-publish, how do I get distribution?

Dan Poynter, the Institute for Small Book Publishers, SPAN, and PMA have all those answers.

What is the Internet route?

It's a service called the Writer's Web. You submit the information product (book, manual, report, et cetera) that you want to sell, and the folks at EDI Technologies, Inc. (EDIT for short) will put a portion of it up on the World Wide Web.

This sample portion can be read for free by anyone who has access to the Web and visits a site called the Reader's Room. EDIT advertises the site and attracts readers.

When the reader visits and reads the sample of your book, they get an invitation to purchase it. Then EDIT takes care of the transaction and delivers the product. You get a check as a reward.

In other words, the marketplace decides whether it wants your book or not. The decision is not left up to any manuscript reader fresh out of college, an agent, or an acquisitions editor at a publishing house—or, for that matter, anyone else at all.

The benefit is, people get discovered in the strangest of places, and you could be the next Brad Richdale or Jay Conrad Levinson!

Do I need to copyright my project before I send it in to the publisher?

Federal statute automatically protects the intellectual property once it's in a fixed form. That means that it's automatically copyrighted the moment you create an original work. On the front page and on each page of your manuscript place:

- A c in circle (©)
- The name of the owner (yourself)
- The year in which the manuscript was created or released

What part of my material can be copyrighted?

For information on this, you should check with your lawyer.

By putting this circle, name, and date imprint on my work, am I *fully protected*?

No, you are not fully protected. Putting these on your manuscript tells everyone it is yours, but it doesn't establish proof of ownership.

How do I get proof of ownership?

Proof of ownership is legally established when you go on public record to show you have created the work. To do this, you need to register your property with the U.S. Copyright Office in Washington, D.C. This formality provides you with a copyright certificate for your records.

Why do I need a copyright certificate for my records?

If you're going to distribute, sell, license, or do anything with your intellectual property, the buyer will need proof of ownership. It protects you, and it protects them.

The certificate proves that it's your property at the time of registration.

How difficult is it to register my property?

It's not difficult at all. You have three choices:

1. Have your attorney register you
2. You do it yourself by calling the U.S. Copyright Office in Washington, D.C.
3. Utilize the services of a professional service, such as Ralph Weinstein's Copyright Connection. He's the person the lawyers hire to do it for them. So cut your costs and go direct

NOTE: A book is as many pages as you want it to be. As with beauty, what makes it a book is in the eyes or hands of the beholder. Share the fantasy; write your book. You have no excuse but yourself.

RESOURCES

Trade Magazines
- *Publishers Weekly*
- *Writer's Digest*

These are available on newsstands and bookstores. Check your library too.

Books
- Dan Poynter has written *The Self-Publishing Manual, Is There a Book Inside You? Publishing Short-Run Books*, and *Book Fairs*. He holds weekend self-publishing how-to seminars in Santa Barbara, California, speaks all over at adult education facilities, and has a helpful fax-on-demand program filled with great resources. Fax-on-demand: (805) 968-8947. He also has a newsletter that is a must. Para Publishing; Box 8206; Santa Barbara, CA 93118-8206; (805)-968-7277; *DanPoynter@ Para-Publishing.com;http//www.ParaPublishing.com/books/para/ 264*
- Marilyn and Tom Ross have written *The Complete Guide to Self-Publishing* as well as *The Encyclopedia of Self-Publishing* (Writer's Digest Books), which contains everything you need to know to write, publish, promote, and sell your own book. It's available in bookstores. This book has an incredible resource list from soup to nuts. Marilyn and Tom can be reached at (719) 395-8659
- *The Insider's Guide to Book Editors and Publishers* by Jeff Herman, St. Martin's Press, 175 Fifth Ave., New York, NY 10010 (212) 674-5151. Herman also has instructions on how to write a proposal
- Writer's Digest Books: (800) 289-0963. Writer's Digest has a catalog of very helpful books about writing all kinds of books and other written word vehicles

Book Proposals
- Wendy Keller (literary agent) gives a seminars called *Get An Agent & Get Sold Now!* 3579 E. Foothill Blvd.,

Ste. 327; Pasadena, CA 91107; (818) 798-0793; fax (818) 798-5653; *Literary Ag@aol.com* Call for a schedule and how to buy the manual and tapes

- *The Insider's Guide to Book Editors and Publishers* by Jeff Herman (literary agent); St. Martin's Press; 175 Fifth Ave., New York, NY 10010; (212) 674-5151. This book has instructions on how to write a proposal

Book Marketing Newsletters

- John Kremer; Book Marketing Update; Box 205; Fairfield, IA 52556; (800) 796-6130 *http://www.bookmarket.com* This newsletter has information on seminars, books, special reports, et cetera. Kremer always lists all the regional, national, and international book fairs as well
- Marie Kiefer; *Book Promotion Hotline*; Ad Lib Publications; 51½ W. Adams; Fairfield, Iowa 52556; (800) 669-0773. Mailing lists and resources galore!
- Dan Poynter; Para Publishing; Box 8206 Santa Barbara, CA 93118-8206; (805)-968-7277; *DanPoynter@Para Publishing.com/books/para/264; http//www.ParaPublishing. com*; fax-on-demand (805) 968-8947

Cover Design

Dunn + Associates; Box 870; Hayward, WI 54843; Phone: (800) 665-6728

Copyright Information

- U.S. Copyright Office, Washington, D.C. for forms; (202) 707-9100; for public information, (202) 707-3000
- Copyright Connection, Inc.; Ralph Weinstein, President; 8824 Southwick St., Fairfax, VA 22031; (703) 280-4767; fax (703) 280-5344

Associations and Organizations

If you self-publish, you're considered a small book publisher, so take advantage of all these organizations. You should also take advantage of them even if you're fortunate to be published. It's always good to educate yourself on what the industry is doing

- American Book Sellers Association; 560 White Plains Rd., Tarrytown, NY 10591; (914) 631-7800. This association presents the famous ABA convention. A must-go-to for anyone thinking of writing a book
- Publishers Marketing Association (PMA); 2401 Pacific Coast Hwy., Ste. 102; Hermosa Beach, CA 90254; (310) 372-2732
- Small Publishers Association of North America (SPAN); Box 1306; Buena Vista, CO 81211; (719) 395-4790
- Institute for Small Book Publishers; 121 E. Front Street, 4th Floor; Traverse City, MI 49685; (800) 706-4636; *http://www.smallpress.com.* The institute was started by Jerrold Jenkins
- Maui Writers Conference; Box 968; Kihei, HI 96753; (808) 879-0061; fax-on-demand (808) 879-6233; *mauicon@aol.com; http://www.maui.com/~sbdc/writers*

Book Publishing Services
These services will take you through the publishing process and do it for you. Not everyone does the same thing, so ask for job descriptions and prices

- Marilyn and Tom Ross; About Books Inc.; Box 1500 G; Buena Vista, CO 81211=1500; (800) 548-1876
- Jerrold Jenkins, Jenkins Group; 121 E. Front St., 4th Floor, Traverse City, MI 49685 (800) 706-4636; *http://www.smallpress.com*
- Yvette McCann, Rhyme Tyme Publications; 2746 Oanbury Dr., New Orleans, LA 70131; (504) 393-7222

Internet
Writer's Web. To see how it works, just visit the site: *http://www.magic7.com/ww*, or call Carl Galletti, One Paddock Dr.; Lawrenceville, NJ 08648 at (609) 896-0245

Software
Make-a-Booklet Software; Paper Direct; (800) A-PAPERS

NOTE: After you publish your book you can turn the manuscript into audiotapes (see the chapter, "Audio Tape Products")

44

PROMOTIONAL PRODUCTS

A great T-shirt is in the eyes of the beholder

Why does my company need promotional products?
Jay Kristal, president of Crystal Kreations, gave me ten very compelling reasons why your company needs them. This is from his webpage:

1. **Client acknowledgment.** Use promotional items as a reminder that your relationship is important and the foundation of future endeavors
2. **Employee recognition.** Express your appreciation for employees, or use promotions as an incentive for those within the organization to reach higher levels of achievement
3. **Competitive advantage.** Promotional products give you a high-impact marketing tool that creates interest and excitement for your company. It is also very cost-effective
4. **New product announcements.** You can capture your audience's attention and innovatively announce your new offering using promotional products
5. **Special events.** Your event becomes even more special when you give your guests a promotional gift—it reminds them of both you and your event
6. **Trade show support.** A unique and useful product will be remembered long after the show
7. **Product development.** Use a promotional product when you are dealing with a corporate sponsor for immediate recognition and brand awareness
8. **New market focus.** Let a clever product help you leave an everlasting impression and create interest

9. **Image development.** Promotional items can be used to emphasize themes of value, service, commitment, quality, and performance

10. **Increase visibility.** Your company name on everyday staples affords visibility and serves to remind clients of your product or service. Promotional products also allow clients to equate your business with practical and easy accessibility

What are some possible business applications?

- Grand openings
- Employee incentives, awards, recognition programs
- Anniversary/birthday celebrations
- Holiday commemorations
- Direct-mail programs
- Thank you gifts
- Convention, conference, and trade show giveaways
- New product/service introductions
- Client/customer traffic builders
- Client/customer appreciation
- Corporate sales and staff meetings
- Campaigns
- Sponsored sports activities
- Relocation announcements
- Expansion announcements
- Travel and sales incentive gifts
- Hotel room amenities
- Travel goody-bag gifts
- Any special event

What should I keep in mind when choosing a promotional product?

Jay says that you must consider these criteria, in this order:

1. Know your budget, its expansions, and its limitations
2. Consider your target market
3. Set down your objectives
4. Know your time frame

At the last trade show I counted 142 different giveaway promotional products. How many are there?

Shirley Palmer, PResident of Shirley's PR Works: PRomotional PRograms, PRoducts & PRemiums, and author of *The PRomotion Insider Newsletter*, told me that she has a list of nearly 400,000 items on CD-ROM computer database. Of these, 8,538 are golf items, 5,143 are mugs, and 7,892 are pens.

How effective are promotional products?

In *The Promotion Insider Newsletter,* Shirley reported on this study done by The Promotional Products Association International:

- Four groups of college professors were chosen.

    1. One group received an imprinted pocket calculator and a thank you note from a major publishing company.
    2. A second group received a highlighter and the same note
    3. The third group received only the note
    4. The fourth received nothing

A mail survey indicated that 33.7% of the professors thought better of the company's sales reps who presented them with the calculator, compared to those who only got the note. The highlighter proved 15% more effective than the note alone

Here are more examples:

- At a popular Southwest fast food chain, $181 worth of promotional products led to a $1,249 increase in sales
- A desktop telephone message holder helped a Texas florist post an 11% jump in ''goodwill standing''
- A sporting goods store found that a sales contest was actually draining profits until promotional products were added to the program. Once they were, sales went up $548 per retail unit

NOTE: If you've used promotional products to get attention, I would love to have the scenario, the facts, and the outcome for my next book.

RESOURCES

Organizations
- The Promotional Products Association International: (214) 252-0404. The association publishes a newsletter
- Specialty Advertising Association: (800) 722-4691. The association publishes a newsletter

Magazine
Promo: The Magazine for Promotional Marketing; 47 Old Ridgefield Rd., Wilton, CT 06897 (203) 761-1510. The magazine's content focuses on product sampling, games, contests and sweepstakes, events, redemption/fulfillment services, direct marketing programs, and interactive services

Experts
- Jay Kristal; Crystal Kreations; 156 Fifth Ave.; New York, NY 10010; (212)-243-5489; Fax (212)-243-6193; *http:// www.crystalkreations.com*
- Shirley Palmer; Shirley's PR Works: PRomotional PRograms, PRoducts & PRemiums: 7947 Amestoy Ave.; Van Nuys, CA 91406; (800) 892-2418. Don't forget to ask her for *The PRomotion Insider Newsletter*

45

LIST YOURSELF IN
EXPERT DIRECTORIES

Being at the right place at the right time

Do people really use directories to find you, or are they a scam?

In their excellent book Big Ideas for Small Service Businesses, Marilyn and Tom Ross, talk about how, as consultants, appropriate directory listings figure prominently in their marketing mix.

"We know that approximately one-third of our inquiries are attributed to this one strategy! This parallels the national average.

"A study by the Association of Industrial Advertisers found that when buyers look for sellers, thirty-five percent find them in business directories. This category leads all others (literature on hand, sales calls, periodicals and direct mail, recommendations, and yellow pages) by a significant margin."

Why is it important to market yourself through directories?

As the saying goes, strike while the iron is hot. Since you don't know when your expertise and talents are needed, when you're listed in a directory you're always in the right place at the right time.

The media are always looking to interview experts for timely news topics. When you sign on as my client, your name automatically goes into all the appropriate directories, and then some. As a result of being listed, my clients are often called upon to lend their expertise when there is a natural disaster, a political upheaval, a legal question, et cetera. By using this opportunity, I am able to market my clients even further.

Speakers such as myself are hired every day from the *National Speakers Association Directory* and the *Speakers Red Pages Directory,* both in print and on-line.

Professionals who register in directories are often called to testify as an expert witness. Take the case of Dan Poynter of self-publishing fame, who is also an expert sky diver. Listing himself in the *National Forensic Services Directory*, he appears all over the world at trials involving skydiving mishaps, and he has developed a good alternative revenue source from testifying.

People registered in directories are asked to sit on boards, hired to give keynote speeches, and recruited from their listings in the multiple versions of the *Who's Who* directories.

Are any services better than others for directories?

It solely depends on the purpose of the directory. Is the purpose to list or to sell you? Is it to represent you and your service, such as the yellow pages, or just to acknowledge your presence like the white pages?

And speaking of the yellow pages, that's another directory you should be in (see the chapter, "Yellow Pages").

And don't rule out community directories. You don't have to have the cream of the crop listing, but you should be present and accounted for.

How do directories charge?

There is usually a menu of options for charging. Each directory has its own menu, so ask. You can choose to have a picture, a bold listing in larger type, just larger type, a bold listing in smaller type, or just smaller type. Some even get down to having an address or just the phone number. Then there is the number of lines of copy.

Some directories are free; others require membership or payment.

What should I include in the copy?

Directory copy writing is the same as writing for direct response ads or the media, where you go for the headline grabber. Don't make the mistake of thinking they're already grabbed, or they wouldn't be shopping in the directory. With directory copy you couple the benefits with the features. Provide the audience with credentials and tell them about your reputation. Fill their needs, fix their problems, and tell them something they need to know. You want them to hire you, so you must provide them with reasons to do just that.

How do I know which directory the call came from?

You can empty the same tracking methods you use for business reply cards, door hangers, or any direct response strategy. Code the response phone number, or use a key word within the reply instructions.

Marilyn and Tom Ross talk about tracking through remote call forwarding in *Big Ideas for Small Service Businesses*. Remote call forwarding is when the calls go to a different number, then are automatically routed to your regular switchboard. The caller never knows the difference, and there is no interruption. You get a bill each month with the time and date of each call. To get this exact record of the number of inquiries, the Rosses say you'll pay around $40 per month plus twelve to twenty-seven cents per call, depending on the vendor selected.

The Rosses offer another interesting tracking approach. They suggest, "You should connect your toll-free number to a dedicated key phone that records who called, for what, and when." Very interesting!

Check with your telephone business office. Technology is changing every day.

Speaking of changing technology, now you can also list your e-mail and World Wide Web addresses. The audiences can have more than a few lines to get to know you. With the many opportunities a Web address affords, you'll have no difficulty tracking the responses (see Part X, "The Internet").

RESOURCES

NOTE: These are the major directory publishers. Your library has some, if not all of them.

National Referral Center of the Library of Congress

Library of Congress; National Referral Center; Washington, D.C. 20540; (202) 287-5680

Directories

- Reed Elsevier, New Providence; 121 Chanlon Rd; New Providence, NJ 07974; (800) 521-8110; *http: www.reedres.com*
- *Radio/TV Report*; Bradley Communications; Box 1206; Lansdowne, PA 19050; (800) 989-1400; fax (610) 284-3704. This directory lists experts for talk shows
- Burrelle's Information Services; 75 East Northfield Rd.; Livingston, NJ 07039; (800) 631-1160
- Bacon's Information, Inc.; 332 South Michigan Ave.; Chicago, IL 60604; 800-621-0561
- Broadcast Interview Source; 2233 Wisconsin Ave. N.W., #406; Washington, D.C. 20007-4104; (202) 333-4904
- New Editions International, Inc.; Box 2578, Sedona, AZ 86339; (800) 777-4751
- Gale Research, 835 Penobscot Blvd.; Detroit MI 48226; (800) 877-4253; *http://www.Gale.com/Gale.html*
- National Forensic Services Directory; 17 Temple Terr.; Lawrenceville, NJ 08648; (609) 883-0550
- Oxbridge Communications: 150 Fifth Ave.; New York, NY 10011; (800) 955-0231; *http://www.mediafinders. com*
- SRDS; 1700 Higgins Rd.; Des Plaines, IL 60018-5605; (800) 851-7737; *http://www.SRDS.com*

Book

Big Ideas for Small Service Businesses by Marilyn and Tom Ross; Communication Creativity; Box 909; Buena Vista, CO 81211; (719) 395-8659

46

PUBLISH AN IN-HOUSE RESOURCE DIRECTORY

Then you can tell the players with your scorecard

Why should I create my own directory of experts?
- If you want to tell your immediate world that you exist
- If you don't have the fees to get in the big directories
- If you only want to stay local

Who can benefit the most from doing this?

Every business can benefit: Profit and nonprofit organizations, businesses, services, service providers, educational facilities, houses of worship, home-based businesses, and even the solo entrepreneur.

- List your employees
- If you're solo list your vendors and consultants
- Identify each department and its function
- List the employees and their specialties
- Note what topics everyone can speak on
- Give three to five tips on each subject listed
- List phone numbers, extensions, and hours of operation at that number

How can an individual create a directory? I thought a directory indicated there was more than one listing.

Since this book is about promoting yourself, I must remind you that coming to a dead halt at guidelines won't get you very far. Think, act, create! Here's what I would do in this case:

- I would list myself and all the appropriate information on my letterhead, then take a sheet of heavy paper used to cover special reports or booklets and staple my list inside. I would fold it over so it looks like a directory. Using a word processor, I would print *Directory of Personnel & Services for* . . . on the outside and send it off to the appropriate place
- List yourself, your vendors, and your consultants. That way you're showing your clients who you are affiliated with and the levels of expertise they will be dealing with. Why not? You're an expert. Show them your style!

What's the purpose of the directory?

Your directory acts as:

- A brochure
- A marketing piece
- A business card

How professional should it be?

It should be as professional as you can make it. Professionally printed would be nice, but if not a good printer will do just fine.

Just remember, your clients will judge your expertise and professionalism by the expertise and professionalism you show them.

To whom or where do I send my newly created directory?

- To the media, Attention: editor of your field of expertise (see the chapters, "Tips, Trends, and Surveys," "Write Articles," and "Newsletters")
- Associations in your field or related fields of expertise (see Part IV, "Relationship Marketing")
- Local business organizations (see the chapter, "Present Seminars")
- Local educational facilities (see the chapter, "Teach a Class")

Should I put it on the Internet?

The Internet and the World Wide Web are great places to

list your directory. Don't forget to register it with all the search engines in order to be fully represented.

What will the recipients do with it?

They will put it on file for future reference when they need an expert in your field. For example, I recently received a call from *Entrepreneur Magazine* in response to just this type of mailing. They were writing an article on self-promotion, checked their files, and there I was, along with the directory release on my expertise and the information I offer.

NOTE: Also send your directory information on disk, both Macintosh and PC. Take it to your local computer consultant and have it converted. Many journalists are putting everything in the computer nowadays. They will thank you for giving them the choice. That thank you registers as one more in the series of imprints necessary to make your image stay in the front of the media.

Part III

NETWORKING

47

THE ART OF NETWORKING

Spinning a web of meaningful relationships

What's the purpose of networking?
- As I see it networking allows you the opportunity to warm call, instead of cold call
- Retail store analyst Brian Dyches looks at networking as a show, tell, and see opportunity
- Gene Call, author of *Word of Mouth Marketing Training*, likes to say that "Networking is better than not working"
- Professional Power CEO Lynn Gabrielson defines it like this: "Networking is demonstrating that you understand and care about people. It's the soft intangible factors that build powerful customer alliances"

Why is everyone so high on networking?
Networking is probably the oldest, most accepted, the best, and the least expensive way to show and tell. It is also one of the best ways to measure how well you're getting your message across, because you are right there in the thick of it when you're representing yourself.

Why is networking a must-have business tool?
Today's marketplace is fiercely competitive, and a personal and professional network can:

- Keep you informed
- Position you in your marketplace
- Help you stay on the cutting edge

How do I make it a successful business experience?

Initially, you must believe that one, networking is power, and two, networking is powerful.

Once you're a devotee of this credo, only then can you three, truly learn the skills that make it a successful experience.

Why are the skills so important?

When you apply the skills then you turn just hanging out and collecting cards into a serious and profitable business opportunity.

- Patti Koltnow took the networking bull by the horns and created her own win-win situation. She took the *Women's Yellow Pages*, targeted her calls, and invited those women in whom she was interested to lunch. Anne Kimbell Relph, the founder of Enterprising Women, gave Patti an opportunity to present a seminar on marketing to the networking group. Anne Kimbell Relph was also the executive director of the USC Orange County campus, and offered Patti a contract as marketing consultant to the office of Exec Ed for their mini MBA program to women
  A year later, Carole Zavala, then the program director of California AWED (American Woman Economic Development), attended an Enterprising Women networking event looking for volunteer trainers and was informed about Patti's marketing expertise. Patti began training at California AWED, became the program director, and when Judith Luther Wilder, founder and executive director of California AWED, left to form Women Incorporated with Lindsey Johnson, former director of the Office of Women's Business Ownership for SBA, they asked Patti to come along as vice president of membership development. All this from one networking phone call
- Gene Call set up a monthly "Soup & Salad" gathering for his data base. But to come you had to bring someone. That way he was able to network his seminars and tapes to new people
- Some people network by putting their merchandise or services in other people's stores that sell similar or compatible products or services
- I was approached at a bookstore by someone who saw me

searching the Internet books. He teaches all levels of classes and was doing his networking. He would sit in the café area and just begin talking to people, asking if they were Internet users

Now what's your opinion on the value of networking?

Are you saying that networking doesn't only occur at formal networking functions?

As my business adviser tells me, "Things aren't always what they seem." There is no hard-and-fast rule that networking must be done in a meeting room with badges, finger foods, white wine spritzers, or any combination thereof.

Networking can take place in elevators, on street corners, at the cash register, waiting in line for café au lait. If there is another person in your immediate space, then the situation is ripe for networking. I sell visibility marketing and consulting services. So I want to know why you are buying that desk, what you are going to do with that briefcase, where are you going to wear the suit. I've gotten many a client from hanging out at a computer store.

How do I approach people?

The best advice is to be aware:

- See what books, magazines, or newspapers people are carrying
- Comment on an article or the headline, and then say, "What do you do?"
- If they have packages look for the store name and start up a conversation

Will people respond favorably?

It depends on the person, the place, and the time. But don't get turned off. My motto is, "Some days you win, some days you lose, and some days you get rained out." I just keep trying. I've gotten some great accounts from just starting a conversation in the lobby while waiting for the elevator that doesn't come. I mention how the elevators in another building are the fastest or the slowest in town. Before long, you're comparing elevator notes, and they or you ask, "How come you know about so many buildings . . . what do you do?'' And the networking has begun.

What if you're shy?

There is help. There are many books, tapes, and seminars that teach how to network for success. I've listed them in the resource section at the end of the chapter. Also, check your local adult education classes. Go to Toastmasters or the National Speakers Association. Take dancing lessons.

You should know that the number one biggest fear of all fears is not death, as you might think, but public speaking. Networking in a broad sense is a form of public speaking. It's all about speaking in public. Maybe one-on-one, but it's the same as speaking, because in networking you are putting forth your ideas.

So know that you're not alone in your fear of networking.

Why is everyone nervous about opening their mouth?

One word: rejection! It's painful enough just putting yourself out there, but having someone walk away in the middle of a sentence, or constantly looking over your shoulder to see who's more important, more interesting, or more helpful, is not in the best interest of your mental health.

How do I get around that fear of rejection?

This is a self-esteem issue, which means you either have to trade yourself in for a new model, or know that in the right arena what you have to offer is interesting, important, and helpful.

As I put on my badge, I repeat to myself three things my parents taught me:

1. ''For every pot there is a cover. Keep looking for that or find a fit that will work for you''
2. ''That's why they make strawberry, chocolate, and vanilla''
3. ''Take what rings true to your heart and discard the rest''

In other words, not everyone in the room is right for you, will like you, will buy from you, wants to talk to you, cares that you exist, and so on. This is not negative thinking. This is pure positive thinking. If you understand this before you go in, you won't be upset when you are rejected or pushed aside or when you're left in the dust.

Don't take yourself so seriously. Keep telling yourself that you are perfect as you are in that moment . . . and work on your networking skills accordingly.

What are some keys to successful networking?

Let's begin with some of the very basics of attention getting, or *grabbers*.

- On the first line of your name tag, put what you do in big, bold letters Then put your company name or your name. This grabber is a fast and great way of inviting a conversation
- Don't hover. Remember that when animals stray outside the herd, they are vulnerable. There is safety in numbers. Go inside the circle and mingle, even if it's with yourself for a few moments until you make contact
- Gentlemen: Wear an interesting tie, then find someone else with an interesting tie and go from there. Ladies: Wear an interesting pin or tie if you so desire
- Have your business card enlarged and laminated. Wear this attached to your name badge. I cut up my book cover, had it sized down and laminated, now I wear that as my name tag. Now that's a grabber!
- Wear bright red or turquoise glasses frames . . . even if you don't wear glasses
- Smile, look interested, give off the vibe that you are approachable. Put out that you have something to offer, and you are willing to exchange it for what they have for you
- Be confident that what you have to say is interesting, and what you have to say *will* be interesting

Lynn Gabrielson, author, speaker, and CEO of Professional Power, offers these twelve important networking rules:

1. Never be late. Be early; it's money in the vault
2. Being late is low priority. Being early is the first step on your financial ladder
3. Time is money. Nonproductive conversation is costly

4. Networking and selling don't mix. Networking is gathering information; selling is making a deal
5. Client or information? Decide what your priority is before the event
6. A question opens a window of information. Prepare and be prepared with opening questions
7. Know who's coming to dinner. Ask for a reservation list before you get there so you can target your networking
8. It's not who talks . . . it's who listens. It's your forum if the audience includes the group of professionals you want to meet
9. Split at the door. Don't sit with your friends. You're there to meet new professionals
10. Always sit by strangers. Reach out. Be consistent and persistent
11. From monologue to dialogue. A communication dialogue is about creating something that causes the customer and prospect to take the next step
12. Understanding the customer's and prospect's needs on a human level

How do I know if what I have to say is interesting?

Very simple—make it interesting. Look carefully for the benefits in what you do. This is called a USP, a unique selling proposition. I call it a unique marketing hook. Copywriter Carl Galletti calls it a unique buying advantage. I've heard it referred to as an emotional buying motive [see the chapter, "Your Unique Selling Proposition (USP)"].

When someone asks you what you do, what do you tell them? The normal answer is the specifics of what you do rather than the benefits. For example, "I'm a travel agent," or "I'm a dentist," or "I sell office systems," or "I'm a personal assistant."

What if, instead of:

- "I'm a personal assistant," you proudly say, "I take away the work gremlins so my boss can climb mountains"
- "I'm a dentist," you proudly say, "I give people the confidence to smile"

- "I sell office systems," you proudly say, "I offer people ways to work smarter, not harder"
- "I'm a travel agent," you proudly say, "I help people fulfill their dreams"

Think of how interesting that would make you. Don't you think people would like to open a conversation with you if you did it that way?

Here are some more examples:

- Shoe salesperson: "I help people point their feet in the right direction"
- Financial analyst, accountant, CPA: "I'm in the numbers racket"
- Consultant: "I give CPR to businesses"
- Car salesperson: "I take people for a ride" or "I give people the ride of their life"
- Insurance broker: "I allow people to sleep at night"
- Contractor: "I build castles"
- Sewing instructor: "I bring out the creative in people"
- Pet shop owner: "I bring smiles to people's faces"
- Ballroom dance instructor: "I make people feel young again"

My answer is, "I bring attention to people, make them famous, successful, and wealthy, but not necessarily in that order."

After that, then what do I say?

After you tell them who you are and what you do, you tell them what you are looking for, what your needs are, and why you are there networking.

Isn't that a rather strong thing to do in a social situation?

Networking, although social, is all business. And as with any business situation you must read the cards before you play the hand. That's what you are there for, to see what they can do for you and you can do for them. Be prepared to bet and call. Otherwise you could lose a very important hand.

How do I know if it's the right time to present my needs?

Ask—that's the only way you'll know. If you find resistance, pull back, smile, and resume the niceties of the day.

Why should I present my needs?

When you present you needs you automatically turn an ordinary social occasion, a chance encounter, into a powerful and meaningful business opportunity. If the other person is there for the same reason and can feed your needs, bingo, a connection. As I say in my speeches, "If you don't ask you don't get. You may not always get what you ask for, but if you don't ask, how will you know what you can or can't get?"

Can you suggest a networking strategy I can follow?

In Gene Call's *Word of Mouth Marketing Training*, he suggests these nine networking strategies:

1. Have goals about whom you'll meet
2. Set your interest compass and your interesting compass
3. Remember your hidden agenda: setting appointments
4. Keep moving . . . circulate
5. Be a host . . . not a guest
6. Focus your attention . . . don't flake
7. Follow up. Follow up. Follow up
8. Make it fun . . . embrace curiosity
9. Engage in the card collection process

What is this business card collection process?

There are two basic schools of thought about exchanging business cards:

1. The first school of thought is that you come prepared to offer your card to all you engage in a greeting. If you're interested in following up with those people, you mark their cards with a word or phrase to remember who they are and why you want to follow up
2. The second school of thought is that you don't bring your cards. Instead, you take their cards, and if there is potential to do business, you either follow up with your card enclosed in a letter, or with a lunch, where you exchange cards. (Always put a few cards in your pocket for that

very special meeting, or to participate in the raffle.) People collect so many cards, yours can end up in a database without any special attention. But if you separate yourself and make yourself stand out, you'll have much more success in making your networking work for you

Just remember what Anne Boe, author of *Networking for Success—How to Turn Business and Financial Relationships into Fun and Profit*, told me, "Become an inverse paranoid; decide the world is conspiring for you."

Network and prosper! As communications expert Marjorie Brody says: "Make this an ongoing life skill."

RESOURCES

- "100 Kaufmann Corollaries," featuring Lynn Gabrielson; Professional Power; 26686 Paseo Tecate; San Juan Capistrano, CA 92675; (717) 240-9269
- *Word of Mouth Marketing Training* by Gene Call; Business for Professionals; 817 4th St.; Santa Monica, CA 90403; (800) 794-7858
- *Is Your Net-Working* and *Networking for Success—How to Turn Business and Financial Relationships into Fun and Profit* by Anne Boe; 607 Summerville Circle; Encinitas, CA 92024; (800) 484-9921
- *Power Schmoozing* by Terri Mandell (First House Press). Terri can be reached at (818) 980-0212

Organization
Women Incorporated; 1401 21st St., Ste. 310; Sacramento, CA 95814; (800) 930-3993 or (916) 448-8898

48

CONSULTING/MENTORING

*Consulting others to be successful
is a very good deed indeed*

What is a mentor-consultant?
A person who shares his or her knowledge for no cost with other businesses or individuals to help them succeed. Mentoring, or helping others succeed in their chosen profession, is an honorable way to promote yourself.

What do mentor-consultants do?
Basically they perform the same duties as a consultant. William Mooney, director and founder of the Center for Consulting & Professional Practices, told me "consultants don't market products or services; they market solutions."

- They provide valuable temporary expertise to companies that can't afford to add such a person to their payroll
- They provide knowledge to create the edge a company needs to win
- They have their finger on the pulse of their industry, seeing it from the outside in
- They provide an overview that might not be seen by those working in the trenches
- They solve problems and create challenges that make a company go forward

Why is being a consultant a good marketing tool?
The more you make yourself and your expertise available to others, the more you are known in the community and your industry. Being a mentor-consultant gets you more business. People talk. Giving gets your name around.

How do I get people to use me?

Sending brochures and expensive mailers is not the best way to introduce yourself. Instead:

- Have someone who is known in your field write you a testimonial or a letter of endorsement (see the chapters "Get Testimonials" and "Endorsement Letters")
- Use referrals. Have someone you know personally introduce you over lunch or cocktails
- Give a seminar on your expertise. Send personal invitations, not brochures, to the companies or businesses you want to attend (see the chapter, "Present Seminars")
- Offer to give an in-house seminar on solutions to basic business needs
- Attend association and organization meetings and mixers. Follow up with those whom you feel might be right for you (see the chapter, "The Art of Networking")
- Draw on companies you've dealt with on the job
- Write articles in the journals and newsletters of your chosen field (see the chapter, "Write Articles")
- Create information products. Write special reports or books. Create audio or video tapes to get your name out there (see the chapters, "Write a Book," "Audio Products," and "Video Products")
- Connect with your religious or service organizations, and let it be known that you are available to mentor others

NOTE: Peter Meyer of The Meyer Group specializes in helping executives and managers get more results with less time, fewer people, and less money. This is what he told me when I asked him about consulting others in the line of service:

"Ever since we started our practice, we have set aside time to help others start theirs. We give advice (only when asked!), run surveys, and distribute the results, and publish our secrets on the Internet. For instance, this year Herman Holtz and I surveyed several hundred consultants to find the barriers that stop them from raising fees. We send the results to anyone who asks.

"We do it because it is the right thing to do, but I have to tell you that it has returned many thousand dollars in revenue. Now, even when we have so little time, requests for surveys or white papers get our full attention. It is good business and good for the community.''

RESOURCES

Books
- *As Iron Sharpens Iron: Building Character in a Mentoring Relationship* by Howard Hendricks (Moody Press)

The following books are available from William Mooney's Center for Consulting & Professional Practices; William Mooney Associates; Box 6159; Torrance, CA 90504; (310) 324-2386; *mooneya@ixs.netcom.com*

- *Consultant's Success* by Howard Shenson and Ted Nicholas
- *101 Proven Strategies for Building a Successful Practice* by Howard Shenson
- *How to Get More & Better Referrals* by Howard Shenson
- *How to Build & Maintain a Profitable Consulting Practice* by William Mooney

Newsletters
- *The Professional Consultant*; Paul L. Franklin; 123 N.W. Second Ave., Ste. 405; Portland, OR 97209; (503) 224-8834
- *Consulting Opportunities Journal*; Consultants National Resource Center; Box 430; Clear Spring, MD 21222; (301) 791-9332

Seminars
- Peter Meyer; The Meyer Group; 883 Cadillac Dr.; Scotts Valley, CA 95066; (408) 439-9607
- Herman Holtz; Box 1731; Wheaton, MD 20915; (310) 649-5745; *HOLTZ@paltech.com*
- Teresita Pena Dabrieo; Success Partnership Network; 1217 Broadway St.; Pella, IA 50219; (800) 943-0012; *teresita@dabrieo.com; http://www./dabrieo.com*
- Paul L. Franklin; National Training Center; 123 N.W. Second Ave., Ste. 405; Portland, OR 97209; (503) 224-8834
- William Mooney; *How to Build & Maintain a Profitable*

Consulting Practice; The Center for Consulting & Professional Practices; William Mooney Associates; Box 6159; Torrance, CA 90504; (310) 324-2386; *mooneya@ixs.netcom.com*

Organizations

- The Center for Consulting & Professional Practices; William Mooney Associates; Box 6159; Torrance, CA 90504; (310) 324-2386
- Academy of Professional Consultants and Advisors; 123 N.W. Second Ave., Ste. 405; Portland, OR 97209; (503) 224-8834
- American Consultants League; 1290 Park Ave.; Sarasota, FL 34236 (813) 952-9290
- Council for Consulting Organizations; 230 Park Ave.; New York, NY 10169; (212) 697-9693
- National Bureau of Professional Management Consultants; 3577 Fourth Ave.; San Diego, CA 92103; (619) 297-2210
- National Consultant Referrals Inc.; 8445 Camino Santa Fe, Ste. 207; San Diego, CA 92121; (619) 552-0111

49

JOIN YOUR CHAMBER OF COMMERCE, SERVICE ORGANIZATIONS, AND TRADE ASSOCIATIONS

A networking business bonanza

What's the purpose of joining my chamber of commerce over any other civic organization?

The phrase "chamber of commerce" tells you quite a bit about its purpose. There are, of course, many civic alternatives with little or no costs involved. However, they don't offer the comprehensive support for the business community that a typical chamber of commerce does.

Are there any restrictions to joining?

Membership is always open to any individual or business.

What are the reasons I should become involved?

Brian Dyches is president of the Laguna Niguel, California–based Retail Resource Group. Prior to launching his consulting firm he was a specialty retailer who found his participation in various chambers an invaluable tool and support mechanism. Brian presented these reasons for involvement from his article, "The Chamber of Commerce—An Organization Worth Joining":

1. It's the voice of your community. It's the central organization in which the business community can join with other organizations to promote projects that benefit people, families, businesses, and the community as a whole
2. It multiplies your effectiveness in the community by pro-

viding the structure, volunteer leadership, professional staff, and full-time office operation to implement an effective program to meet the needs of the business community

3. It's your sales manager for selling community businesses, products, and services in a targeted, business-to-business atmosphere

4. It answers your mail through replying to scores of inquiries about the surrounding area, about your business, and you

5. It's your spokesman to local, state, and national representatives

6. It's your advocate to the community for promoting the understanding of our free-enterprise system of business

7. It's your information bureau for data on other businesses and community services

8. It's your goodwill ambassador for people coming to the community who might be in need of your goods or services

If you were to put a dollar figure on the publicity, referrals, business and political contacts, marketing and research information, et cetera, it would certainly exceed the membership dues to be part of your local chamber of commerce.

Upon joining your local organization you will be added to the business directory, usually receive publicity in an upcoming newsletter, and most importantly have an opportunity to volunteer for committee work. It is the willingness to serve, and even eventually chair a committee, that gives you the chance to help your business community grow and prosper. If a committee doesn't exist in your field of expertise, become proactive and establish one.

Advisory councils provide a forum for members to gather together and work for the benefit of the retailing and service community. This committee is usually one of the more influential, as it represents the many small businesses that typically comprise the majority of the employment force for a given area. Remember—small, not large, businesses make up the backbone of the community.

There are many other committees on which you can serve. There's the continuing education committee, where ideas for seminars and training programs originate. Programs on such topics as preventing shoplifting, trends in employee benefits, advertising options, and taxes are typical offerings, all great subjects to involve you and your staff. This group usually works closely with local trade schools and other institutions of higher learning. It often utilizes professors who offer their expertise to conduct round-table discussions or seminars. What a great opportunity to have a trained professional review your business plan or simply give free advice. Finally, this also presents a great opportunity for you to teach seminars on subjects that you feel particularly well versed in—such as color and fabric trends, for instance.

Other groups include the legislative committee that deals with governmental issues at both the local and state level. Quite often this group will make recommendations to the chamber's board of directors as to how it should stand on particular political issues. Take the recent debate over increasing the minimum wage as a typical issue facing this committee.

Another popular group is the leadership development program at some chambers of commerce. This program inducts ten to twenty local up-and-coming businesspeople into a year-long series of seminars and retreats, where they learn from established business leaders. They are taught myriad skills ranging from public speaking to negotiating. There are other groups and committees that might be active at your local office, so I encourage you to inquire.

Take the time to check out your local chamber of commerce and discover how it can be a relationship worth paying for.

RESOURCES

Consultant
Brian Dyches; Retail Resource Group; 26 Stern St.; Laguna Niguel, CA 92677; (714) 249-7840. Brian is a speaker and author on the subject of how to redesign your store into a money-maker

50

TAKE THEM OUT FOR LUNCH

Breaking bread—the ties that bind

Have you ever heard the terms power lunch or power breakfast? Either of these, or having a traditional cocktail hour, is still one of the most acceptable and fruitful ways for personal marketing.

When people take their meetings in a place of business, business is what prevails before, during, and after the meeting. Phones are ringing, people are passing in and out and around. There is no freedom to be yourself.

At a meal or in a quiet after-work setting, people relax and are more open about themselves.

Why is dining out a good marketing tool?

It's not so much the dining atmosphere that makes it a good marketing tool, it's the act of follow-up and wanting to know someone better that is. Dining is secondary. It is the atmosphere of the dining arrangement that makes the follow-up more pleasant and personal.

Who picks up the check?

Paying the bill can be a power play. Normally, if you absolutely must insist on paying the bill, arrange this beforehand with the waiter. Give up your credit card in private before you sit down. That way there is no discussion at the end of the meal. You simply say, "I've taken care of it; thanks anyway."

If, on the other hand, the guest insists, it's your call. You can let him or her pay and say, "I'll get it the next time."

Just make sure you don't ruin the pleasant networking meal by arguing about the bill.

How should I follow up?

This is a business networking arrangement, not a date. You don't have to send flowers or candy. If you wish to continue this business friendship, then call, fax, or e-mail your delight in meeting this person, with a mention of "we have to do this again soon."

Will they think I'm being pushy?

Not if the time lag is spaced properly. You might also suggest that you have a friend you would like them to meet who might be helpful in their business. Ask them if they also want to bring someone along.

NOTE: I'm a Gemini, and every time I met a Gemini I would take them out to lunch, no matter what line of work they were in. I was always taught that you never know who people know, where they know them from, and where they'll end up knowing more people. Eventually these lunches evolved into a small Gemini birthday party. The next year I asked those same Geminis to bring a Gemini friend. The next year those friends brought Gemini friends, and so on and so on for eight years. Here's the interesting thing. Many a time I would show up for a social or business event, and when introduced, total strangers would say, "Aren't you the woman who throws that great Gemini party?" I've gotten some very fine referrals from complete strangers, people I would never meet in a lifetime, all because I started taking people to lunch.

51

SIT ON THE BOARDS OF ORGANIZATIONS AND ASSOCIATIONS

Top bananas get more sunshine

How do I get to be a board member?

Sometimes it's as easy as asking. Many organizations use board positions for fund-raising, but many pay a fee to board members. I sat on the board of a ballet company and a halfway house, and I contributed several thousand dollars for the privilege to both.

I didn't know I could contribute my way into a seat. How do I find that out?

You simply ask the organization, "What are your requirements to be a board member?" You'll know soon enough what they are, and if the organization wants you.

How do I find out if they pay you?

Exactly the same way. Ask.

Why would the board want to pay me?

If your name and position is advantageous to have you listed on their board, the organization will go after you to sit on its board. I have several friends who derive their sole income from sitting on boards and the consultation fees they get from that networking opportunity.

Can I contribute my service in lieu of contributing money?

Absolutely. Again, ask. It could be your lucky day. For eight years I was on the board of the entertainment industry's T. J. Martell Foundation, a children's leukemia, cancer and

AIDS research group. In turn, I did the publicity for its Rock 'n' Bowl, the annual dinner, and on occasion research announcements for the foundation's Mount Sinai Hospital's laboratory.

What if the organization doesn't pay or want money, but wants time?

If the people are right for growing your business, and you feel the organization is true to your heart, find the time. It will be most rewarding in many ways, on many levels.

NOTE: Volunteering is becoming big in business. Many employers have instituted programs in which they encourage a certain time off during the workweek for you to volunteer at your favorite charity.

52

START AN ORGANIZATION, A CLUB, OR A SALON

Find a void and fill it

Who founds organizations other than industry groups and professional associations?

- People who are passionate about what they believe in and want to share it
- People who want to be the center of attention
- People who can't find an organization to meet their needs, so they start one
- People who have a message to get across
- People who love people and want to share experiences
- People who are looking for companionship of like minds

- People who want to teach others
- People who want to learn new things
- People in need of support

What are some examples of organizations started by people like me?

1. **International Boost Your Self-Esteem Month.** This promotion was started in Boston by author and speaker Valla Dana Fotiades. She has a Self-Esteem Newsletter, a list of Self-Esteem Recommended Readings, her Favorite Self-Esteem Quote, Tips To Boost Self-Esteem, and an Official Self-Esteem Definition. Dana also has a name for the people who support and carry on the tradition of International Boost Your Self-Esteem Month. They are called EBs, for Esteem Boosters, and she even has silver and blue stickers for their stationery needs.

   Here's how it works. Valla proclaimed February as International Boost Your Self-Esteem Month (see the chapter, "Proclamations and Celebrations"). This is her message from her promotional materials:

   "Melt winter blahs and negatives that impede personal and professional growth with a Perfect Solution! As winter winds down and people crave seasonal change, boost morale in businesses, corporations, clubs, schools, organizations, your own life, and your own family by springing into self-esteem programs. Inspire yourself and others to seize new challenges. Ignite personal potential. Make dreams a reality."

   There are no dues, no reporting in, no paperwork, no nothing. And people can set their guidelines as they wish. What a way to have an organization!

How has this worked as a good marketing tool for her?
- Valla listed International Boost Your Self-Esteem Month in *Chase's Calendar of Events* and John Kremer's *Celebrate Today*
- The media call her when February comes around
- It's a great hook to get speaking engagements
- She hosts a TV talk show
- She has written a book

- She is a frequent guest on national radio and TV talk shows

2. **Berkley Square Bench Club.** Mel Bloom was so enchanted by the storied English garden in London's Berkley Square that he bought a bench from the city's bench program four years ago and placed it in the garden. Prompted by friends who visited and sent back photos of them sitting on the bench, he formed the Berkley Square Bench Club, an elite but nonexclusive collection of those who summarily perched on the Bloom Bench.

   There are no dues or obligations. Members receive a club pin designed by his wife, Andi, and an invitation to the club's annual grand tea.

3. **Women Empowered™.** In 1990, Nicole Rhodes, a skilled facilitator and business coach, formed a by-invitation-only forum in which successful women peers meet to learn, grow, and contribute within a confidential setting. This yearlong learning program meets once a month in groups of ten to twelve, with a professional facilitator and an expert resource person. There are peer and facilitator coaching sessions, and critical issues sessions. They share a commitment to resolve the most important issues in their personal and professional lives.

   The forum now has three modules in California. Nicole is always interested in sharing the Women Empowered™ experience with anyone who would like to facilitate a module.

I'm not a speaker or an author. How do I start an organization?

Because you know the target market, you can jump right in:

- Rent mailing lists from like-minded local organizations
- Rent local demographic names from magazine mailing lists
- Ask your friends for referrals
- Give a talk or a networking event, then put the information in the newspaper

- Collect cards at like-minded mixers, meetings, lunches, et cetera.

And don't forget to list your organization in any and all local directories. Call the chamber of commerce to see what community directories are in existence. Also call the mayor's office and ask the same question.

NOTE: For additional information, see the chapters, "Present Seminars," "Teach a Class," "Be a Toastmaster," and "Developing Your Own Mailing Lists," as well as Part VII, "Using the Media to Get the Word Out."

RESOURCES

Organizations
- Valla Dana Fotiades; International Boost Your Self-Esteem Month; Box 812-W. Sd. Stn.; Worcester, MA 01602-0812; (508) 799-9860
- Nicole Rhodes; Women Empowered™; 353 Puerta de Lomas; Fallbrook, CA 92028; (619) 732-0200

Books
- *Chase's Calendar of Events*; Contemporary Books; Dept. C; 2 Prudential Plaza; Ste. 1200; Chicago, IL 60601-6790; (312) 540-4500
- *Celebrate Today* by John Kremer; Prima Publishing; Box 1260 BK; Rocklin, CA 95677; (916) 632-4400

53

VOLUNTEER

What goes around, comes around

What's your overview of volunteering?

Retail consultant and mentor Brian Dyches said it brilliantly when I asked him that question: "The many issues that have faced our world community these past few years—mergers and acquisitions, AIDS, ozone depletion, ocean pollution, and so on—have spawned a curious side effect—civic volunteerism. Not in recent memory has the number of people volunteering their time been as high. This giving of time in a world so often short of time is itself an anomaly. Just take a look at the Suzy column in *WWD* and you'll see a whole slew of designers giving their time and millions to various causes. Could it be that civic pride and responsibility are making a comeback?"

How does volunteering make a good marketing tool?
- Volunteering is a great way to network, and we all know that networking is a great way to market oneself
- Volunteering is great for name recognition

What should I consider when choosing an organization or charity to volunteer time, effort, and money to?

Choose your volunteering as if you were selecting your marketing campaign. Besides choosing an organization or cause with which you resonate, check who is on the board and how they can be of service to you. Volunteering, when there is a business purpose involved, is a calculated science. As with planning your marketing campaign, volunteering can pay off.

If I volunteer, will I only see the people I'm helping? If so, how does that help me market myself?

You might think you're only coming in contact with the people you're helping. You really are coming in contact with many more people, especially those on the level you're trying to network with. It might only seem that you're only seeing those on the receiving end.

But in reality you're networking with the other volunteers, the families of those you're helping, and most of all the board members who are, in most cases, the community movers and shakers.

Aside from the yearly Christmas party, how can I be in contact with these movers and shakers?
- Show an interest; ask if the board meetings are open
- Invite them to breakfast or lunch to discuss how you and your resources can best serve the project
- Determine their birthdays or anniversaries and send a card
- Send holiday greetings
- Reach out to them

NOTE: Making time for others is more than marking time; it's being in time itself.

RESOURCES

Retail Expert
- Brian Dyches; Retail Resource Group; 26 Stern St.; Laguna Niguel, CA 92677; (714) 249-7840. Brian is a speaker and author on the subject of how to make your retail store a money-maker

Part IV

RELATIONSHIP MARKETING

54

JOINT VENTURING

When two heads are better than one

What does joint venturing mean?
It's about joining forces and having a relationship with a like-minded business to increase each other's bottom line. Other names for joint venturing are:

- Satellite marketing
- Consignment marketing
- Strategic alliances
- Host-parasite

Where can you find these power partners?
Terri Lonier, author of *Working Solo*, told me the best way to do this is to "begin by developing an awareness that you may find a partner anywhere—from a local business meeting to a national conference. It may be through a referral, or even an on-line connection. The world is brimming with partnership possibilities—waiting for your discovery."

What is an example of a joint venture?
My client was a juvenile clothing and toy store. Their next-door neighbor was a mattress store. What a joint-venture marriage.

I suggested to both that we place mannequins dressed in pajamas, and dolls and cuddly teddy bears, in the mattress store on consignment. The mattress store didn't buy them, it just provided the space.

On one hand, it made the mattress store looking a bit more homey and lived in, and it also gave some life to its merchandise. On the other hand, it could:

- Take a percentage of the sale
- Rent the space for a small fee
- Barter goods or services
- Do an exchange of products

In return, my client benefited from:

- A branch store without paying rent, taxes, and employees
- Word-of-mouth marketing
- Networking
- A chance to display its merchandise to a target market

What are some other examples?
- Shoe stores can display their shoes and hosiery in a clothing store
- Clothing stores can dress up mannequins for automobile showroom cars
- Sporting goods stores can put up travel agency posters
- Jewelry stores can do a joint venture with any apparel store, or dress up almost any window to point up a lifestyle motif
- Wine, flowers, and candy can go in any display
- Books on any subject can go in any display

What about services?
- Car care businesses, such as oil change shops, can sell anything that goes in a car, including stereos
- Chiropractors and health care facilities can do a joint venture with aromatherapy companies, massage therapists, nutritionists, spas
- Hotels can offer personal security systems, nature sounds, yoga mats, and kennel care

How do customers know it's my merchandise?
Part of the relationship should be that you're allowed to tag or sticker your merchandise. If there are display windows ask if a tasteful card can grace your items, such as "Shoes compliments of Mary's Footery."

NOTE: Once you understand joint venturing you'll never be able to go into a store or office again without seeing the possibilities. Don't be shy. Suggest it to the owner or manager. And it's great networking.

RESOURCES

Working Solo by Terri Lonier; Box 190; New Paltz, NY 12561; (914) 255-7165; fax (914) 255-2116; *solonews@workingsolo.com; http://www.workingsolo.com.* Call (800) 222-7576 to order Terri's book, audiotape, print newsletter, or electronic newsletter

55

GET TESTIMONIALS

Ask and ye shall receive

Why are testimonials important marketing tools?

When you ask people to give you a testimonial, you are asking them two things:

1. To lend their names to your data base
2. To tell their data base about you

For example, if you want people to eat at your restaurant, it definitely would be better to have someone other than you or your family recommend your fine dining establishment.

Where would you eat? A place that said, "Eat at Joe's— Great Food!" signed by Joe, or one that said "Eat at Joe's— Great Food!" signed by community leaders and neighbors?

When someone else gives you advice, they are an impartial observer, saying basically the same things you're saying in your marketing materials, but it's not coming from you. Sometimes the horse's mouth is not the one that should speak.

It's called third party endorsement, and it works. It can attach value to a person, place, or thing.

Why do testimonials work?
Testimonials, like endorsements, promote honesty, believability, and trust. And these three promote loyalty. A loyal follower is a thing to behold and hold on to.

Isn't using a testimonial or an endorsement blowing my own horn?
Just the opposite. They are used to get other people to sell and tell for you.

What are the different types of testimonials?
- Testimonials and endorsements can be an affirmation used to publicly tell others about the faith another person has in your product or service
- They can be a tribute, a means to compliment an interaction
- Testimonials and endorsements can be not only tied to products or services but also to ability and character
- They can give support

What are some specific examples that illustrate how I can best put a testimonial to work for me?
- Each time a client, customer, patient, or patron tells you how nice you are, how great your service is, or how much they enjoyed what they bought, ask them if you can print that compliment in your newsletter or flier
- Put those comments in your brochure
- Put those comments on your stationery and send them along in any package carried or mailed
- When you send your special report, ask for comments. Put those comments and testimonials on the back or on the inside page of the next printing
- Keep a tape recorder handy. When someone gives you a testimonial, ask if you can record and use it. Incorporate it into your hold button message
- If you have an in-store video marketing system, set up a video camera. Follow people through your store or have

it situated at the cashier. Ask them if they mind giving a testimonial

• When people write you thank you letters, put them in plastic sleeves and keep them in a notebook. Keep them in your waiting room or at your sales desk. Display it open so people will feel comfortable reading it

Is there a way to word my request for a testimonial so I get what I need it to say?

• Ask for reasons why people shop with you or your business
• Ask for emotions or feelings they encounter with you or your business
• Ask for problems solved
• Ask for needs met
• Ask for things you taught them
• Ask for things they learned from you

What if they ask me to write it for them?

This is often the case. Don't be shy. Ask the above questions, then draw up three paragraphs that say basically the same thing, starting from the subtle to the roar. Let them choose the one that makes them feel the most comfortable.

What lends itself best to testimonials?

Any business, place, person, idea, talent, or thing. There are no restrictions.

NOTE: In chiropractic school doctors are taught to say to their patients, "If you like how you feel when you leave here, who are you going to bring along with you on your next appointment so they can have that feeling too?" Now that's a testimonial come full circle.

56

GIVE TESTIMONIALS

Give and ye shall receive

Why is giving testimonials an important marketing tool?
As with endorsements, when you give your name and support to another person you are getting free recognition of your own name as well. There it is, right out there for everyone to see. That makes it one more audio or visual imprint. And we all know that we need all we can get. And it doesn't cost anything.

For example, when Orvel Ray Wilson (*Guerrilla Selling*) and Tony Parinello (*Selling to VITO*) heard I was writing this book, they asked me if I wanted a testimonial before I could ask them. Why? Of course they wanted to support me and add their credibility to my product. But also because they're smart. They know that hundreds of thousands of people will read my book and will also get to see their names and book titles. This is not only a visual imprint, it is an endorsement from me that could encourage you to go out and buy their book. And in return, Jay Conrad Levinson, Orvel Ray Wilson, and Mark S. A. Smith asked me to give a testimonial for their book, *Guerrilla Trade Show Selling*.

How do I go about giving a testimonial?
It's basically the same procedure as getting a testimonial, only in reverse. If you like someone's product, service, or talent, write him or her a letter on your company stationery. It could end up in a testimonial book, a special report, a brochure, a newsletter, an infomercial, or a book.

Write a letter to a local talk show host. More than likely it will be read on the air.

Dan Kennedy always includes people's comments in his *No*

B.S. Marketing Letter. There's that old third party endorsement at its best.

Don't forget to talk about the problem they solved for you, the need they filled, or any other reason you felt you were compelled to want to write the testimonial.

NOTE: Giving testimonials is a win-win situation. Don't be shy; it could mean you get in the face of thousands of people who might not be clients of yours . . . yet.

RESOURCES

Book
Guerrilla Trade Show Selling by Jay Conrad Levinson, Orvel Ray Wilson, and Mark S. A. Smith (John Wiley)

Consultant and Newsletter
- Dan Kennedy; *No B.S. Marketing Letter*; Empire Communications Corporation; 5818 N. 7th St., #103; Phoenix, AZ 85014; (602) 997-7707

57

ENDORSEMENT LETTERS

Support and conquer

How does an endorsement letter differ from a testimonial?
A testimonial is usually a sentence or brief paragraph. An endorsement letter is a letter you write that supports:

- A product
- A place

- An idea
- A person

This can be the only piece in the envelope, or it can be a cover letter to a marketing mailing piece.

How long is an endorsement letter?
As long as it needs to be to get the job done.

- It can be just a one-page note briefly describing to the recipient why you support and sanction this person, place, product, or idea
- It can be many pages going into great detail, with stories, examples, bullet points, reasons, et cetera
- It can be a lift off, i.e., a small piece of paper clipped to or stuck on the promotion piece. When the recipient reads the marketing piece, the endorsement can be lifted off so as not to take attention away from the piece

Why does an endorsement letter work?
It's the Eat at Joe's, signed by someone other than Joe principle. It's all about that sought-after third-party endorsement that makes it better, more accepting, more magical.

How does an endorsement letter impact readers?
It's the value added concept.

- If the return address is from someone they know, then opening the mailing piece and finding someone else praising a person or a product is something extra they didn't expect
- If the return address is not from someone they know, but the letter talks about someone they know, again it's a little something extra they didn't expect

It's another way to get an AHA!

Does it matter if the recipient knows the person who writes the endorsement letter?
No, because the letter will fully document that person's credentials and why the letter is being written on his or her behalf.

If I write that endorsement letter, how do I benefit?
- When you mail to the recipient's data base, who you are and what service you provide puts you in front of a new universe of potential business prospects
- When you endorse to your own data base, you're perceived as helping someone, and as we all know this is good for your image

Who pays for the printing and mailing costs?
Either the person who asks for the endorsement, or, because both parties are benefiting, you could split the cost.

Are there any less expensive ways to do this?
Try a postcard mailing:

- Use the front to display the person, product, place, service, or idea, and write the endorsement on the back, opposite the address
- Use the front for the written endorsement, and put the picture on the back

See the chapter, "Postcard Campaigns" for an in-depth discussion on the merits of postcard marketing.

58

COMMUNITY INVOLVEMENT

Love your neighbor, and you'll love yourself

Is community involvement like volunteering?
No. Instead, this is when a business forms an alliance with a community project or a nonprofit organization for social responsibility. In a way, it's another form of a joint venture.

How do I benefit?

Although the benefits to the business usually remain tactfully unspoken, they are a factor in the business's community involvement. There is nothing wrong with that, unless the what's-in-it-for-me attitude overwhelms the giving. That is, if the name is bigger than the project.

Benefits include name recognition, customer loyalty, and goodwill in the community.

What are some examples of what you mean by community involvement?

- Universal Studios's community outreach programs to educate youth and provide the human touch to retirement centers
- Arbella Mutual Insurance Company and The Medical Foundation of Boston's Perils of Teen Drinking and Driving campaign
- Nordstrom's in-store and mall mammogram clinics
- Saturn's city pocket parks program
- Greyhound's Teen Runaway Hot Line—Free Ticket Home program
- Eastman Kodak, Xerox, Bausch & Lomb, and the University of Rochester's summer science camp and after-school science program for city school children
- Home Depot's Beautification Day and School Refurbishing programs
- Radio Station KXPK's Random Acts of Kindness projects
- Crest Toothpaste's sponsorship of Dr. Jack Miller's Tooth Mobile
- Clinton, Massachusetts–based NYPRO's robotics student intern program in cooperation with the National Science & Invention Organization

What can a smaller business do?

The little guy can take a look at what the big guy is doing and modify the program's design to meet its own needs.

- Group 3, a New Jersey insurance company, teamed up with its local National Alliance for Excellence. Group 3 offers local students scholarship programs in science technology

- A dry cleaner in Santa Monica, California, earmarks one dollar per bill to Heal the Bay
- Il Cielo restaurant in Los Angeles printed a box at the bottom of the check. If their customers checked the box, $1 would be added to the total. This dollar is donated to local food banks

Are there resources that will help me create a project I can participate in?

- Banks and hospitals have community outreach programs. Contact them and see if you can partner with them
- Contact any public relations or marketing company. Hire a company to find you local or national involvement. That's right up its alley
- Read your newspaper. It is always reporting on nonprofit programs that could use a financial handshake

As a public relations and visibility marketing specialist, I've created many alliances with my clients and nonprofits for community outreach.

- I suggested to my children's shoe store client that we place a large barrel at the front door. On top of this barrel we put a sign requesting patrons to bring in their children's used or outgrown shoes. These outgrown items would be donated to homeless shelters. All donations were rewarded with a $5 discount applied to their next purchase
- I represented an eyeglasses store. I arranged for the county to donate used frames to the needy. Patrons buying new frames would be given a discount if they donated their old frames
- I ask all my entertainment clients to take an hour or two off their busy schedules when they are on tour to visit the local children's hospital. If they can't go in person, I arrange for a conference call from the local TV or radio station, or club where they are performing. Contact your local music club. Ask if the artists can give a few minutes of their time to call the children's ward of your local hospital
- I partnered my soap opera clients with the ASPCA. Once

a week my clients, armed with dogs, cats, and birds, would visit elder care residential homes

How can I involve my employees?
- Ask your employees what they would like to do. If it's volunteer time they want, give them a few hours off a week or a month
- Use the old suggestion box for ideas. Perhaps they have favorite charities that have programs you could sponsor
- If there's a Special Olympics or a marathon or a Habitat for Humanity Day, ask your employees if they would like to represent the company in a collective effort

NOTE: Your employees will think more of you, you'll help others, your image in the community will shine a little brighter, and in the long run you'll get back what you put out.

59

CONTINUITY PROGRAMS

Keeps them coming, and coming, and coming . . .

What is a continuity program?
It's a strategy for developing return business.

What kind of businesses does it work well with?
Any business that offers a repeat service, and basically that's any business. Car washes, hair salons, restaurants, dry cleaners, et cetera are the ones that come to mind. But carpet cleaners, exterminators, and plumbers also want your repeat business, even if you only need them once or twice a year.

What do I have to do to make it work?

Establish a system or a reason for your target audience to give you repeat business.

What's at the heart of a continuity program?

A program that promotes customer loyalty. If you love 'em they won't leave you.

Is a membership card a continuity program?

A very good one, in fact. I set my yoga teacher up with a member's coupon book. Clients that bought ten private sessions got $20 off the regular price of each session.

I did the same for my massage therapist client. Because she does energy balancing, acupressure, and jin shin jytsu, she now gives a coupon book made up of all these coupons. Educating my client's audience to the fact that she provides several services broadened her image and increased her word-of-mouth marketing. Now when they recommend her, she's not so one-dimensional, and she draws in clients with different treatment preferences.

Marketing experts Alan and Brad Antin reported this interesting continuity program. They told of a gas station that added an automatic brushless car wash. The smart owner started giving customers special membership cards to his Wash-a-Week Club.

This is how it works: Club members get a free car wash with no strings attached every week. All they have to do is come in on their assigned day (noted on their membership cards) to get their free car wash.

"Guess where the line for the car wash started?" Brad asked me. "That's right, right in front of the gas pumps. Not only did he sell a ton more gas, but he also offered car wash options like hot wax, under spray, and wheel and tire cleaning. Most people bought gas and one or more of the options. But most importantly they came in almost every week."

The car wash membership outcome? Alan told me that "the station owner soon opened several more stations. Where do you think he got the money?"

Do I have to offer memberships?

Continuity programs are not only based on memberships.

Here's an interesting way to carry on a joint venture continuity program with your competition, no less. This one comes from marketing geniuses Glen Osborne and Judith Kendall of KOMG Marketing.

Here is a high profit/low cost continuity program. Readers can use it to get male and female patrons to come back. Judy Kendall and Glenn Osborn of the Millionaire Mastermind Marketing Association created a Continuity Referral Program for a test client who owns four restaurants. During their visit to his city patrons return to the restaurants they frequented before or are referred to another restaurant. Diners receive two reports at each restaurant. Women get "Fifteen Second Relationship versus One Night Stand Dating Test" and "How to Use the Sixty Second FBI Truth Test on a Dating Prospect," while men receive "Bartender's Guide Quiz on How to Pick Up Women" and "Eight Dating Mistakes Men Make." At the end of each report are the names of two more reports diners receive *if* they eat at the restaurant across the street. The reports have pizzazz because they're based on Bryan Redfield's *Bartender's Guide* books for men and women. The results: continuous referrals!

What are some less complicated ideas?
- My health spa gave me a coupon for a free massage after every five visits
- I received a free coupon for a large dairy cream after I purchased ten foot-long hot dogs at Annapolis's pride and joy, Anne's Dairy Creme
- My hairdresser gave me a free coupon for a color rinse after twenty-five haircuts
- The garden center offered me a two-for-one sale the next time I bought a plant
- The bookstore gave me a discount coupon after I purchased ten books

Why are continuity programs a good marketing tool?
Aside from giving good customer service, continuity programs promote word of mouth. Word of mouth promotes referrals, and referrals promote new business. Put the new business on a continuity program, and you'll have more people

coming back time and again. And what did it cost you? A glass of wine, a car wash, a color rinse job?

If you figure out what it costs to get and keep a customer, your ROI (rate of investment) continuity programs are definitely a win-win.

RESOURCES

- KOMG Marketing Group; Glenn Osborne and Judith Kendall; 116 W. University Pkwy; Baltimore, MD 21210; (410) 235-6789
- Brad and Alan Antin, *The Antin Marketing Newsletter, Secrets from the Lost Art of Common Sense Marketing*; 11001 Delmar, Ste. 1200; Leawood, KS 66211; (913) 663-5775; fax (913) 663-5552; *antin@tyrall.net; 75706.2523@ CompuServe*. The Antins offer six audiotapes and a 205-page, three-ring training binder. Great seminars and consulting, too!

60

CONTRIBUTE TO OTHER INDUSTRY NEWSLETTERS

A tip here, a tip there can tip the scales in your favor

Why would another newsletter be interested in my material?

Newsletter publishers are always looking for the right tip, the right list, the right survey. Contributions that make their readership successful, happy, and add to their overall well-being are always welcome.

How do I find these other newsletters?

Ask your local library for these resources:

- *Hudson's Subscription Newsletter Directory* (800) 572-3451
- *Newsletter Directory:* Oxbridge Communications, (800) 955-0231
- *Newsletters in Print:* Gale Research, (800) 877-4253

There are newsletters for every industry, profession, and then some.

What are the benefits?

The main reason is to inexpensively market your name or business name to current or potential markets.

If your tips, trends, surveys, lists, et cetera, are accepted, the publication prints your name, phone, and a description of what you do . . . *for free.* Would you turn that down?

Can I submit material to newsletters that aren't on my specialty?

Absolutely. If you are a chiropractor, for example, you can create material that fits the needs of a gardening magazine. You could discuss the best way to bend or lift a sack of dirt without blowing out your back or knees. Indeed, every profession or industry can use information on how to:

- Save money
- Save time
- Eat healthy
- Enjoy life
- Feel better
- Do better
- Get more from what they're doing
- Get a loan
- Pick a house
- Save for a rainy day
- Not be stressed

- Dress for success
- Get a raise
- Be a better person
- Sit properly
- Shake hands
- Travel light
- Travel safe
- Travel with children and survive
- Organize their life
- Organize their desk
- And so on . . .

Will readers call for services from a newsletter article?
Absolutely. I'm living proof. In the last two years I've gotten at least ten consulting jobs and sold more than 100 books and tapes from the articles I placed in three newsletters. And those consulting jobs resulted in more recommendations that turned into profitable situations.

- Twice, my top ten tip list on "How to Get the Editor to Publish Your Top Ten List" resulted in a well-paying speaking engagement
- Excerpts from my audiotapes *How to Do Your Own Publicity, an Insider's Guide to the Publicity Game* resulted in a request to create customized tapes for a doctor's collective

So yes, people do read your articles, and yes, you can get work from them. It's worth the effort.

RESOURCES

NOTE: There is an in-depth newsletter resource list at the end of the chapter, "Newsletters."

61

CULTIVATE REFERRALS

You scratch my back; I'll scratch yours

Sally Wright, consultant, workshop leader, CEO, and founder of MarkeTeam, teaches a wonderful course on referrals. She was gracious enough to share information from her article, "Focusing On Referrals."

What are referrals?

When you get a new customer, and that customer has heard about your service from someone else, that's called a "referral."

Why are they important?

Many say that 90% of all business comes as a result of referrals. This is especially true for those who offer a service. Some people call it word-of-mouth marketing. No matter what you call it, you can't ignore a marketing technique that brings in as much as 90% of your business.

If referrals are so important, what about conventional marketing, such as brochures and advertising?

Not to worry! Don't go out and throw away your brochures and cancel your advertising. These are important, partly because those who refer business to you are influenced by these very things. It may be that your brochure or your advertisement captivates that certain person who is almost ready to recommend you, and tips the balance, causing them to make that phone call, give that recommendation. On the other hand, if your brochure is mediocre, often the potential referrer would be reluctant to pass it on to your potential client.

How do I get referrals?
There are three sources of referrals:

1. Your current client
2. Your inactive client
3. The person who is in contact with many of your potential clients and can influence them to use you

None of these sources will come to you until you have met six conditions. These conditions are:

1. Your influencer must be in contact with your targeted customer
2. Your influencer must be respected by your targeted customer
3. Your influencer must know what you do
4. Your influencer must know your targeted customer profile
5. Your influencer must trust you
6. Your influencer must be motivated to refer other clients to you

How do I know if these conditions are all in place?
Here's how to do it: Take one person whom you think should be sending business your way. Ask yourself each of the six questions listed above. Does that person meet these conditions? If he or she falls short in one of these areas, then you have identified the very area that you need to work on!

The key to successful referrals is making sure that you unequivocally provide stellar client satisfaction. Without this, you are almost guaranteed that no referrals will come your way.

NOTE: The Pareto Principle. There is an internationally known marketing principle. As it was told to me, it basically states "that eighty percent of your business will come from twenty percent of your existing data base. And so too will eighty percent of your complaints come from twenty percent of your data base."

Referrals are important for many reasons, but the biggest

one is to replace the numbers that drop out of your data base so you can stay in business.

RESOURCES

MarkeTeam; Sally Wright; 5902 Monterey Rd., Ste. 252; Los Angeles, CA 90042; (213) 227-6667; fax (213) 225-8228; *marketeams@aol.com*. Sally offers consulting and workshops

62

HELP LINES BUILD CONNECTIONS

If you light just one candle . . .

WHAT IS A HELP LINE?

It is a situation where people can call in live, ask questions, engage in a dialogue, and exchange information with an expert or a panel of experts. You might know it as a hot line or a call-in line.

WHY IS THIS A GOOD MARKETING TOOL

It presents you as an expert in your field. When marketed properly your name and service can be seen and heard by thousands of people.

HOW WOULD I MARKET THIS HELP LINE?

- Fliers
- Newsletter announcements
- Newspaper articles
- Calendar items
- Being a guest on local talk shows
- Direct-mail pieces
- Broadcast fax
- Postcard campaigns

See all these chapters for more information.

What are the benefits of a panel of experts versus going solo?

Putting together a panel is about combining experts in non-competitive, similar fields of interest.

- Potential prospects from sharing mailing lists
- Image enhancement
- Expanded media coverage to different but related sections
- Introduction into field-related newsletters and journals
- Broader outreach into the community for name recognition

What are some examples of a noncompetitive panel makeup?

- Pediatricians, child psychologists, teachers, social workers.
- Stress experts, cardiac specialists, nutritionists, yoga instructors
- Plumbers, architects, building inspectors
- Disability board members, compensation experts, PI lawyers, chiropractors, doctors
- CPAs, tax experts, IRS representatives
- Acting coaches, child labor people, agents, former child actors

How do I set up a help line?

Call the business office of your local telephone company. Tell the people there that you want to set up a live call-in telephone hookup. They'll give you all the charges and details, and they'll make it happen.

What does the telephone company need to know?

- Where you want the lines set up
- How many lines
- What phone number you want to use
- What time
- How many hours
- How many days

What if no one calls?

If you've done the marketing plan described above, someone will call. And if they don't, look at all the name recognition you got from the visibility marketing.

How can I use the calls and the answers in another form?

- Tape the entire event, then have it transcribed. Use the transcription for your newsletter
- Use the tape as a gift to people on your mailing list or as a giveaway on your hold button message
- Write an article for your newspaper based on a list of the most asked questions

What if not enough people call?

Do what legitimate theater does: Paper the house. In other words, write out questions you know are important, give them to friends, clients, and relatives, and when there is a lull have them call in. This will beef up the taped version and keep you busy during those downtimes.

NOTE: Buy time on a local radio station and broadcast the help line (see the chapter, "Host Your Own Radio Show").

63

MARKETING WITH CELEBRITIES

Sometimes it really is "who you know"

Utilizing celebrities is a tried-and-true method of getting good visibility and excellent name recognition for your marketing needs.

Products, places, and ideas can all benefit from celebrity endorsements. Whether it's charity event, parade, political cause, or the opening of a shopping mall, people will stand in blinding rain and blizzards just to see their favorites. I know this firsthand. Since the beginning of my company in 1979, my client roster has included daytime TV personalities, comedians, rock and roll and jazz giants. Many of them have been asked to press the flesh, grip 'n grin, and sign the name, all in the name of visibility.

Are celebrities expensive to get for a function?

Up-and-coming celebrities will often come free, just for the exposure. And there are certain charities that certain A-list celebs will also do at no charge. The price depends on whether you want them for an evening, a weekend, a spokesperson for a year, or for commercials or product endorsements. And yes, the agencies that provide them to you charge a percentage on top of the star's fees.

Celebrities usually get two first-class round trip tickets, hotel, meals, and a limousine.

Why would anyone pay to have a celebrity at an event?

When the big city marathons first began, it was rumored the organizers paid the champions to come and run. Why? It brought status, credibility, and a more global scope to the event. The same with charities, private parties, parades, et cet-

229

era. The right celebrities, whether they are local or international talent, can:

- Expand publicity efforts
- Add to the organization's cachet
- Make the posters stand out
- Sell tickets
- Increase fund-raising totals
- All but guarantee a successful event
- Create good word of mouth that can last a long time, or at least until next year's event

How can I get them to come to my event?

Getting to the celebrity gatekeepers is not as difficult as you'd think:

1. Contact the specialized celebrity placement agencies
2. Contact managers, agents, or the celebrity's public relations person
3. Contact the teams, TV and radio stations, or film studios where they work
4. Contact the ad agencies that create their commercials

What are some of the agencies that recruit celebrities?

There are two very reputable agencies in Los Angeles that I recommend: Celebrity Connection, Barry Greenberg, president and founder, and The Celebrity Source, Rita Tateel, president and founder. They recruit and coordinate celebrity involvement for any type of event.

Can you give me examples of the kinds of events?

The scope of these two agencies' work runs from getting Jane Seymour to act as spokesperson for Ralston Purina's Fit and Trim National Rib Check Day campaign, to hiring Elliot Gould to be the keynote speaker at United Jewish Appeal (UJA) dinner, to getting ten celebrities for a private party to kick off the Kentucky Derby.

That's right. When you see those parties on "Entertainment Tonight," E!, or CNN's "ShowBiz Today," in many cases those celebrities were there because they were hired to be there. Not always, but it's a good bet most of the time.

Rita told me how she was hired by James River Paper Products to put their environmentally friendly toilet paper in the hands of caring celebrities so they would spread the word about the product.

What if a charity can't afford to hire a celebrity?

You can contact the celebrity's manager, agent, or PR agent directly and ask for availability. It's a long shot, but it has been done before. This is how you find out who the agents are:

- For television: Call the network the show is on and ask for programming. Tell programming you want the name of the celebrity agent, manager, or PR person. If the show is on location in another city or produced by a private production company, you will be given that information and you call there
- For movies: Call AMPAS, the Academy of Motion Pictures Arts and Sciences. (AMPAS puts on the Academy Awards.) Ask to be connected to *The Players Guide*, a directory. You can also call the Screen Actors Guild (SAG). You're allowed to ask for three celebrities at a time. SAG will give you the celebrity's agent's name. But what you need is the manager or PR person's name, because an agent gets a fee for booking his or her client. If there is no money in it for the agent, he or she won't pay any attention. So you call the agent and ask for the manager or the PR person's name and go through them. You must follow up with a call to the manager or PR person. They will not call you back unless it is a request for something like an appearance at the White House
- For music: Call the celebrity's record label. Most record labels are in New York or Los Angeles, so check information for the number. There are a number of resource books for the music industry; check with your local library. If you can't find the celebrity through any of the directories, then call NARAS, the National Academy of Arts and Sciences. (NARAS puts on the Grammies.) The problem here is not all artists are NARAS members, but NARAS can tell you where to go next
- For athletes: Call their teams. If you know the city they

play in, call information to get the team number. The team office will direct you to their responsible agent

What about using local celebrities?

Local actors, commercial personalities, politicians, television news anchors, and talk show hosts are a very good draw. I connected my juvenile furniture store and video store clients and marketed a Child Safety Day. To give it some celebrity attraction, we asked the local news anchors to host the day and high school athletes to help out. It was a media success and people admitted that they came not only to get their child videotaped but to meet their local celebrities.

What about hiring a celebrity impersonator?

Celebrity impersonators are fun and do get you noticed, but you need to make certain that they are licensed to appear as that celebrity.

Is there anything else I should be careful about?

- Federal Trade Commission regulations say, "Endorsements must always reflect the honest opinions, findings, beliefs, or experiences of the endorser." They also say that "the endorser must have been a bona fide user of it at the time the endorsement was given"
- Learn as much as you can about the celebrity's reputation. An incompatible past can mar your event with unwanted publicity

NOTE: Don't be scared off by the thought of paying celebrity fees. Call Barry or Rita and find out what the fees are. If your organization can't afford the fees, maybe you can solicit a sponsor to contribute the necessary funds (see the chapter, "Sponsor an Event").

RESOURCES

Networks

- NBC-TV: 30 Rockefeller Plaza; New York, NY 10112; (212) 664-444

- CBS-TV: 51 West 52nd St.; New York, NY 10019; (212) 975-4321
- ABC-TV: 77 West 66th St.; New York, NY 10023; (212) 456-7777
- FOX-TV: 205 East 67th St.; New York, NY 10021; (212) 452-5555

Directories
- Film and TV: *The Player's Guide*; Academy of Motion Picture Arts and Sciences (AMPAS); 8949 Wilshire Blvd.; Beverly Hills, CA 90211; (310) 247-3000
- Music: National Academy of Recording Arts and Sciences (NARAS); 3402 Pico Blvd.; Santa Monica, CA 90405; (310) 392-3777
- Screen Actors Guild (SAG); 5757 Wilshire Blvd.; Los Angeles, CA 90036; (213) 954-1600
- *The Standard Directory of Advertising Agencies*; National Register Publishing; (800) 521-8110. This directory lists ad agencies by location, size, and accounts. Use it in the library

Celebrity Source Agencies
- Celebrity Connection; Barry Greenberg, president; 8306 Wilshire Blvd., #2659; Beverly Hills, CA 90211; (213) 650-0001
- The Celebrity Source; Rita Tateel, president; 8033 Sunset Blvd.; Los Angeles, CA 90211; (213) 651-3300

Magazine
The Licensing Book (Adventure Publishing Group). Call (212) 575-4510 for a sample copy. This weekly trade magazine looks at celebrity and product licensing

- Check your library for celebrity resource books
- Check your local bookstore chains

64

MULTICULTURAL MARKETING

Joseph had a coat of many colors; so could you

Advertising and public relations expert Lynne Choy Uyeda told me that the most important advice one could have is, "Fear of failure and fear of making a mistake begin with a lack of understanding. Don't be inhibited by fear of the unknown." From her seminars and articles here are her ten Steps to Gaining a Better Understanding of Marketing in a Diverse Market:

1. **Don't overcomplicate.** People are people, regardless of ethnic origins. They want to see a sincere effort to communicate in terms they find relevant
2. **Don't oversimplify.** Never lump all ethnic audiences into a "minority" category. All of us are products of our environment and life experiences. Ethnic audiences respond to the same messages. Understanding this is the key to understanding ethnic audiences
3. **Don't be afraid to ask what they want and need.** Find people who represent the specific audience you want to target. Ask them how they would respond to a given message. This rule applies to focus groups, phone surveys, and mall interceptions—the same as you would do for mainstream audiences
4. **Educate yourself.** Invest the same time, effort, and thought into learning the cultures. Throw out the stereotypes, and *never* make assumptions—no matter how obvious!
5. **Mix and mingle. Observe and learn.** Attend cultural festivals, exhibitions, fairs, parades, and other ethnic events. Observe activities, ask questions. You might be

surprised at how eager and proud they are to share their customs and heritage

6. **Find reliable sources.** Add to your Rolodex a university professor, a government official, or a community leader who may have expertise in ethnic and cultural issues. Establish a relationship with that person. Use the person as a sounding board. You may have to pay a small consulting fee, but it's well worth the expense to gain the necessary insights

7. **Learn the ethnic media outlets in your area.** Work with the media. You don't have to speak Spanish or an Asian language to do this. They speak English. Establish a relationship built on trust and respect

8. **Enlist community support.** The community will feel a sense of participation and ownership if its leaders are involved. Keep them involved through the planning and execution stages of your marketing campaign

9. **Get feedback.** Are your messages being received and understood? Is your message having the desired effect? Get feedback from your audiences. Be prepared for candid criticism. Don't be discouraged if you hear some negative remarks. Use it as a learning experience to avoid future pitfalls

10. **Hang in there.** Don't expect instant results. Trust is the basis of all relationships. Trust is never given freely— trust is earned. Demonstrate your solid commitment and be willing to stay the course

How do I find the ethnic media in my community?
- Ask your librarian
- Look in the yellow pages
- Ask your chamber of commerce
- Call your local government offices
- Call an advertising or public relations company
- Call Lynne Choy Uyeda

Because translations don't always represent the intended meaning, how do I know that what I'm writing in English will come out the way I intend it?

Language accuracy is of critical importance. The best way to see this one through is to have your brochures, USP, handouts, and media releases all written in the language, not translated into the language.

Where do I find these people?

Check your local yellow pages under Translators and Interpreters. Make certain that they don't just translate word for word, but rewrite. Before you invest in the printing and postage, have several people do a reverse translation for you. Have them translate the text to you. Listen to how the words and ideas come out, and adjust appropriately.

RESOURCES

Expert

Lynne Choy Uyeda; 1871 S. Cloverdale Ave.; Los Angeles, CA 90001; (213) 933-2398; fax (213) 933-2448

Media Distribution

- Derus Media; 500 N. Dearborn, #516; Chicago, IL 60610; (312) 644-4360. Derus is a media service that issues scripts and electronic media kits to radio and television. It offers a full-service division for the Hispanic market, including rewriting your materials in Spanish to assure language accuracy
- Rancho Park Publishing; 2203 Balsam Ave.; Los Angeles, CA; (310) 470-7488; *http://www.Earthlink.net/~rpptranslation*. Rancho Park accurately translates, edits, and typesets your existing packaging, labels, press releases, advertising, user manuals, and software into any major language
- Media Distribution Services; 8592 Venice Blvd.; Los Angeles, CA 90034-2549; (800) 637-3282; (310) 836-6600. This full-service media fulfillment house mails advertising, marketing, and media materials. If there's a newspaper, MDS has it in their data base
- Interviewing Service of America; 16005 Sherman Way, #209; Van Nuys, CA 91406; (818) 989-1044; fax 818-989-5043

Part V

MARKETING WITH
TELEPHONE TECHNOLOGY

65

800 AND 900 NUMBERS

Good numbers to bet on

Why are 800 and 900 numbers important marketing tools?

Because 800 and 900 numbers give you or your business an anonymous profile, which gives you the opportunity to do business.

- No one knows your race, creed, religion, or color
- No one knows if you're a large or small business, or how many people you employ
- No one knows if you're geographically undesirable
- They make it easy to do business; they're user friendly
- Having one tells your audience you care about wanting their business
- They provide you with the opportunity to establish a broader awareness
- Your image is elevated. You appear global, more expansive, more able to rise to the occasion
- They provide twenty-four hours of outreach, a value-added service to your customers, clients, or patients
- It grabs the attention of the consumer without much time or effort

What are some examples of how I can use the numbers to my business advantage?

You can use the number to:

- Capture all kinds of profile information
- Search for potential markets
- Promote a trial campaign

- Distribute your catalog
- Get feedback on your advertising, direct mail, infomercials, in-store promotions, inserts, door hangers, cable commercials, et cetera
- Tack on additional services to the primary call
- Update your "ads" without graphics charges
- Use it for mail order
- Give free samples
- Offer tips on the benefits of your product or service
- Use it as a lead qualifier

How do I tell people I have an 800 or a 900 number?

Use your business cards and stationery, and advertising, marketing, and public relations efforts to promote your number.

What are the benefits of 900 numbers?

- 900-number callers are more interested callers than 800-number callers, because they have spent money to reach you. This makes them qualified prospects instead of seekers or the simply curious
- Because the callers are qualified prospects, you can build a more accurate data base for your offerings
- You can service a very special market with a dedicated information line, such as a psychic hotline, soap opera updates, sports scores, a performing arts calendar, weather reports, financial information, et cetera.

What are the drawbacks?

- You're responsible for the bills if your callers don't pay. This can put you out of business with you left holding the bag
- Calls to a 900 number are fewer than a toll-free 800 number
- Because of its shady past with pornography and scam artists, 900 numbers have a tarnished image. Only education about you and your product will help this situation
- Because the call costs money, make certain the cost of the giveaway is a break-even or winning situation
- Because of the cost of doing business, only mass market outreach gives you the best payoff

What are the benefits of an 800 number?
- You make it easy to do business with you
- You please the consumer by giving them something for free

What are the drawbacks?
- You open yourself up to people who call just because it's free
- You have to pay for wrong numbers

What are the benefits of using a catchy name for the 800 number?
- It's an attention grabber
- If it applies to the business, it can be easy to remember
- If it describes the offer, it could help sell it

What are the drawbacks of using a catchy name for the 800 number?
- People may remember the name, but not how to spell it. Since it looks easy to remember, they might rely on their memory and then forget. It's better to have people write down the number
- Many times the word or name doesn't match the offer or the person doing the offering. The person trying to remember doesn't have anything to hang it on, so the number is easily forgotten
- Users get turned off when they have to figure out the corresponding numbers. Always provide the numbers when using a keyword

RESOURCES

900 Number Service Providers
- Americall 900: (800) 453-1453 or (913) 338-1545
- AT&T MultiQuest Express 900 Service: (800) 382-0202
- Sprint Gateways: (800) 735-5900

800 number and 900 number Service Bureaus

These companies will set you up and handle your incoming calls. Many of them will also do product fulfillment. Compare prices and services

- Audio Communications, Inc. (ACI): (800) 828-9414 or (818) 883-0441
- Call Interactive: (800) 428-2400
- Infotouch: (800) 239-4636
- Interactive TeleMedia: (800) 441-4486 or (818) 788-4784
- Scherers Communications, Inc.: (800) 356-6161
- Simtel Communications: (818) 706-1921
- Network Telephone Services, Inc.: (800) 727-6874
- UCI Enterprises: (818) 784-1058
- VCI Technologies: (512) 472-5391
- West Telemarketing Corporation: (800) 841-9000

Also check your yellow pages

Other Resources

- Robins Press; 2675 Henry Hudson Pkwy., #6J; Riverdale, NY 10463; (800) 238-7130. Robins publishes a wide variety of voice/fax processing publications. Call for free catalog
- *900 Know-How & Money Making 900 Numbers* by Robert Mastin; Aegis Publishing Group; (800) 828-6961; fax (401) 849-4231
- *The Power of 900* by Rick Parkill; InfoText Publishing; (714) 493-2434. This book is from the publishers of *Info Text*, the magazine of interactive telephone marketing
- *The 900 Guide* by Madeline Bodin; (800) LIBRARY
- *The 900 Source Reference Guide*, edited by Michael Landers; Robins Press; (800) 238-7130
- *How to Get Filthy Rich in 900 Numbers* by Michael Glaspie; (313) 683-6060 or (800) 368-1277
- *1-900 Opportunity* by Michael Glaspie; (313) 683-6060 or (800) 368-1277. This audio set has six tapes plus two packed three-ring binders
- *900 Number Video*; Equity Ventures; (800) 825-7719 or (719) 590-7575

- *Info Text* magazine; 201 E. Sandpoint Ave., Ste. 600; Santa Ana, CA 92707; (714) 513-8400
- *VoiceNews,* edited by Bill Creitz; Stoneridge Technical Services; (800) 238-7130. This is a monthly publication on voice processing technology and its applications

66

BROADCAST FAX

The world is your marketing oyster

Does broadcast fax have anything to do with combining a fax with radio or TV?

Close, but not in the technical sense. It has to do with combining the same purpose that radio and TV has—that of spreading the word. Only it does this task over the facsimile (fax) machine.

What's the purpose of having broadcast fax capabilities?
- Broadcast fax allows you to simultaneously send a common fax to many recipients
- It's a great way to let everyone know about specials, limited runs, one-day-only sales, overstocked items, slightly damaged cans and crushed boxes sales
- You can use it to survey data bases

What are the marketing advantages?
- Create, update, and download files from your PC applications for immediate access by customers and off-site personnel
- Offer information on upcoming sales, new merchandise, et cetera
- Send out seasonal and holiday greetings, et cetera

- Use it to distribute your newsletter
- Send financial reports
- Provide survey results

Is it expensive to send all those pages?

It's considerably less than conventional printing, postage, and mailing costs, plus it's immediate, and you know it's been received without having to confirm by calling.

Nonetheless, how can I save money?

Arrange your broadcast data base into local and long distance phone numbers. You can send the local phone numbers yourself, but hire a broadcast fax service to send the long distance numbers. This service will save you time and money, not to mention wear and tear on your machine.

I recommended this to a client who averaged a two-page mailing to 500 people eight times a year. By using broadcast fax instead of a conventional mailing, he figured he saved more than $700.

Where do I find a broadcast fax service?

- Broadcast fax companies are listed in the yellow pages
- Mailing list houses have broadcast fax capabilities
- PR media release services will send your releases via broadcast fax to regional, national, and international outlets

If I'm sending my message out to hundreds or thousands of people, what will make them pay attention to mine?

As Gene Palmer, strategist for Advanced Communication Technologies counseled me: "They have to be intrigued with you and your services enough to call you back." If your written materials are positioned correctly and your offer is a good one, your phone should be ringing off the hook that very same day.

NOTE: The sky is the limit. I'd be interested in hearing about the applications you come up with. Try it and let me know.

RESOURCES

News Releases By Broadcast Fax
* PB Newswire: 1515 Broadway; New York, NY 10036; (800) 832-5522 or (212) 596-1540
* Business Wire: 1990 S. Bundy; Los Angeles, CA 90025; (310) 820-9473
* News USA: 8300 Boone Blvd., Ste. 810; Vienna, VA 22182; (800) 355-9500 or (703) 827-5800

Broadcast Fax Services
* Fax>>Direct: 5221 Blackpool Rd.; Westminster, CA 92683; (800) FAX-1GURU; fax (714) 894-6052. Fax-on-demand demo: (800) FAX-2SEL. Fax>>Direct calls it publish-and-mail-on-demand, and it includes faxing photos, too
* Check your yellow pages under Fax Transmission Services. Page ads will list this service if available
* Ask your local fax equipment dealers

67

FAX-ON-DEMAND

A free twenty-four-hour receptionist

What is fax-on-demand? What are the benefits?
For customers, clients, and patients who are not on-line:

* Fax-on-Demand, or FOD, is an easy-to-use, cost-effective fax and voice processing system that employs both telephone and facsimile technology to help businesses be

more responsive, professional, and profitable
- Not only does this system give you an opportunity to share your services and products with the world, but it does it most economically. No brochures, no printing, no mailing costs, and no tying up employees' time until necessary
- It's an ideal solution if you're swamped with telephone requests for information, and you find you can't effectively meet those demands in a cost-effective way without giving up good customer service

What kind of businesses can best benefit from this technology?

Those that have:

- Something to sell
- Information to offer
- A personal service to provide
- Price lists to show

How is FOD used?

Let's say I am presenting a seminar on 101 ways to promote yourself. Afterward there's a book and tape signing. Because the line is long, people might decide they would rather network or go to a session. Instead of losing the sale, I give them my fax-on-demand phone number, from which they can get a printed brochure and order form any time, night or day.

By pressing different extensions they can get my seminar and retreat schedule, my bio, and a list of people resources I talked about in the seminar. Also, they can access special reports, articles I've written, even tips on how to make life better. The list of offers is endless. And so are the sales.

Here are some more possibilities:

- You have a catalog house but don't maintain a twenty-four-hour switchboard. With fax-on-demand your clients can call in at any hour to order
- You're a retailer, and a physically challenged customer saw your ad. With fax-on-demand the customer can dial in any time, request in-depth printed information, and place an order without having to come into town
- You're a research company that's closed for the weekend,

and you need information for a client immediately. With fax-on-demand you can order up the statistics and be a hero to your client

- You're a consultant. I have your brochure and would really like more in-depth conversation on your services, but I'd rather not be sold to in person. With fax-on-demand I'll be able to fill in the details I'm missing and be prepared when we have our meeting

Does FOD serve the same purpose as a home page on the World Wide Web?

In essence, yes. But a majority of your clients, customers, patients, and patrons don't have Internet capabilities, so why lock them out of the market?

Do enough people have fax machines at home to make the service worthwhile?

With the growth of home-based businesses, you would be surprised at the number of households that have fax machines. I have friends who even use the fax to send and receive personal correspondence.

Many places offer fax capabilities as a value-added customer service. If you take a survey of your neighborhood, you'll find faxes available at drugstores, bookstores, banks, copy shops, and mailbox and packaging stores. Even my Laundromat has added a limited business center that includes a fax. I use it while waiting for my laundry.

How much will this system cost me?

Assuming you already have a computer, the specific FOD software on the market today runs as low as $500, and continues to go down.

What do I need to participate in fax-on-demand?

1. A fax modem for your computer
2. Fax-back software

Do I need a separate computer?

You don't need a separate computer, but it is a good idea to have an independent system, referred to as a stand-alone. If you install fax-on-demand on your only computer and you start getting great response, it might present problems with your normal computer usage. As inexpensive as computers are, you might want to think about that, along with installing a dedicated phone line.

What is the procedure for calling up fax-on-demand?

Most fax-on-demand systems work similarly according to the instructions below. Just in case they do not, listen carefully each time you dial up someone's system.

1. Dial the number
2. Listen for the menu of choices
3. Enter the fax number to which you would like your documents sent. Include the area code. Listen to the instructions to begin the transaction. **Note:** The number must be a dedicated fax or computer modem line. The system will not respond if it receives a voice answer
4. The system will repeat your number back to you and ask if it is correct. Follow the voice prompts to accept or reenter your fax number
5. Listen to the brief instructions, and press the digit document number of the report you would like to receive. Press 1 if you do not want any more reports. This will end your call
6. If you would like to receive additional reports, press 2 and repeat step five above
7. The reports you requested will arrive within minutes on your fax machine

If you don't have a fax, the system could be set up for you to get the documents by instructing you to call voice mail.

How can I make good marketing use of the caller's information?

Because FOD provides you with the caller's fax number, you have a new entry for your general marketing data base and broadcast fax system (see the chapter, "Broadcast Fax").

How can I make money using my FOD system?

As marketer and self-publishing expert Dan Poynter does,

you can give some information away, but you use it to sell your reports, tapes, catalogs, and newsletter subscriptions.

How will people know I have an FOD system?
Add that information to your marketing tools. Put your number on your stationery, business cards, and brochures. Include it in your advertising. List it alongside your Web page information.

RESOURCES

Books and Advice
Robins Press; 2675 Henry Hudson Pkwy., #6J; Riverdale, NY 10463; (800) 238-7130. This very helpful publishing company specializes in telecommunications, computer telephone, and voice and fax applications. Ask Marc Robins for the voice and fax processing library

Newsletter
Sarah Stambler; 370 Central Park West, Ste. 210; New York, NY 10025; (212) 222-1713. Sarah offers seminars and a newsletter on all phases of fax and Internet technology

Fax-on-Demand Numbers to Sample and Order From
- Dan Poynter: (805) 968-8947 (see the chapter, "Write a Book")
- Maui Writers Conference: (808) 879-6233
- Sarah Stambler: (303) 575-1554 (see the chapter, "Broadcast Fax")
- Fax>>Direct: (800) 329-2735 or (800) FAX-2SEL

68

HOLD BUTTONS

Turn your silent downtime into a smart business marketing tool

Jeff McNeil of On-Hold Marketing Systems told me that while 94% of all ad budgets is spent to induce calls, only 6% is spent to handle the call that is made. His statistics show that:

- The average American executive spends more than sixty hours a year on hold
- Eighty-eight percent of all business callers will hang up when forced to hold
- Thirty-four percent of hang ups won't call again
  He's found that with on hold marketing:
- Eighty-five percent of callers placed on hold will keep listening to hear the message

How can a message on a machine be a business marketing tool?
- I changed my chiropractor's deafeningly silent hold button into a time to educate her callers. She now gives out a chiropractic tip of the week, an exercise, a fact, a quiz that gets them a session or information on nutritional products. It's prompted her patients to ask for specific tips for specific needs
- I suggested a bookstore read passages from its latest arrivals or those on the best-seller lists. This suggestive selling technique increases customer awareness, and customer awareness translates into cash
- For a cooking store client I designed cooking classes. The store announces the class calender along with tips on how

to use its imported herbs and spices. The classes bring increased foot traffic into the store, and at the same time bring an increase to the bottom line
- A wine store client offers callers lessons in the differences between wines, which wines to serve with which foods, definitions, and hints on the proper way to uncork a bottle. Educating customers makes for more comfortable and more knowledgeable browsers
- An out-of-the-way hotel now gives directions, pointing out interesting landmarks and natural attractions to look at while on the way. The hotel also recommends places to stop while going through town, and the location of phone booths in case someone is hopelessly lost. The guests arrive less stressed and much more appreciative

Can I use other people's tapes or information instead of a message I generate myself?

If you would rather not toot your own horn, you could play self-help, humor, or business tapes from the masters. If the material is copyrighted, that is if it has a © and a date, you need permission from the owner to use it.

How can I use this as a marketing tool?

Depending on your goal, the message can be used to:

- Advertise
- Qualify
- Close
- Inform the caller of product knowledge
- Give service or merchandise updates
- Promote sales specials
- Promote word of mouth
- Offer customer service
- Show good public relations

How do I set up the service?

1. Utilize a full-service professional production company to script and produce a customized audio marketing message

2. Use a voice-over production house to produce what you've designed
3. Script and produce your own marketing message

When using a professional production company first, do I have to write the message and give them the music?

If it's a full-service company such as Hallmark Audio or On-Hold Marketing Systems, they do everything. They write the script, find the right music, provide the announcing talent, and produce the finished product. You fill out their questionnaire and send along any promotional materials that provide the bigger picture.

What do they need to know?
- Business hours
- Slogans, mottoes, or special sayings
- Special services you offer
- Special items or products
- Your location
- Anything else you want your public to know

Do they provide music?

Yes, and usually you can have your choice of styles. A good production company will consult with you and help you pick what's best for your image.

Do I need special telephone equipment?

You provide a telephone system that has music on hold capability; they provide the digital playback equipment and the message.

How much will this cost me?

Basic costs depend on two things:

1. What goes into the making of your message
2. The update and changes fee schedule

Grant Robison of Hallmark Audio told me that Hallmark's minimum digital message on-hold programs could cost you as little as $2.27 a day. I have to agree with him when he says,

"Not a bad price to pay for a full-time, twenty-four-hour employee."

Hallmark Audio has a wonderful free audiocassette brochure that gives you examples of what you can expect from the company.

On-Hold Marketing Systems has a killer phone message that gives more than ten examples of what to expect, as well as fax-on-demand. The company also has an audiocassette of what to expect.

What if I can't afford a full-service production company?

Susan Berkley, president of Berkley Productions, Inc., is a wonderful resource for accomplishing your goal in this arena. Her professional voice has sold more than $50 million worth of products and services.

She takes the three-to four-minute script you've written (for a little more she'll write the script), adds music, and gives you a finished product that you can play on your phone. But she doesn't provide the digital equipment.

Can I save money if I produce my own on-hold message?

Yes, but be aware that it won't be that much cheaper than the professionals, and it may not present you in the best light. It's also time-consuming. But if you want the experience, here are the details:

- Hire a recording studio. The yellow pages lists recording studios. Make sure the studio understands your recording needs. Cost: $40-plus an hour
- Choose the style of music. If you use recorded music off the air, cassettes, or CDs, you're required to pay licensing fees. Cost: could be more than $1,000 and could require yearly renewal fees
- Write the script yourself or use a copywriter. Cost: up to $500 an hour or more
- Lease the digital equipment. Cost: up to $100 a month or more, plus down payment

Do I need to pay a licensing fee if I want to use someone's music in my production?

Absolutely. Unless you get free clearance (permission) to

use the composition, you are required by law to pay a licensing fee. It's the same principle as licensing the right to produce someone's image, toys, apparel, books, art, et cetera.

The law in this case is U.S. Copyright Law Title 17. Should you choose to ignore payment, the term is willful infringement, with penalties that can go as high as $100,000 per composition.

How would anyone know I've used the music?

Believe it or not, there are professional listeners who check to see if you are pirating music. A friend was relaxing in a spa when the soothing spalike music stopped. That's right. A performing rights checker showed up and literally pulled the plug. Songwriters who call businesses and hear music have been know to check with their performance rights agency to determine if the music is properly licensed.

How do I find out the cost of the licensing fee?

Fees and collections are handled by a performing right licensing organization. There are three of them in the United States: ASCAP, BMI, and SESAC. Each has an office in New York, Los Angeles, and Nashville. Songwriters, musicians, and music publishers belong to only one of the three, and it's your responsibility to call and find out which one.

If I still don't want to go a message company, are there companies that provide music without all the fuss?

Yes. There are companies that have already taken care of the licensing fees. You have four options:

1. **AEI Music and Muzak.** They license original music and provide the service through cassettes, CDs, or satellite dish transmissions. The standard contract is for five years. The cost depends on update schedules. You've heard their music service in elevators, lobbies, rest rooms, stores, and restaurants

2. **Music Libraries.** These wonderful collections exist for your every musical want, need, or desire. Anything from symphony sounds to a dog barking to a door creaking. The industry term for this type of service is needle drop music; it comes from the old days, when there was a

needle to drop and a record to drop it on. The good part about libraries is the enormous variety of available music. The not-so-good part is you have to pay a usage fee. You don't own needle drop music, you only rent it

3. **License free compilation music audiotapes or CD-ROMS.** You can buy these and make your own music library. You can find these companies listed in the back of most computer and music magazines. Unfortunately the price doesn't always denote the quality of the music, and the compositions are usually limited in creative scope. The good thing about this is you pay once when you buy them, and nothing ever again

4. **Create your own music.** Any musician can do this for you. Fortunately, I was referred to McKinley Marshall, president of Brave New Media, a multimedia and music production studio. She consulted with me on image requirements and came up with various sound options to choose from. The advantage of doing your own music is you *buy it out*, and then own it to do with as you please

It is my recommendation that unless you are in advertising, are a great copywriter, or have a state-of-the-art studio and a wonderful on-air voice, let the professionals do the work.

RESOURCES

Performance Right Licencing Organizations
- ASCAP; One Lincoln Plaza; New York, NY 10023; (212) 595-3050
- BMI; 320 W. 57th St.; New York, NY 10019; (212) 586-2000
- SESAC; 55 Music Sq.; Nashville, TN 37203; (615) 320-0055

Recorded on-Hold Music
- AEI; 900 East Pine; Seattle, WA 98122; (206) 329-1400
- Muzak; 2901 3rd Ave., Ste. 400; Seattle, WA, 98121; (800) 331-3340

Message on-Hold Programs

- Hallmark Audio; 1014 S. Westlake Blvd., #14-145; Westlake Village, CA 91361; (800) 6 AUDIO 7 or (818) 880-2980
- Marketing On-Hold, 13023 Polvera Ave.; San Diego, CA 92128; (800) 466-4653; *http://pages.prodigy..com/voicepro*
- Berkley Productions, Inc.; 780 Piermont Ave.; Piermont, NY 10968; (800) 333-8108
- Brave New Media; 11511 Sawtelle Blvd., #333; Los Angeles, CA 90025; (310) 450-7918

Copyright

Copyright Connection, Inc.; Ralph Weinstein, President; 8824 Southwick St.; Fairfax, VA 22031; (703) 280-4767; fax (703) 280-5344

Part VI

RESPONSE MARKETING

69

WRITING DIRECT MAIL AND SALES LETTERS

The aristocracy of the marketing highway

I thought *advertising* was the aristocracy of the marketing highway.

I surveyed ten marketing experts with this question: "What marketing tool is the most effective for product and service sales results?" All ten, without hesitation, replied, "A direct response mail campaign."

Why does it work so well? What does it have over everything else?

Direct mail is a targeted effort directed to a specific population with the intent to get the exact kinds of customers, clients, patients, and patrons you want. When executed properly a great direct-mail letter duplicates, in an envelope, the sensation of what makes in-person sales and customer service successful.

We talked about how to create your own mailing list and how to rent mailing lists. Marketing experts agree that the list is the most important part of the process. But after the list has you at the door, then the envelope design has the recipient interested in opening the letter. But it's what's printed inside that gets the reader to do what you want.

The end result is what fuels the offer. It's why you took the time, expense, and effort to send the direct-mail piece in the first place.

What are the most important parts of a great direct-mail campaign?

There are four:

1. The list
2. The offer
3. The copy
4. The creative tools to enhance the offer and the copy

What can I ask the reader to do for me?

You can offer anything that needs a response. You can ask them to:

- Buy something
- Attend a seminar
- Join an organization or club
- Sign a petition
- Come to an event
- Sample a product
- Donate money
- Subscribe to a newspaper, magazine, or newsletter
- Order from a catalog
- Support your symphony or theater arts

What makes for a great direct-mail letter?

The industry calls this *the creative*. Generally speaking, there are three parts to the creative:

- The copy
- The graphics
- The format

To make my customers take my offer, what do I need to keep in mind when writing?

Carl Galletti, consultant and seminar leader on the art and craft of writing effective ads and sales letters, graciously agreed to share these twenty-seven powerful points from his Copywriter Protégé Program.

27 POWERFUL POINTS TO KEEP IN MIND WHEN WRITING COPY FOR YOUR ADS, SALES AND DIRECT RESPONSE LETTERS

1. **Take the best, most powerful, most effective thing you can say and move it to the beginning.** If you lose your readers because of uninteresting ho-hum stuff in the beginning, they will never get to the good stuff. So put it up front. It will excite your reader, and have residual effect, so when they get to the less interesting stuff, they will still be paying attention. Of course, you should always try to make *all* of it interesting. But there will always be some of it that is better, more powerful, and/or more effective. Put it as close to the beginning as possible

2. **The headline is the most important part of the ad.** This is the device that newspapers and magazines use so their readers can pick out the articles they are interested in reading. No one has time to read all the articles. So the headline helps the reader pick out what is of interest. In the same way, your prospects will pick out your ad to read by scanning the headline. This is something they are used to doing. It is a habit. Take advantage of it and use the headline to pick out your audience. The copy is what gets them to buy. The headline is what gets them to read the copy. Treat it with importance and respect. Spend a lot of time studying and understanding how to construct good and effective headlines. Then spend a major portion of your ad-writing time developing the headline for your ads and sales letters

3. **The headline is the first thing you see.** I define the headline as the first thing the reader sees. So, if you put "teaser" copy on the outside of the envelope for a sales letter, *it* becomes your headline. If you leave out the headline in your ad, then whatever catches your reader's attention first becomes the headline. Take my advice: It's more effective to put the headline in and control

the selling experience than to haphazardly let the "headline" establish itself by accident

4. **The best way to get the reader's attention is to speak directly to them.** This means using a lot of "you" and "your" versus "me," "my," "we," and "I." Say "You can make a lot of money . . ." rather than "a lot of money can be made" or "we know a lot of money can be made." Readers don't pay much attention to what you say about yourself until after you say something that interests them. Treat them as the most important person by addressing them directly, and you will have their interest

5. **Use proof, endorsements, and testimonials.** The hardest thing to do in advertising is to be believed. Testimonials, endorsements, and other instruments of "proof" (such as bank statements, sworn statements, et cetera) go a long way toward making your promotion more believable

6. **Know your prospect.** The more you know about the people you are addressing, the better your chances of having something effective to say. Do your research. Find out what they really want. Then you'll know what to sell them, what to say to them, and how to present your sales message

7. **Prove the points you make.** Just because you say it doesn't mean it's true. And if you prove what you say by citing an example, telling an anecdote, demonstrating it to them, or showing them how to demonstrate it for themselves, you will go a long way toward bringing your readers closer to becoming buyers

8. **Use specifics.** Specifics are more believable than generalities or rounded-off numbers. "Ivory soap is 99 and 44/100 percent pure" is much more believable than "Ivory is 100% pure." Why? Because the assumption is that it was actually measured, whereas the rounded-off 100% figure sounds more like a brag or boast without any actual measurement involved. People realize that in real life figures seldom come out that even. Therefore, it must be a lie if it is an even number. And the truth is, it probably *is* a lie. If the best you can do is an estimate and the estimate comes out even, it is

better to lower the figure to a more believable one. For example, 73% would be better than 75%, because the latter figure is such an even amount. Actually, 73.6% would be even better yet

9. **Use examples to demonstrate your points.** Examples often clarify points that are unclear in your descriptions. Check out the examples given in this document and note how they clarify points. When you are giving an example, all you need to keep in mind is to make it practical—i.e., describe a real-life application

10. **Offer something** *free!* The best way to make your offer compelling is to give something that has a high perceived value to your customer, yet costs you very little. People have been known to buy products just to get the free bonus. Information products are very good as free bonuses, because it is easy to make them valuable while their cost remains low

11. **Demonstrate the major buying advantage of the product.** If you were selling a weight-loss product, you would show a "before" and "after" shot—the major buying advantage being that by using the product you would have a similar result as the person in the pictures, namely that you would lose a bunch of weight and look great

12. **Picture with pleasure.** Associate your product with the pleasure the customer will get by using your product. Put the reader in a situation where he or she is using the product and reaping the benefits. For example, if you were selling a vacation package to Hawaii, you would describe the experience. It would go something like this: "Imagine yourself on the white sandy beaches of Hawaii; you're on a comfortable lounge chair laying back soaking up the rays (which are warm but not hot, because the ocean breeze is gently rolling in and keeping you comfortably cool). The sounds of the surf are gently lulling you into a serene and peaceful bliss, while a beautiful, hula-clad waitress or handsome waiter brings you a cool drink . . ."

See what I mean? The thing to do when "picturing with pleasure" is to use the senses in your description, and to keep in mind that you are putting your reader in a pleasurable experience where the benefits of the product (in the above case, a trip to Hawaii) is extolled in the description

13. **Thoroughly research the product.** Oftentimes you will come up with break-through insights by researching your product thoroughly. Claude Hopkins, the father of effective advertising, was famous for this. By doing his research he found little-known facts that would bring tremendous response. One time he was researching his client's beer production facility and made note of how the beer was processed. By using what he had learned, he generated ads that brought the client, Schlitz, up from sixth to first place within six months.

Another classic example is when David Ogilvy discovered something in an engineer's report and exploited it to create one of the most effective and often-quoted headlines in history: "At sixty miles an hour the loudest noise in this new Rolls-Royce comes from the electric clock."

14. **Establish an effective central selling concept.** Your product may have many benefits and features. One will be more effective than all the rest at generating sales. If you discover what it is and focus your ad or sales letter on it, you will dramatically improve your response.

The way to find out which benefit produces the best response is by testing. One benefit will be significantly better at producing results. Play *that* one up as the central selling concept and use the others as supporting benefits

15. **Make it personal.** Write to your audience in the most personal way possible. Use common language. Make it read like something a friend would write to them. When you do this the rewards are great in terms of increased sales and profits

16. **Apply these three questions.** Write your ads and sales letters as if your readers have the following questions in mind while reading: So what? Who cares? and what's in it for me? If your copy is so exciting and interesting that these three questions do not rear their ugly heads, then you've done your job well. Otherwise, you need

to rewrite until the situation is corrected. Sometimes the problem is with the product or offer. In the former case, change or enhance the product. In the latter case, enhance the offer (usually with bonuses)

17. **Tell the whole story.** Claude Hopkins believed that any time you got the attention of your reader, you should give him your whole story and not depend on him ever reading anything else. I believe the same thing. And all the tests I've been privy to have supported this position. What it means is that you may have to write a long letter instead of a short one. So do it. Just remember that making it long without making it interesting is cheating. It must be long because it tells all the reader wants to know to make an informed buying decision. You always get a better response by telling more. The adage is: "The more you tell, the more you sell"

    Warning: Inexperienced people almost always fight me on this one. After we get done testing, *they always lose*. But don't take my word for it. Test it yourself. Just keep in mind that *what* you test must be a *good* sales letter/ad, and writing a good one is not like writing an interoffice memo. Start by following the guidelines in this section:

18. **Use simple words and short sentences.** Be a student of powerful words and sentences. If you do, you will note that most of them are short and simple. Compare these two sentences: "The financial projections for personal income will escalate to twice previous conditions" and "You will double your income and put a lot more money in your pocket." Which is more powerful? If you said the latter you are right on track. Otherwise you are either kidding yourself or you need a lot more practice at evaluating the reactions of your reader

19. **Make them an offer they can't refuse.** I like to refer to this as the Cosa Nostra school of marketing. Make the offer *so good* that the only way they can reject it is to be insane or stupid. To make your offer better, add bonuses, lower the price, improve the terms of payment, or anything else you can do to make it more attractive

20. **Let the PS be your second headline.** In a sales letter, oftentimes the second thing a person reads is your PS

(postscript). The reason for this is that they always want to know who sent the letter. So they turn to the end to see the name and drop their eye down to the PS. Therefore write your PS accordingly. Make it say something that will intrigue them enough to get them to go back to the beginning and read your entire letter.

I try to avoid this reader reaction of them turning to the PS by putting a letterhead on the first page that says who and where it came from. My theory is that this retards the "look at the PS" reaction, and therefore gives me better control of the reading sequence. In other words, the sequence I want the reader to follow is to read from beginning to end in the order I intended. It works better that way. Nevertheless, I still write the PS as if they cheated and looked at it second—just in case

21. **Restate your offer.** After you get through describing everything the customer will get, you have often gone on for several pages, especially if you do it right and especially if it is a significant package. If this is the case, just before ending the letter summarize your offer. Then ask for the order (again).

Another place to do this is on the order form, which you should try to call something else—such as application or enrollment form

22. **Ask for the order.** Don't be shy. Ask for the order or die. And just to be sure, ask for it once more (no extra charge for the rhyming)

23. **Establish value.** Don't assume your readers automatically know the value of what they are buying. Spell it out to them in detail. Compare it with other similar things. For example, in one promotion for a copywriting course I sell, I compare what it would cost to hire a professional copywriter to write a promotion for you versus doing it yourself with my course. I also compare what it would cost to pay someone to personally tutor you to get the same skills. My course is a bargain in comparison

24. **Use reason why advertising.** Ads and sales letters are *always* more effective when you give your reader a reason why. John E. Kennedy, Albert Lasker, and Claude Hopkins first discovered this, and they made a fortune

with it in the early days of modern advertising. It still works today

25. **Reward quick action, penalize procrastination.** Tie your bonuses and discounts to prompt action. "If you order within the next ten days . . ." "You save an extra fifty dollars if you order before the date stamped on the application form . . ." "Order by June seventeenth to avoid the price increase . . ." "We only have twenty-three in stock, so order now. All orders received after present stock is sold will have to be returned unprocessed"

26. **Reverse the risk.** Buying is risky, especially if done through the mail. So ease your prospect's mind by taking the risk on yourself. You do this by offering strong guarantees or by delaying payment or accepting credit terms

27. **Keep the graphics simple.** The Grand Canyon is aesthetically very beautiful, but hardly anybody *ever* uses the thing. Don't let your ad or sales letter suffer from the same plight. Most of the time the pretty-looking graphics just do not get read as much as the plain-Jane stuff. So keep the graphics simple. Don't get too fancy. Or you'll find your ads and letters receiving awards but not generating any sales

   BONUS: Benefits versus features. The difference between a benefit and a feature is that the benefit is an advantage to the buyer, whereas a feature is a characteristic of the product. Customers usually make their buying decisions based on the benefits, and justify their decisions based on the features. Use both to support each other. Put yourself in the "reader's" shoes

What do I need to remember when designing my direct sales piece?

- Bullet point laundry list. A very important part of a direct-response pitch is the *laundry list* of benefits. Quick and easy to read, it is the ultimate grabber in the copy
- Mail your letter in a nine-by-twelve envelope. It looks more impressive and doesn't have that fold along a sentence so you can't read it

- Hand address if you can. Just another way to make it look more personal
- Use a real stamp instead of the postage meter
- Continue the last sentence of your paragraph on the next page. This is called a cliff-hanger. Ask a question or give a solution. That way they'll have to turn the page, if only to finish the thought
- Copy drives graphics. Curb your clip art finger. If you have to, use pictures instead of graphics
- Keep the layout simple. Leave your indent, underlining, centering, and subhead finger outside the door
- Don't justify your right margins
- Use paragraph headings like mini-headlines. These should be in the same color as your letterhead. It will make them stand out like bulleted points but without being so exact
- Use Courier typeface. It's the easiest to read and still out-pulls all other typefaces

Finally:

- Use color stationery and good paper stock. Aside from the fact that it's classy, it's unusual and it won't look like junk mail or a solicitation piece

If I do what the experts tell me, why might people still not go for the offer?
- Because they can't afford it
- Because they don't need it
- Because they have never heard of you and don't trust you
- Because they weren't convinced they should act now

How can I avoid this?
Advertising and promotional copywriter Erin Thomas Palmeter summed it up with these five keepers from her booklet, "Copy Writing That'll Help Your Promotions Deliver":

1. **Have a plan.** This may sound trite, but it's crucial. Know what you want to accomplish with everything you produce. What do you want this piece to do? How will it be used? Your answers will set the tone for the copy. All of your printed materials should sell you and your ser-

vices. If they don't you're wasting your money. The *way* in which they sell can vary from blatant to subtle, but they all should sell

2. **Know thy reader.** This is a well-worn phrase but an important one. If you aren't sure who'll be reading the material you're creating, don't proceed until you do. Get inside the mind of your prospective clients. What are they looking for? What do they want? How can you appeal to their needs? You are attempting to communicate with them. It helps to know who they are

3. **Get to the point.** Too many brochures and mailers never make their point. This wastes the reader's time and your hard-earned money. Direct copy without a lot of "fluff" is more effective and will result in more business

4. **Draw them in.** Being direct doesn't have to be boring. Tell a story using examples. Make your message compelling and persuasive. Tell the reader why they should be doing business with you. Share your credentials in an interesting way. Did you save a client money? Did you meet an impossible deadline? Did you help the client form a strategic alliance with another company that, in turn, helped their business?

5. **Educate as you sell.** Whenever you can, educate. Don't just rattle off dry statistics. Give your readers useful information that makes them say, "Hey, I didn't know that," and helps them see you as a valuable resource for their company

NOTE: A good direct-mail piece saves on salespeople and turns prospects into customers. Try it. If you need help, call an expert. It's worth it.

RESOURCES

Books
- *The 100 Greatest Sales Letters of All Time* complied by Richard Hodgson (Dartnell)
- *The Golden Mailbox* by Ted Nicholas (Enterprise Dearborn)
- *Mail Order Magic* by Herman Holtz (McGraw-Hill)

- *Do-it-Yourself Direct Marketing* by Mark S. Bacon (John Wiley)
- *Mechanics of Mail Order* by Mike Rounds and Nancy Miller; CPM Systems; 6318 W. Ridgepath CT.; Rancho Palos Verdes, CA 90275; (310) 544-9502. This book contains fourteen pages of sources for everything you'll need to do mail order

Experts
- Carl Galletti; One Paddock Dr.; Lawrenceville, NJ (609)-896-0245; fax (609)-896-2653; *carl@edit.com*. Carl offers copywriting seminars and courses, and the Internet site Writer's Web
- Erin Thomas Palmeter; The Palmeter Group; 12071 Alta Carmel Ct., #88; San Diego, CA 92128; (619) 485-5181

Organization
Direct Marketing Association (DMA): 11 W. 42nd St., New York, NY 10036-8096; (212) 768-7277

Magazines
- *DM News:* 19 W. 21st St., 8th Fl.; New York, NY 10010-6888; (212) 741-2095, *http://www.dmnews.com*
- *Direct Magazine*, Box 4949; Stamford, CT 06907; (203) 358-9900
- *Direct Marketing Magazine*; 224 Seventh St., Garden City, NY 11530-5771; (516) 746-6700

70

USING ENVELOPE TEASER COPY TO PROMOTE THE INSIDE

But you can judge a marketing piece by its cover

How is using the outside of the envelope a good sales and marketing tool?

Teaser copy is another way to say attention grabber. It's copy that invites, questions, commands, informs, hints at, or just plain tells you what you'll get when you open the envelope.

In *The Levison Letter: Action Ideas for Better Marketing Communication* expert and copywriter Ivan Levison offers "15 Things You Can Put on the Back of the Envelope" (you can put them on the front, too).

1. **A note from the president of the company.** She or he can talk about the guarantee, the special offer, you name it

2. **What they'll find inside the envelope.** "Inside: Your choice of two upgrades and three FREE bonuses!" Don't make them guess what the payoff is. Give them a good reason to tear open the envelope and start reading!

3. **A restatement of the bonus offer.** "Yours FREE: the most terrific strategy game on the market!" Never underestimate the power of a bonus offer to boost sales. If you have something neat to give away (and I hope you do), say so loud and clear!

4. **Several ad shots with captions.** Go easy on this one. Unless you've got something really interesting going on, save them for your flier

5. **A photo of everything that comes in the box, including all disks and bonus items.** It's a nice way to increase the perceived value of your offer. This works particularly well if you have something interesting to show, such as special hardware that comes with your software
6. **Rave review quotes.** These can carry a lot of weight with readers! Three to five reviews are enough. If you include too many, they won't get read
7. **Customer testimonials.** They can be powerful, but make sure you choose people from highly regarded companies. No anonymous testimonials, please
8. **Award logos.** If you've got them, flaunt them! Obviously, they build confidence and overcome skepticism
9. **Box shots with bulleted lists of features.** A little dull unless you've got a clearly superior product
10. **Product contents lists**
11. **Product uses**
12. **A long list of satisfied customers.** If the related company names are recognized by your readers, go for it. Note: A bunch of companies that no one has ever heard of won't do you a lot of good
13. **Examples of products output: drawings, reports, banners, menus, layouts, diagrams, et cetera.** Don't forget to say "Actual Output!" or something like that
14. **The offer expiration date.** Make your readers worry that they're going to miss out on a terrific opportunity
15. **A list of what's new.** You don't have to wait until the letter to let readers know what's hot

What are some examples of teaser copy?

On Steven Dworman's *Informercial Marketing Report* envelope promoting the upcoming conference:

URGENT
ONLY TWO SPACES REMAIN!

- On an envelope for chiropractor Robert Hochstein (written by Randy Gage) in bright red, the envelope turned on its side:

AN IMPORTANT MESSAGE FOR DADE COUNTY PBA MEMBERS

- On the front of the Institute for Noetic Sciences' membership mailing:

WANT TO MEET THE MOST INTERESTING,
EXCITING PERSON YOU'LL EVER KNOW?

On the back: a green, white, and lilac–colored box offering Norman Lear's book *Wherever You Go, There You Are* . . . FREE With Your Membership

- On an envelope for KCET Public Television: the first line, all caps in bright red letters, the second in black, lower case:

Funding crisis over? Think again.
your favorite TV programs still need *you* . . .

- On the back of a teal-colored square with off-white lettering on a white envelope in bold, one-inch letters, for a charter subscription to *Essential Facts: Employment*, available through Warren, Gorham & Lamont:

LAST YEAR,
PAT G.'s
$19,000-A-YEAR
SECRETARY
HAD TO BE PAID
$178,000.
IS YOURS NEXT?

- On the front of an envelope sent by author and speaker Mark Victor Hansen; A blue screened picture of Mark's smiling face with the message:

You're
Special to
me and I
want to
prove it to
you!

- On a black background envelope, with red and white printing, for *Exec*℗ *Magazine:*

DEMAND
A RAISE!
(AND ACTUALLY GET IT)
TOP MANAGERS REVEAL:
⇒Best clothes to wear!   Address box
⇒Best time of day!
⇒Best mood for the boss to be in!
⇒Best way to state your case!
⇒Best way to turn "no" into "yes"!

- On a large white envelope for a travel agency, on the far left, a three-by-three black-and-white picture of a marina and villas, ringed in light blue with the message:

WISH YOU WERE HERE?
Picture
GETAWAY IDEAS INSIDE . . .

Do all copywriters agree on using teaser copy on the envelope?

No, and there are an equal number of marketing experts who don't think you should put copy on the envelope, front or back.

Alan Antin of *The Antin Marketing Letter* told me that the way to get a direct response letter opened and not tossed into the wastebasket is to:

1. Hand address if possible, or have it impact addressed, not ink jet addressed
2. Use real stamps, not metered postage
3. Don't put any writing on the envelope

Alan told me that "the personal-looking letter, one that asks the question who sent it, is the one that gets their curiosity. That's the one they want to open over a letter that looks like it might be junk mail."

Expert copywriter Carl Galletti suggests that if you decide to go the outside of the envelope route, have a copywriter do it, or at least look it over. This kind of copy really counts, and can make or break the entire offer.

RESOURCES

- *The Levison Letter: Action Ideas for Better Direct Mail and Advertising;* Ivan Levison & Associates; 14 Los Cerros Dr.; Greenbrae, CA 94904; (415) 461-0672; *http:// www.levison.com; ivan@levison.com*
- Carl Galletti; One Paddock Dr.; Lawrenceville, NJ, 08648; (609)896-0245 fax (609)896-2653; *carl@edit.com*
- Alan and Brad Antin; *The Antin Marketing Letter: Secrets from the Lost Art of Common Sense Marketing*; 11001 Delmar, Ste. 1200; Leawood, KS 66211; (913)663-5775; fax (913) 663-5552; *antin@tyrell.com; 75706.2523 @CompuServ*

71

MAIL ORDER

Having what you want without getting dressed

People who get rich overnight are a small percentage on one extreme end of the curve, as are the people on the other end who have been working at it for thirty-five years and still haven't broken even.

Nobody can guarantee you overnight success, but with the right technique you can get into the 68% norm of people who are making billions of dollars in the direct response marketing business.

What are the different categories of the mail-order business?

1. People who buy and sell other people's goods and services
2. People who sell their own goods and services

How do I pick a mail-order winner?

- Sell what appeals to people and will move through your warehouse
- Stick with goods and services you know
- Sell things that don't break
- Select a product that is inexpensive to mail with no special packaging
- Select products that can stand a good markup
- Repeat buys are better product investments than trends

In *Mechanics of Mail Order*, Mike Rounds says that "too many people have been persuaded to get involved in business deals that they knew nothing about. More importantly, didn't understand or even like the products that they had to sell. They saw others doing well with the products and the program, and decided that if somebody else could do it, they could, too."

What are good categories for mail order?

- "How to" information: books, special reports
- Gardening supplies
- Clothing
- Specialty food items
- Items from foreign countries
- Sports equipment

What's the best way to deliver an order?

1. Send it out yourself
2. Use a fulfillment house

When approaching a fulfillment house what should I ask about?

Most importantly: Make sure you find out exactly the services it provides. The total needs picture could include:

- A twenty-four-hour toll-free number
- Operators to take credit card orders with the fulfillment house's merchant number or yours
- Operators that will answer questions from a script you write
- Mailing your product
- Capturing all the names, addresses, and numbers per inquiry and per purchase
- Sending you a daily list of calls and purchases by e-mail, fax, or mail

What are the disadvantages of using a fulfillment house?
The only real downside is the loss of the personal touch of vendor to consumer.

How can I remedy this?
Use this opportunity to have the fulfillment house place a personalized thank you note or letter in the package. You can also add any other product news, special articles you want to share, tips, trends, surveys, et cetera (see the chapters "Inserts," "Write Articles," "Send Special Reports," and "Tips, Trends and Surveys").

How do I enter the mail-order business?
1. Register for a business license at your city or county clerk's office
2. Obtain a seller's permit from the state board of equalization
3. File a fictitious business name statement, known as a doing business as (DBA) with the county clerk
4. Publish your fictitious business name statement notice in the newspaper
5. Get a merchant account to take credit cards
6. Get an 800 number

How do I tell the world I have something to sell?
- Use classified ads
- Do display advertising on radio and television, and in newspapers and magazines
- Have a World Wide Web site
- Hook into a cybermall

- Use the yellow pages
- Send out catalogs
- Do door hangers
- Participate in coupon packs and card decks
- Create a presence at a trade show
- Do outdoor advertising

Check out each of these chapters for in-depth success details.

What do I need to be aware of?

Mike Rounds shared these six Tips to Be Aware of in Direct Mail from the book, *Mechanics of Mail Order*, with me:

1. Mail-order sales are governed by rules of the Federal Trade Commission (FTC), various state laws, and postal regulations
2. Warranties and exchanges are a matter of policy rather than a matter of the law. The law states that you must live up to the representation that you make. If you don't live up to that representation, you are in breach of contract
3. You must ship your order within thirty days of receiving it, unless the advertisement clearly states it will take longer
4. If you can't make the shipping time, you must notify the customer in writing in advance of the promised date, giving a new date and offering the opportunity to cancel the order
5. By law you must refund charges from canceled orders within seven business days
6. You cannot substitute merchandise without consent

RESOURCES

Books
Mechanics of Mail Order by Mike Rounds and Nancy Miller; Rounds Miller Associates; 6318 W. Ridgepath Ct.; Rancho Palos Verdes, CA 90275; (310) 544-9502

Merchant Account for Credit Card Approval
(other than banks)
Axin Financial Services, Inc.; (310) 694-0565

Fulfillment Houses
- Promotional Distribution Services Worldwide; 82 South St.; Hopkinton, MA 01748; (508) 435-0001
- Motivational Fulfillment & Packaging Services; 5959 Triumph St.; Commerce, CA 90040; (213) 723-0997
- ICT Response; 800 Town Center Dr.; Langhorne, PA 19047; (215) 757-0200
- Check your local yellow pages for companies in your area

72

CATALOGS

Multiplying your presentation options

Should I publish my own catalog or put my products in other people's catalogs?
If your product lends itself, I recommend both options.

What's the most important thing I need to know before I try to place my products in a mail-order catalog?
The most important thing to know is that you must be a manufacturer or the *exclusive* supplier of the products you're offering. If not, and the catalog owners think the product you've submitted has potential, they'll take your product and go directly to the supplier.

How do I get my products considered by mail-order catalogs?

There are two ways:

1. Do it yourself
2. Hire a catalog broker

How can I do it myself?

Mike Rounds, co-author of *The Mechanics of Mail Order*, offers these suggestions:

1. Write out a good, clear description of your product. Describe the market that you think it's best suited for, as well as the kinds of people whom you think will want to buy it
2. Check out Ad-Lib Publication's *Directory of Book, Catalog and Magazine Printers* and Oxbridge Communications' *Natural Directory of Catalogues*
3. Find the section that lists the kinds of catalogs that handle similar or identical products to yours. Use your imagination a little bit here. You'll be better off offering your products to companies that are marginal in their similarity, rather than deciding that they're not interested
4. Copy down the names, addresses, and telephone numbers of each of these firms
5. Call them first to determine if they're looking for products like yours, and who the buyer will be. While you're talking to them also ask them what their current policies and procedures are for submitting new products for their consideration
6. Send them your submission package. This may include descriptions, literature, samples, pricing, or similar items
7. Call them again to follow up. This is critical! *You must follow up!*

Don't assume simply because you've sent the package that they're planning on calling you. Take the initiative and do the work yourself. Once you find interested firms you'll open your negotiations, and you're off and running.

What kind of deals are open to me?
There are two basic deals:

1. You can buy the ad space in a catalog
2. They can buy your products in bulk at a discounted price

How do catalog product brokers work?
They take the time and effort to search for the right catalog. Some take a fee and others work on a commission basis, in which you pay them only for the orders you receive, much like a per order situation (see the chapter, ''Per Order/Per Inquiry'')

Do catalogs do the fulfilling?
1. Some will do the entire fulfillment
2. Others will handle the paperwork, give you the names, and then you do what is called *drop ship* the merchandise
3. Others will have the replies come directly back to you, leaving the mailing company the job of only preparing and mailing the catalog

What if I want to do my own catalogs? How can I compete with the big ones and make it successful?
- Find and define your niche market as closely as you can. Start with your own list and ask for referrals
- To compete with the big boys, make your catalog and the ordering experience as personal as you can
- Positioning in the marketplace is a key factor
- Make your graphics and your pictures interesting, artful, creative, different
- Employ a creative copywriter
- Make it convenient and easy to order
- Cultivate a relationship with your customers. Know everything about them, including their birthdays, and send cards
- Make your catalog an extension of your own personality

Is writing catalog copy the same as writing ads and sales letters?
The premise is the same. Study the chapters, ''Writing Direct Mail and Sales Letters,'' ''Yellow Pages,'' ''Card Decks,'' ''Couponing,'' et cetera.

RESOURCES

Books
Mechanics of Mail Order by Mike Rounds and Nancy Miller; Rounds Miller Associates; 6318 W. Ridgepath Ct.; Rancho Palos Verdes, CA 90275; (310) 544-9502

Directories
- *Directory of Book, Catalog and Magazine Printers*; Ad-Lib Publications; 51 W. Adams; Fairfield, IA 52556; (800) 669-0773
- *Facts on File*
- *National Directory of Catalogues*; Oxbridge Communications; 150 Fifth Ave.; New York, NY 10011; (800) 955-0231; *http://www.mediafind.com*

Catalog Product Brokers
- Catalog Solutions; 521 Riverside Ave.; Westport, CT 06880; (203) 454-1919
- Direct to Catalogs, Inc.; 6600 Coffman Farms Rd.; Keedysville, MD 21756; (301) 432-4410
- Call your favorite catalog and ask what brokers they do business with

Catalog Product Fulfillment
- National Fulfillment Incorporated, 507B Maple Leaf Dr.; Nashville, TN 37210; (615) 391-0196
- Call your favorite catalog and ask which fulfillment houses they do business with

73

CLASSIFIED ADS

Good things come in small packages

What kinds of businesses do well with classified ads?

Any business with information, a service, or a product to sell can effectively utilize classified ads. And that's just about everyone.

Do people actually buy from classifieds?

Yes, but I'm told that classifieds pull much better for lead generation than for sales.

What's the difference between a classified and a display ad?

A classified ad has words; a display ad has pictures.

What do I have to do to make my ad stand out from all the rest?

- Offer something free. A brochure, audio or video tape, a special report, a sample, a taped message
- Pump up the benefits
- To attract attention quickly, print your headline in CAPITAL LETTERS
- Be direct. Use simple language. Get to the point fast
- Use 800 numbers, not 900 numbers, even if it's a local call
- Even English-speaking people have difficulty with ad abbreviations. Spell things out
- Say everything you need to say. You don't get a second chance on an impulse buy
- Utilize multiple section placement
- Test what days are best

- Place your classified ad under several different compatible categories

RESOURCES

Newsletter
Classified Communication; Box 4242; Prescott, AZ 86302; $29 a year

Placement
- National Response Corporation; 3511 W. Commercial Blvd.; 2nd Floor; Fort Lauderdale, FL 33309; (888) 672-4237. This company will place your ad in multiple circulation
- American Publishing Company; Box 1049; Kirksville, MO 63501; (800) 748-8249. This company will also place your ad in multiple circulation

Newspaper Directories
Your local library has these directories. All directories offer list rentals on labels or CDROM.

74

YELLOW PAGES

That's right, "Let your fingers do the walking. . . ."

Why should I use the yellow pages?
- Marketing consultants Brad and Alan Antin tell me that if you don't already trade with a business that sells what you need, most people check out the yellow pages first, before any other comparable source
- The Advertising Research Corporation reports that on any

given day, 23.5% of the population of the United States refers to the yellow pages. If the population of the country is about 260 million, that would be more than 60 million people a day. Eighty-four percent contact a business listed in the yellow pages, and 49% actually go on to purchase something from that contact
- Brad and Alan Antin also report that 74% of the people who check the yellow pages do not have a specific company in mind when they look

What if I'm in a business that doesn't lend itself to yellow pages advertising?
There is no business that doesn't lend itself to yellow pages advertising. What you might need is some special attention with the wording, page setup, and pictures, but every marketing person I have spoken with tells me that everyone can benefit from advertising in the yellow pages.

What works best, listings or display ads?
Eighty-four percent of the people who look at the yellow pages respond to a display ad rather than a listing alone.

If yellow pages advertising is one of the most powerful ways to market, why do my friends tell me their yellow pages ad didn't work for them?
Two very important reasons:

- They were not written by experienced copywriters
- They were not tested

Advertising consultant Barry Maher listed "The Ten Deadliest Yellow Pages Mistakes to Avoid" in *Business 95* magazine:

- Mistake #1: letting your rep whip up a quick ad
- Mistake #2: putting your name first (not what your business does)
- Mistake #3: "A picture is worth a thousand words" (either not using one, or using the wrong one)
- Mistake #4: errors of omission (include the hard factual information your customers need)

- Mistake #5: saying too much
- Mistake #6: buying the wrong size
- Mistake #7: buying the wrong color
- Mistake #8: being in the wrong place
- Mistake #9: white pages advertising (think about a bold listing to make it easier for customers to find you)
- Mistake #10: not reviewing proofs

What are some yellow pages do's?

Brad and Alan Antin published "What Are Some Yellow Pages Do's?" in *The Antin Marketing Letter: Secrets from the Lost Art of Common Sense Marketing*:

- Make your ad a compelling sales pitch for the prospect to call or go see you
- Talk about a specific offer in your ad
- Make certain your ad has a "call to action," words that tell the prospect exactly what to do next
- Use a strong, attention-getting, benefit-driven, newsy kind of headline
- Include your USP, or as the Antins call it, your SOB, statement of benefits. And try to utilize it in your headline
- Sell your integrity. Use testimonials
- Educate them all about your product or service. Show them what an expert you are
- Build rapport and trust
- Tell the reader why you are better than your competitors
- Tell your readers why they will benefit from picking up the phone and calling you . . . now!

Should I use fancy graphics, drawings, logos, or pictures?

The copywriter's consensus is graphics, drawings, and logos take up a lot of valuable selling space, and usually don't add much to the persuasiveness of the ad. If your logo is part of your name, then by all means use it.

Pictures meaning photos, not drawings, are the one exception to this rule.

A good photo:

- Points up your credibility
- Can add personality to an ad

- Can show what it is you actually do
- Can show you performing the service that the reader wants to buy
- Can show that you're a caring, compassionate person, not just a building with a sign outside

Is there an advantage to having a bigger ad?

The Advertising Research Corporation statistics show that, with all other things being equal, simply enlarging your ad will increase its pulling power by a larger percentage than its added cost.

How can I test my ad before committing to a full year's cost of running it?

The Antin brothers have stellar advice. "Test! Come up with two or three or more ads and test them to see which pulls the best. Simply run all three ads in your local newspaper (at different times, of course), and carefully track the results. The one that pulls best is the one you put in the yellow pages. Test different headlines, appeals, rationales, offers, et cetera. Find the combination that works best, and use it."

RESOURCES

Newsletter

- *Secrets of the Lost Art of Common Sense Marketing* by Brad and Alan Antin; 11001 Delmar, Ste. 1200; Leawood, KS 66211; (913) 663-5775. The Antins offer six audio-tapes and a 205-page three-ring training binder. Great seminars too!
- *Getting the Most from Your Yellow Pages* by Barry Maher; Barry Maher & Associates; Box 2126; Santa Barbara, CA 93120; (805) 962-2599

Books

- *Yellow Pages Industry Facts Booklet*, published by the Yellow Pages Publishers Association; 820 Kirts Blvd. Ste. 100; Troy, MI 48084; (810) 244-6211. $2.95

Magazine
- *Business 95* magazine; Group IV Communications; 125 Auburn Ct., #100; Thousand Oaks, CA 91362; (805) 496-6156. The name of the magazine changes to reflect the current publication year

75

POSTCARD CAMPAIGNS

A picture is worth a thousand words

What's the purpose of a postcard campaign?

To maximize the exposure of your name, service, or product to your target audience in a less expensive manner than traditional letter and envelope mailings.

What are some ways I could conduct a picture postcard campaign?
- I used a picture postcard campaign for a photography studio client who wanted magazines to hire him. It went for fifty-two weeks. Each month was a theme. We sent four oversize cards a month, each featuring a different aspect of his talents. The front of the card showed his photographic expertise; the back had helpful hints on what was pictured on the front. Each card announced next month's theme.

For example:

- Front: food. Back: recipe
- Front: hair. Back: tips on hair care
- Front: wine. Back: tips on buying wine

It got so that photo editors were calling with their specialty requests. We found out that the oversize cards were being saved as works of photographic art. Yes, he got hired, a lot. The campaign worked.

- *Biz* magazine conducted a postcard testimonial contest. The magazine contacted its subscribers for testimonials (see the chapters, "Give Testimonials," "Get Testimonials," and "Endorsement Letters"), and picked a winner.

  To announce the winner the magazine took a picture postcard from the winner's city and sent that to all its subscribers and advertisers.

  That winner's name and testimonial appeared on the postcard along with the question, "Never been to Matthews, Louisiana?"

  Then *Biz* offered another contest to track this one. If you mailed back the postcard, you were entered in a drawing to win a basket of tasty foods made in Louisiana. The postcard asked you to "Simply fax this card back by a certain date."

  The fourth offer asked if you were curious about the magazine. You were provided with the name and number of the associate publisher and were told to mention this card to receive an additional 10% off your first ad in the magazine. At this point you were reminded that this was a $3,000 value.

  I received five of these postcards. I never won the drawing, but I was so impressed with the magazine that I gave it as gifts.
- A recording company was changing its name, so it came up with a campaign to celebrate the death and burial of the old name. The company held an actual burial ceremony at a famous cemetery, followed by a wake. The campaign consisted of four postcards with photos of famous funerals. The postcards were your invitation to the funeral and the party

How long is a campaign?

As long as you want it to be. One mailing can be considered a campaign in the eyes of the beholder.

What else could I use a postcard campaign for?

- Saying thank you
- A new product announcement
- An upcoming sale
- Just to keep in touch
- A special events promotion
- Announcing a new staff addition or your promotion
- To develop or continue a relationship
- Announce a new location
- To chronicle a celebration
- Feature a contest winner
- Contacting advertisers or prospective advertisers

Do people really consider postcards weaker than a letter?

I don't know anyone who doesn't like getting postcards. They're not as official or threatening as letters. People won't open what they think is a junk mail envelope, but they do read what they think is a junk mail postcard.

How can I make mine stand out?

- Make it one size over the regular size. If you can afford the extra postage, it's worth it
- Use cartoon graphics to convey your message
- Use a picture postcard from a different city
- Use color
- Very important: hand address it

RESOURCES

Commercial Postcard Design Companies

- Carl Sebastion Colour; 436 E. Banister Rd.; Kansas City, MO 64131; (800) 825-0381
- Superior Business Cards; 8025 N. Division St., Ste. F; Spokane, WA 99208; (800) 745-9565
- Daicolo Corporation; 21203A Hawthorne Blvd.; Torrance, CA 90503; (800) 772-9993 or (310) 543-2700
- U.S. Press; Box 640; Valdosta, GA 31603-0640; (800) 227-7377
- Call local advertising agencies. They use postcard campaigns for their clients

• Look in your yellow pages under Photography. Most photo labs will tell you who makes postcards in your area. Many of them send the work out to the above names

76

BULLETIN BOARD MARKETING

A more personal classified ad

Bulletin boards, such as those in supermarkets, Laundromats, and health food stores, are another way to do word-of-mouth marketing that brings results.

Bulletin boards market to the inner reaches of the mind and address your needs just like the expensive printed stuff. That's why people stop to read those three by five cards and tear off the paper fingers with the phone numbers.

Why are bulletin boards an effective marketing tool?

Curiosity is a human quality. Curiosity governs our daily actions in ways we don't ever think about. It mostly has to do with the what's-in-it-for-me attitude we all have, but don't always want to admit to.

When you pass the bulletin board, your mind immediately goes into the mode of asking yourself if maybe there is something on the board that might:

• Benefit you
• Give you an edge
• Make you a better person
• Bring you more happiness
• Offer you the opportunity of a lifetime
• Advance your status
• Teach you something you need to know

How can I find them?

Just start looking in the places you shop. I've seen them in print shops, bakeries, on college campuses, in libraries, markets, libraries, health food stores, hair salons, and so on.

Think of where your current and potential clients, customers, patients, and patrons go, and put up your messages: "Do you need" or "Are you looking for . . ." or "Free samples," et cetera.

Because not everyone carries a pen and paper, how can I pass along my number?

From tear pads. These are far more effective than just a three by five card. People actually take home your phone number and information.

Put your contact information on the bottom of the paper in boxes or what are called fingers. Cut around the three sides, leaving the information attached to the body of the paper. If your message is compelling, and people want to contact you, they can tear off the information without removing the entire flier.

Another kind of tear pad you can make up is called a peel off, made from removable self-stick notes. It's like the 3M Post-It packs. Your printer can make these up for you. If you're strapped for money, take a Post-It pack and handwrite each one with your contact information.

Can I market on electronic bulletin boards the same way I would on cork bulletin boards?

No, not exactly in the same way, because you're not allowed to market on-line unless you pay for it. But if you're clever with your wording, you can tell people about your product or services.

For example, if I wanted to inform bulletin board readers about *101 Ways to Promote Yourself*, I would word my message like this:

- Looking for self-promotional stories for the sequel to my book *101 Ways to Promote Yourself*. E-mail me at *ZenOfHype@aol.com*
- Looking for PR or promotional examples to add to the 101 categories in my book *101 Ways to Promote Yourself*.

Anyone have anything interesting to share? E-mail me at *ZenOfHype@aol.com*
- Can anyone give me suggestion on where to place classified ads to add to the directory of resources from my new book *101 Ways to Promote Yourself*? E-mail me at *ZenOfHype@aol.com*

NOTE: Grab yourself a fist full of thumbtacks and go to it. Remember that great lists are made one person at a time.

77

BOUNCE BACKS

Great qualified lead generators

What is a bounce back?

Have you ever received a coupon or a postcard with an offer to buy or try something, and all you had to do to get that offer was peel off a preprinted mailing label, put it in the box marked *put label here*, then mail it?

That card or coupon with the peel-off, preaddressed mailing label is what the direct-mail industry calls a bounce back. They bounce it to you, and you bounce it right back to them.

Why is this a good marketing tool?

It's for data base capture. The reason this is such a great marketing tool is it's designed for only the eyes of the addressee. The precoded, prelabeled, preposted reply card is set up so that only the recipient can retrieve the offer. Once you send the offer, the addressee can give it away to someone else, but the person's name will still be captured by the data base.

When people respond to the offer, their names get checked off and moved further up your list as a potential hot prospect.

And how do I get addressees to return the card?
- Give a great offer that grabs their attention
- Give them great copywriting to convince them to take the offer and return the card (see Ivan Levison's list in the chapter, "Business Reply Cards")

What makes a great offer?

A great offer includes at least one of the universal law of supply and demand:

1. Does it fill a need?
2. Does it solve a problem?
3. Does it tell them something they don't already know?

The more of these you can incorporate in your offer, the better your chances you'll get the card back and make a sale.

NOTE: So while you're going about making it a great day, make it a great offer too!

RESOURCES

Newsletters
- *The Antin Marketing Letter: Secrets from the Lost Art of Common Sense Marketing* by Brad and Alan Antin; 11001 Delmar, Ste. 1200; Leawood, KS 66211; (913) 663-5775; *antin@tyrell.com; 75706.2523@CompuServ*
- *The Levison Letter: Action Ideas for Better Direct Mail and Advertising*; Ivan Levison & Associates; 14 Los Cerros Dr.; Greenbrae, CA 94904; (415) 461-0672; *http://www.Levison.com*

78

BUSINESS REPLY CARDS (BRCs)

A way to get the horse to drink

What is a BRC?
Here are two types:

- Nestled on top of your catalog purchase is a postage paid card, much like a postcard, telling you about a wonderful bonus closeout promotion. The card directs you to "fill in this card and send it back"
- Or, if you log on to America OnLine and there is an offer to buy the new Web Pages Dictionary or an atlas, and in the text you were prompted to choose the order box or the cancel box, this is an electronic version of a business reply card

Where else can I use BRCs?
- Sales letters
- Fund-raising letters
- New product announcements
- Business openings and moving notices
- Direct mail
- Anywhere you want to capture someone's name

Should I use a postage paid card?
Postage paid cards speed up the decision-making process by eliminating the step of getting out and putting on the stamp. Business reply cards appeal to the impulse of the moment, and you want to encourage that moment, not destroy it.

For maximum return opportunities, yes, use a postage paid card. But there are two ways to do this:

1. Pay for postage up front
2. Set up a return postage due account, in which you pay postage only when a reply card is returned

Why should I use business reply cards?
1. To promote another sale
2. To enhance customer service
3. To keep recipients in the loop
4. To have another means of keeping your name in front of your target market

What are the guidelines for writing a business reply card?
- In *The Levison Letter; Action Ideas for Better Direct Mail and Advertising*, Ivan Levison, copy writing and newsletter expert for the software industry, wrote these "Guidelines for Writing a Business Reply Card":
- State the offer clearly. Once people are ready to order, they want you to cut to the chase. Don't disappoint them. Let them know what's for sale by getting to the point
- Avoid writing like a lawyer. A lot of BRC copy often sounds stilted and legalistic. Try to make your copy sound as if it was written by an accessible human being
- Write with energy and personality. When you are writing selling copy, keep the benefits in the reader's face
- Stress that the offer is risk-free. Restate your guarantee on the BRC
- Include check boxes. If there are ordering options, check boxes are a must. If there are no options put a prechecked box in front of the "Yes"
- Remember to punch up the 800 number. You hope that all readers will call rather than send it back. You shorten the sales cycle and strike while the iron is hot. That's why you must say, "To order now, call (800) 123-1234" right on the card
- Don't put important information on the reverse side. The back of your BRC can have a supportive message, but don't put the key elements of the offer there. Make certain that everything important goes on the front
- Use visuals to spur action and guide the reader. A well-placed red arrow can point to key copy (and higher return rates)

- Attach a stub. BRCs often get better results when there's a stub perforated along the edge of the card. What should go there? How about a copy of the money-back guarantee that the buyer can retain for his or her records?
- Give your business reply card an appropriate title. Instead of calling your BRC an "order form" or "order card," try "action card" or "preferred customer upgrade card"

RESOURCES

Newsletter

The Levison Letter: Action Ideas for Better Direct Mail and Advertising Communications; by Ivan Levison & Associates; 14 Los Cerros Dr.; Greenbrae, CA 94904; (415) 461-0672; *http://www.Levison.com*

79

CARD DECKS

There's safety in numbers

What is a card deck?

A card deck is a pack of cards that offers free samples and is sent through the mail. This is a well-respected way to get your message out. It's another way to enter the direct response market. Cards that ask for your contact information rather than offer a generic coupon are a good example of a BRC, a business reply card.

There are two basic card decks:

1. Business to business
2. Business to consumer

Eighty percent of card decks are targeted business to business, not consumers.

Why is the consumer percentage so small?

Consumers do better with couponing, coop mailings, and package inserts.

How do card decks work?

- Each card has a pitch on one side and the address on the other
- Depending on the target market, there can be up to 200 cards
- There are more than 1,000 specialized card decks that target your market
- Most companies use them for lead generation, but some companies do use them to promote sales
- Double-sized cards and folded cards bring in a better response

How much does participation cost?

The cost per piece is very low, about three to four cents per double-sided card. The rollout, depending on the list, can cost you thousands of dollars. But this is still less expensive than if you mail a promotional postcard, flier, or sales letter.

Is there a less expensive way to participate?

There are companies that will, instead of a fee or flat rate, agree to a per inquiry or per order rate (see the chapter, Per Order/Per Inquiry). This is a win-win situation, because you can pay as you go. But be aware if you do this. In many cases you will need to leave a deposit. Ask the company for its policy, and watch out for the fine print.

What kinds of results can I expect to get?

Don't forget that the people on the other end haven't requested your information, so they are not expecting you.

The response rate is lower than 2%, which is the average response rate to most unsolicited efforts. This doesn't make it great, but in this medium those 2% are usually considered good prospects. They have so many cards to choose from, if they've responded to yours, they could very well be qualified leads.

If you can offer an 800 number with a warm body at the other end who can talk intelligently and creatively about your offer, then your response numbers will increase.

Who benefits most from using card decks?

People whose profit margin is high can afford this method. Surveys show those that benefit most are:

- Catalog houses
- Magazine subscriptions
- Charities
- High-priced items such as jewelry, furs, cars, et cetera

What's the downside?

The downside is in expecting bags filled with responses, especially on your first time out.

How can I improve the downside?

- Testing, as with all direct response marketing. Test your offer, the copy, the color, the headline. Take advantage of the expertise at the card deck company. The company knows what works and what doesn't
- Make certain you have a great headline to pull attention away from the other cards
- Have a picture of the product, preferably in use
- Make sure there is a call to action so recipients will mail back the card. Offer a free sample, a gift, or a discount

Are all card decks reputable?

Most are, but no, they're not all reputable. I've been told by several users that the quality of the list determines the quality of the card deck. (Familiarize yourself with the questions in the chapter, "Using Commercial Mailing Lists.")

- Ask about the source of the names
- Ask when the list was cleaned and corrected
- Ask to see samples of several months' card decks. Look for repeat names; these are people who are hot prospects
- Call several of the advertisers and ask about the service

If you're serious about card decks as a medium for you, read *DM News* (available on newsstands). It describes the new companies and the new decks.

Also, if you need advice, Jay Conrad Levinson and Seth Godin, in their *Guerrilla Marketing Handbook*, tell you to call Leon Henry, Inc. "His service is invaluable—we don't recommend advertising in a card deck without consulting him."

RESOURCES

Card Deck Companies

- Leon Henry, Inc.; 455 Central Ave.; Scarsdale, NY 10583; (914) 723-3176
- Venture Communications; 60 Madison Ave., 3rd Fl.; New York, NY 10010; (212) 684-4800. Venture comes highly recommended by Dan Kennedy
- Lifestyle Change Communications, Inc.; 5885 Glenridge Dr., Ste. 150; Atlanta, GA 30328; (404) 252-0554. This company has a great data base of people in the thick of life: new parents, new marriages, new homes, new cars, and is also recommended by Dan Kennedy, Jay Conrad Levinson, and Seth Godin
- *SRDS*; 1700 Higgins Rd.; Des Plaines, IL; 60018-5605; (800) 851-7737; *http://www.SRDS.com*; SRDS has the most comprehensive list of brokers, along with descriptions on who they target

Magazine

DM News; 19 W. 21st St., 8th Fl.; New York, NY 10010-6888; (212) 741-2095; *http://www.dmnews.com*

People Resource

Dan Kennedy; Empire Communications Corporation; 5818 N. 7th St., #103; Phoenix, AZ 85014; (602) 997-7707; fax (602) 269-3113. Kennedy publishes *No B.S. Marketing Letter*.

Book

The Guerrilla Marketing Handbook by Jay Conrad Levinson and Seth Godin (Houghton Mifflin)

80

COUPONS

Clip and ye shall buy

What's the difference between coupons and card decks?
Card decks are primarily for the business-to-business community. Coupons are for the consumer market.

How cost-effective is couponing?
Very effective. In fact, it's almost unheard-of not to break even. Look at it this way. Even a break-even campaign has a built-in bonus. Now you have the names to go after for referrals and repeat business.

What type of results should I expect?
Marketer Dan Kennedy notes in his *No B.S. Marketing Letter* that depending on your offer and your service, "There's a pull of 2-1 to 4-1 return on the investment, including big ticket service providers like doctors, dentists, and lawyers."

He goes on to say that "generally speaking, as with card decks, an uncomfortably large chunk of those responding will be very poor quality leads or customers. But there should be enough quality sifted out of the quantity to get you to break even or better."

How do I maximize my results from the first mailing?
• Repeat it in the same zip codes several times
• Send your own direct-mail letter for support recognition
• Do other forms of publicity for support recognition

What are the advantages of coupons?
This method is limited in what it can do, but it is:

- Affordable
- Effective
- Less expensive than your own efforts
- Won't take up your time and effort

What format does the best?

Two-sided coupons, full color, and even larger inserts folded down to fit the standard coupon size pull better than the usual one-sided, one-color standard size.

What are the rules of success for couponing?

In *No B.S. Marketing Letter*'s "And a Dozen Quick Thoughts About Direct-Mail Coupons," marketing expert Dan Kennedy writes:

- Ask for first-time advertiser and test discounts, free color, and other concessions for testing, split testing, buying more than one zone, et cetera
- Split test two different coupons within the same zone. Once you have a *control*, a coupon that works consistently and repeatedly, you can start testing against it
- Most coupons can be dramatically improved just by creating and using a strong, compelling headline
- Photos often help, especially a story that shows a story and has a caption that is a second headline
- Print the front like an ad and the back like a letter, using an advertorial format
- The rules for yellow pages ads and postcards apply to these coupons
- You can also joint-venture advertise in this medium. Maybe a chiropractor, dentist, optometrist, et cetera could go together on an eleven by seventeen insert, half filled with helpful health information from each; the other half with their coupons. Create something with enough informational value that it might be kept and used. How about all the stores in one strip center or little shopping center going in together on a coupon?
- Even with ordinary look-alike coupons, many businesses can get break-even or better results from this medium consistently, repeatedly, and frequently
- The medium works best for common businesses that peo-

ple already instantly understand, periodically need and use, and often are price driven. Fast food, carpet cleaning, auto painting, dentistry, hair salons

What if I use several programs? How do I know what comes from where?

All marketing experts will encourage you to use more than one program. If you do, make certain each program's coupon is tagged with appropriate identification so you can test which one originated the response.

Don't shy away from this medium just because you aren't a dentist, a rug cleaner, or an oil change shop. You have an advantage if what you have to offer is unusual to the coupon program. Typing services, seminars, bookstores, consultants to consumer needs—all can do well in this medium. Remember, with downsizing, many consumers opening the envelope are now members of home-based businesses. If your product or service can appeal here, then advertise in this manner.

Again, remember that no one way will provide you with the complete win you are looking for. I often talk about combining multimedia efforts to promote yourself. With coupons, ask the distributor to provide you with print overruns. You may have to pay a little extra, but then you have them to put in your direct-mail piece, your package insert, your envelope stuffer, or your news release to the media.

RESOURCES

Mail Marketing

- ADVO; 1 Univac Lane; Windsor, CT 06095; (860) 285-6100
- Val-Pak; main address is 6456 S. Quebec St., Bldg. 5, Ste. 550, Englewood, CO 80111; (970) 843-0943. Local brokers are listed in the white pages under Val-Pak
- Money Mailers; 201 Park Pl., Altamont Springs, FL. 32701; (407) 831-0022. Call this main office and they will give you the phone number of your regional representative
- Lifestyle Change Communications, Inc.; 5885 Glenridge Dr., Ste. 150; Atlanta, GA 30328; (404) 252-0554
- SRDS; 1700 Higgins Rd.; Des Plaines, IL; 60018-5605;

(800) 851-7737; *http.//www.SRDS.com*. This directory is also available in the library

Expert
Dan Kennedy; Empire Communications; 5818 N. 7th St., #103; Phoenix, AZ 85014; (602) 997-7707; fax (602) 269-3113. Kennedy publishes the *No B.S. Marketing Letter*, holds seminars, and is the author of eleven books on marketing. Go to your bookstore or call Dan direct

81

DOOR HANGERS

Unwanted maybe, but not abandoned

What are the benefits of door hanger marketing?
- If your business is geographical, this is a great way to deep farm the area
- Printing costs are much cheaper than mail and brochures
- It's an in-your-face direct-mail piece. It requires no opening envelopes, no reply cards, and very little reading time
- You can use door hangers for sampling, too

How can I encourage people to keep them around?
Make one side the offer, and on the other put:

- A calendar
- A list of emergency telephone numbers
- A collection of famous sayings on success, mothers, fathers, love, et cetera
- Local government agency names and phone numbers
- A schedule of local sports events

If you do put the keeper information on the other side, make sure you only print down as far as the coupon so they don't have to tear into the text. And don't forget to print your name, address, and phone number on the keeper information side so they always see your name, coming and going.

Think about making the calendars, directory names, et cetera the giveaway gift when they take advantage of the offer.

Is copywriting for door hangers different than it is for BRCs or bounce backs?

Not really. But this medium is more prone to be tossed out than the others. It's on your door, you didn't ask for it, and it's often thought of as littering. So the headline and the layout of the remaining wording have to be a *big wow grabber.*

The technique is no different than any of the direct response pieces we've talked about. The headline must be short and to the point. It must fill a need, solve a problem, or tell them something they didn't know.

Check over the copywriting for other direct response pieces, then study the door hangers you've saved. If you don't have a door hanger file, ask any local printer. I'm sure they do.

A very important note: If you're in a neighborhood that doesn't know you or your reputation, use testimonials in your copy (see the chapter, ''Get Testimonials'').

How do I distribute them?

Put a notice in a penny saver circular, ask a friend's children, put a notice on the bulletin board at the Laundromat or supermarket. Get the Boy Scouts and Girl Scouts interested. The best way to pay them is based on a percentage of responses. That way they won't skip doors or toss them in a friendly wastebasket.

There are companies that do door hangers. Look in your yellow pages or ask your printer, or see the following resources list.

How do I test them?

Door hangers are easy to test. Just code each one and track the results. You can code by numbers, color, the alphabet, campaign names, initials, et cetera.

How do the results compare to those for other direct-mail pieces?

Typically it has been found that door hanger results are much higher than most other direct response methods. If the geographical area needs what you have, door hangers average a 15% return. The only method that gets higher response rates is:

1. Using your own list
2. Using your own list and following up with a telephone call

What is the marketing value of door hangers?

My client wrote a book listing gourmet restaurants that prepared meals to go. Besides an innovative media campaign, we also suggested door hangers.

First, we designed a medium-sized shopping bag to look like the book. Into the bag we packed several of the restaurants' samples in takeout containers, a plastic bag stuffed with a book brochure, a business reply card order form, and a discount coupon from a bookstore chain. Armed with trays and baskets, we handed them out during rush hour at train and bus stations.

Door hangers were distributed in the suburban neighborhoods where the buses and trains deposited the people who got our packages. For tracking purposes when ordering, we instructed the callers to speak to a code name. Each neighborhood had a specific code name, so tracking was easy.

NOTE: Be sure door hanging is legal in the neighborhoods you want to target.

RESOURCES

Alternate Postal Delivery; 1 Ionia SW; Grand Rapids, MI 49503; (800) 438-9430. This company does sampling bags

82

PER ORDER-PER INQUIRY

Perfect purchasing power

What's a PO or a PI?

POs and PIs are one of the best-kept marketing secrets. Normally you pay the media for advertising space. With a per inquiry (PI), you make a deal to pay the media a set amount for each caller who responds to the print ad or the electronic message. With a per order (PO), you strike a deal to pay the media a set amount for each caller who orders the offer.

What product or service works well with PI-PO marketing?

Any business, product, or service works well with this type of marketing, but mass appeal is what gets you through the door.

Why is this a good marketing tool?

- You get to put out your message without draining your budget
- You can run a lead-generating campaign with no money up front
- You can test a new medium with your existing advertising without risk

Does every newspaper, magazine, radio, or TV station participate in this form of marketing?

No, they don't. The major media don't need to, because they can sell their ad space. You're better off going with local or regional media that have a harder time filling their ad spaces.

If you do get a no from the local or regional media, they

might be saying no because it's not the right deal. Everyone would rather make sure money and sell the space. But if they have open space and the PI-PO will bring in revenue, they might go for your deal. So if they say no, try digging a little deeper to determine if the no is really a maybe with stipulations.

Is one easier than the other to get the media to take?

I've been told that a PI deal is easier to achieve than a PO, simply because it's based on leads rather than getting orders. Depending on the item offered, leads can be easier to attract than orders.

What's the best medium for PI-POs?

Marketing surveys show that card decks and television are the best avenue for good PI-PO deal making.

How much do I have to give them on each item?

There are no rules on this one. It's up to the media and you.

How do I determine what price to negotiate?

In *The Antin Marketing Letter: Secrets of the Lost Art of Common Sense Marketing*, experts Brad and Alan Antin suggest that you:

1. Determine what you're willing to pay for a qualified lead. This is determined by the selling price of what you plan to sell to these new leads, and the gross profit you expect to make from a sale
2. Add in the intangible of what each lead might bring you through back-end marketing (back-end marketing includes everything you sell customers after they make the first purchase)

Will the media act as the fulfillment house for the orders on the PO?

I have never known the media to be responsible for fulfillment. You need to have your own setup in place. Since honesty and accuracy are very important with these transactions, I would ask the media who they have a good working relationship with. That way both parties will feel more comfortable all the way around.

What guidelines should I follow for the business side of the offer?
- Use an 800 number
- Give prompt and courteous service
- Pay as much as you can to the media
- Make sure your offer is irresistible
- Keep very strict records
- Track results
- Honor the guarantee you offer

RESOURCES

Magazines
- *Response TV:* (800) 346-0085. This magazine covers the teleshopping industry, including how to get your products on the air. The publisher also puts out *Response TV's Industry Directory*
- *Electronic Retailing:* (800) 624-4196. This magazine provides information on teleshopping, direct response TV, and more

Experts and Newsletters
The Antin Marketing Letter: Secrets of the Lost Art of Common Sense Marketing by Brad and Alan Antin; 11001 Delmar, Ste. 1200; Leawood, KS 66211; (913) 663-5775; *antin@tyrell. net;75706.2523@CompuServ*. The Antins offer six audiotapes and a 205-page, three-ring training binder. Great consulting and seminars, too!

83

POINT OF PURCHASE MATERIALS

*POPs: getting a bigger bang
for your promotional dollar*

What's the purpose of point of purchase (POP) materials?
Point of purchase materials:

- Create name and brand awareness
- Provide a motivation to buy
- Are an in-your-face reminder that the product is there
- Make the product stand out over everything else on the shelf
- Provide critical decision-making power
- Drive life into sales
- Catch your attention
- Say "buy me, not them"

Most importantly, they are the only medium that places your customer, product, and advertising together at the same time in the same place for the same purpose.

Why should I use point of purchase materials?
Next to value, consumers respond most to visual and auditory appeal. Visual and auditory point of purchase materials heighten awareness and therefore translate into increased returns and revenue.

What importance do point of purchase materials hold in the market?
Brian Dyches, president of the Laguna Niguel, California–based Retail Resource Group, told me that "point of purchase is taking on new importance today as it joins more established

forms of marketing as means to drive new life into product sales. From 1981 to 1991, annual investment in POP has exploded from $5.1 billion to $15.2 billion. Today's figures are estimated to be around $20 billion.''

- The average sales increase attributed to utilizing POP is a whopping 244%!
- Combining the display and feature activity of a specific product can result in an additional sales increase of 128%
- Eighty percent of the decision to buy is made at point of purchase

What are the different applications for point of purchase?
Close your eyes and pretend you're walking around a store. Picture all the ways the message buy me jumps out at you. These are POPs . . . point of purchase displays:

- Demonstrations
- In-store music
- In-store videos
- ''Attention Kmart shoppers'' type announcements
- Packaging
- Signs
- Pull offs
- Fixtures
- Stand-alone displays
- Take ones
- Interactive displays
- Modular displays
- Product displays
- Countertop dispensers
- Stickers
- Hang tags

Where do I get these materials?
Some will be provided by your vendors while others can be purchased from display and fixture distributors.

What colors should I use?
Tia Potter is the editor of *WWD, A Business Newsletter for Specialty Stores*. She printed an extensive article on color in

visual marketing by Martin M. Pegler, S.V.M., author of *Visual Merchandising & Display*. Pegler feels that color is one of the strongest forces in attracting shoppers and enticing them to buy. For many customers, color is the most important factor when deciding to buy, even more important than style or price.

Study colors and what they mean before you go out and design your display materials.

How can a small business afford POPs?

- Start small, but start
- Make your own signs. Barter for services. Put signs up yourself
- Do your own in-store demonstrations. The massage man is at Wild Oats market giving $1-a-minute massages
- Offer an in-store clinic on your products or services
- Offer tips
- Make friends with the stores. Courage is appreciated and oftentimes honored

Overall, do the best you can with what you have. I go around to bookstores, take my book, which is displayed spine side out, and turn it around to face full front. Most stores have "signed by the author" stickers. I also shamelessly announce myself as the author and proceed to sign all my books with flourish. I also ask if I can do a book signing. When I'm on the road speaking, I call ahead to bookstores and ask to set up a signing. I ask if I can give a minilecture on the floor.

NOTE: If you can demonstrate that you can increase sales of your product by whatever POP you're using, you'll get the store's attention. Then it's up to you to get the attention of the consumer.

RESOURCES

Consultant

- Brian Dyches; Retail Resource Group; 26 Stern St.; Laguna Niguel, CA 92677; (714) 249-7840. Dyches is a speaker and author on the subject of how to make your retail store a money-maker

Organization
Point of Purchase Advertising Institute (POPAI); 66 North Van Brunt St.; Englewood, NJ 07631; (201) 894-8899

Magazines
- *POP & Sign Design*; 7400 Skokie Blvd.; Skokie, IL 60077-3339; (847) 675-7400
- *Retail Store Image*; 6151 Powers Ferry Rd., N.W.; Atlanta, GA 30339; (404) 955-2500

Custom Display and Packaging Companies
- Tag-It!; 3820 S. Hill St.; Los Angeles, CA 90037; (213) 234-9606
- Ruszel Woodworks; 2980 Bayshore Rd.; Benicia, CA 94510; (707) 745-6979
- The Concept Group; 459 West 15th St.; New York, NY 10011; (212) 989-1616
- Innovative Designs; 17401 Nicholas St., Unit K; Huntington Beach, CA 92647; (714) 848-0588

Newsletters
- *WWD, A Business Newsletter for Specialty Stores*; Fairchild Publications; 7 West 34th St., New York, NY 10017-0298; (212) 630-4199; fax (212) 630-4201
- *Merchandising Insights*; N83 W13330 Leon Rd.; Menomonee Falls, WI 53051; (800) 678-5880

84

TAKE ONES

The offer of a lifetime could live inside

What is a take one?

You see these at least once a day in every place of business you go in and come out of. It's that stand-up box on the counter, the door, the wall, even in the bathroom that's filled with information about the business and how it can benefit you.

What are the real benefits of take ones?
- The people are already in the store, so you don't have to do any hard selling
- It's an opportunity to keep them in the store and keep them coming back without much of a dollar investment
- It's like silent word-of-mouth marketing
- It's an opportunity to get the last word
- It's an opportunity to tell them exactly what you want them to know, in case you forgot to personally tell them

How can take ones be used?

The sky is the limit. Here are several possibilities:

- A brochure
- A flier
- A product card
- A sale announcement
- Testimonials and endorsements
- Discount coupons for the next visit
- Famous sayings
- Calendar cards
- Menus

- Special reports
- Trial memberships or subscriptions
- Thank-you-for-shopping-here notes

How fancy should the take ones be?

It's not a matter of fanciness; it's a matter of professionalism. Take ones may be the first and last thing seen, so you want them to make and keep the impression you try so hard to establish.

How fancy should the holder be?

Once again, fancy is not what we're dealing with. It's what's appropriate. If you're not creative get something plain and easy so the material can be removed without ripping. But if you want to be creative, go for it. It will add to your presentation of who you are!

- Shoe store: Cut down the front of a boot
- Florist: Put them in an unusual vase or wreath
- Automotive shop: Cut up an oil can or nestle them in a piece of tire
- Dentist: Use a large display tooth
- Restaurants: Get a fake cake and hollow out the inside
- Plant stores: Use a hanging basket

How can I capture the names of the people who take one?

You can offer a drawing. You could call it a Give and Take! Use a box or a bowl next to your take one display. Follow up with a letter on who won, and offer a discount coupon to those who didn't.

Can I put my take ones in other places than my own?

Absolutely. Offer an exchange. It's sort of like a box bulletin board. I was in a health food restaurant where they had a whole cork board wall filled with mounted boxes.

What are the guidelines for designing a flier?

- If you use colored paper use it wisely. Be careful of red, orange, and dark green. The eyes have difficulty reading the black print first
- Make sure your logo or name is in big letters. You have

a brief moment to capture peoples' attention, and they should see your name
- Make sure the headline is brief and direct and meaningful. You don't have time to be cute
- Include your offer, your marketing call to action

See the chapter, "Fliers."

Are there companies that design and distribute take one displays?
Yes. You can find them in the yellow pages under "Advertising." Many times the same people who do coupon packs and card decks do this too.

NOTE: Take ones are inexpensive advertising, very savvy marketing, excellent customer service, and brilliant public relations.

85

INSERTS

They go along for the ride

What are package inserts?
There are two types of package inserts:

1. Advertisements on services or products your business has to offer. Bloomingdale's, Spiegel, and my local deli all provide me with more pictures and print on what to buy, enjoy, test, or taste. What a great way to market. When I worked in my father's shoe store, he called it suggestive selling. Because it comes in a package you've already bought or a piece of mail you're expecting, they have

you captive, so why not utilize your time and their package?

2. Information and offers from other sources outside your business that you wish to share with your data base. For example:
   - Health and medical professions with a pharmacy or health food store
   - Gardeners and interior designers with plant nurseries or florists
   - Temp agencies, CPAs, or lawyers with business furniture or business supply companies
   - Business consultants with business books or business furniture stores
   - Travel agencies with luggage shops or boutiques selling cruise wear
   - Baby-sitters, nanny agencies, baby nurses with juvenile furniture stores, diaper services, or clothing stores
   - Candy shops with home or office entertainment system stores
   - Swimming pools, dive shops, ice-skating rinks, and ski resorts with sports equipment stores
   - Car washes, oil change stores, and even eye doctors and eyeglasses stores with automotive supply stores

How can I convince someone to include me?
The biggest reason is called value added. In other words, you're adding value for their customers.

- Give a discount
- Give a free sample
- Offer a trial period
- Offer them your mailing list to add to theirs
- Offer to tell them if you get a lead so they can do the right customer service thing
- Offer a percentage

NOTE: Package inserts are another source for response mail pieces. Another name for inserts of this type is ride alongs. They ride along with something else. Samples or information pieces in magazines are also considered ride alongs.

86

STATEMENT STUFFERS

Cushioning the billing blow

What are statement stuffers?
They're the buy-me offerings that come in the envelope along with your payment statement.

Why are they a good marketing tool?
To begin with, if it is in your envelope, the postage is free, the people already know you, they have bought from you, and in most cases they are loyal consumers.

What do I put in the statement stuffers?
Show and tell them:

- Something they don't know about your service
- Something new
- Announce a contest
- Introduce a new line, product, or service
- Introduce a new approach
- Announce a sale
- Sell something only available in the stuffer
- Inform them about your favorite charity
- Ask them to support a community campaign

How can I advertise in other people's stuffers?
I did the viz-ability marketing campaign for Nashville's second annual Tin Pan South festival. In order to reach people intimately, I suggested we include a statement stuffer in the American Express regional billing cycle. All it took was a telephone call, and American Express was happy to be a part of the festivities.

It became a sponsor and absorbed the mailing costs for hundreds of thousands of mail pieces. We included a partial schedule of events and an order form. American Express customers were given a 10% discount if they purchased tickets from the statement stuffer.

If the company you're approaching loves the idea, and it provides value to the people at the other end of the list, placing a stuffer can be that easy. Just like the chapter on coupons, find services you are compatible but not competitive with, and ask if you could be an insert in their bills.

If you donate a portion of the sales to a charity, your sales response will increase. And if the charity is the choice of the host of the mailing list, it's even more of a win-win situation.

Part VII

USING THE MEDIA TO
GET THE WORD OUT

87

SEND A MEDIA RELEASE

"George Washington slept here!"

When should I send out a news release?
When you want to announce:

- An event (seminar, party, conference, luncheon, et cetera)
- The release of a new product or product line
- That you're rolling out a marketing campaign
- To prospects and customers that you've changed your location or that you're opening a new branch
- That your company has made staff promotions or signed a new partner
- Quarterly and year-end reports

How do I construct a news release?
- It should be no more than 250 words, or one page, double spaced
- It should have a headline that summarizes the story, helps the editor find the lead, and organizes the story
- It is written in the third person, never the first person
- A great release tells the story in only four paragraphs
- Each paragraph should be less than thirty words
- The purpose of each of the paragraphs is to move the story along
- Include a contact name and telephone number in case the media require more information or clarification
- Always put the date on the release
- If it is for immediate release, print those words after or below the current date. If the release is to be held for any length of time, mark the appropriate date

What makes up each of the paragraphs?
- Paragraph 1: the basic facts, the who, what, where, when, and why
- Paragraph 2: a slightly broader explanation of the basic reason for the release
- Paragraph 3: This is where you place the quote from the CEO, or testimonials
- Paragraph 4: more information on the reason for the release

Put the least important facts at the bottom. That's where the editors cut first, even without reading.

Where do I send it?
- If it's local, call the paper and ask for the name of the section editor you're targeting
- If you're going to send it out nationally and you don't know the newspaper or the magazine editor's name, just put the section name in which you want it to appear (Style, Business, Health, et cetera). It's always best to know the specific editor's name. If the list you've gotten is more than a month old, chances are the names are no longer valid. If you don't have time to check the names, sending it in care of Editor, Business Section is safer than naming someone who is no longer there, is on vacation, or is now in another department
- Use media distribution services. For a small fee they'll use their data base of appropriate section names
- Rent labels from any of the media directories
- Have it sent out over PR Newswire or Business Wire

RESOURCES

Books
- *You Can Hype Anything: Creative Tactics for Anyone With a Product, Business, or Talent to Promote* by Raleigh Pinskey (Citadel Press)
- *The Zen of Hype, An Insider's Guide to the Publicity Game* by Raleigh Pinskey; 1223 Wilshire Blvd., #502;

Santa Monica, CA 90403; (310) 209-0990; *Raleighbk@ aol.* An eight-audiocassette home study kit

Mailing House
Media Distribution Services; 8592 Venice Blvd.; Los Angeles, CA 90034; (310) 836-6600. Ask for Eileen

Newswire Services
- PR Newswire: 1515 Broadway; New York, NY 10036; (800)-832-5522. For as little as $230 for 400 words, this company will send your news release to 1700 newspapers
- Business Wire: 1990 S. Bundy; Los Angeles, CA 90025; (310) 820-9473. This company is similar to PR Newswire
- News USA: 8300 Boone Blvd., Ste. 810; Vienna, VA 22182; (800)355-9500 or (703) 827-5800

Label List Rentals
- Ad-Lib Publications: (800) 669-0773
- Bacon's Information, Inc.: (800) 621-0561
- SDRS: (800) 851-7737
- Reed Elsevier, New Providence: (800) 521-8110
- Oxbridge Communications: (800) 955-0231
- Burrelle's Information Services: (800)-631-1160
- Gale Research: (800) 877-4253
- New Editions International, Inc. (800) 777-4751

Media on Disc
Publicity Blitz Media Directory-On-Disc; Bradley Communications; Box 1206; Lansdowne, PA; 19050-8206; (800) 989-1400. 20,000 print and broadcast media contacts; 75 subject categories

88

FEATURE STORIES

Seeing is believing

Hundreds of proposals for stories cross editorial desks every week. Only a handful of those are from people the writers know.

Contrary to popular belief, there's no magic to becoming the subject of a feature. No smoke and mirrors. Just pay attention to the wants, needs, and desires of the media, and you'll be in print in no time.

How should I contact editorial departments?

Even if you call and tell your story briefly to the editor, he or she will tell you to send it in writing. So:

- Write first
- Call later to follow up on the status of your request for a story
- Don't be surprised if they can't find your materials and ask you to send another set

What should I put in my request for a feature story?

Logically, you would ask to have a story written on your product, service, talent, or concept. But, unfortunately, if you ask the editors to write a story based on that request alone, they might just tell you to take out an ad.

So, instead, follow these two rules when writing your pitch letter:

1. Editors know you want a story, and they'll do one if it is interesting, valuable, or entertaining for their readership. They'll listen to you if you give them something in return

2. You must tell them what makes your product, service, talent, or concept different, exciting, interesting, amusing, informative, important, necessary, or unique

How long should my pitch letter be?

The shorter, the better. The attention span of the media is no different than yours while you surf radio or TV channels or open your mail. You know within four seconds if you want to move on or throw it away. Limit your request to no more than 100 words, or be prepared to have it tossed.

The trick is, also include pictures and backup materials for an in-depth show-and-tell. This show-and-tell is called a media kit or a presentation kit. (Many people call it a press kit. The traditional term "press" is used for print media only. Since you'll be sending this kit to radio and TV, it should rightfully be called a media kit and a media release.)

What should I include in my media kit?

- Pictures of you, the product, or service
- A brief backgrounder (biography) on you and the company. It should contain only professional information; personal information only if it pertains to the professional
- A Q&A (question & answer) on the company, you, and/ or the product or service
- Reprints (copies) of any articles or transcriptions of talk shows
- Stat sheets (statistical and technical information sheets) if appropriate
- Testimonials from clients or vendors

Do I need a fancy cover to put this in?

There's no room in the file drawer for covers. Usually the editor or journalist pulls out what information they need and then scans it into the computer. Fancy or not fancy, covers get thrown away.

Unless you're a movie studio and the cover will become a collectors' item, then your cover should only be a simple folder that holds the material together. You decide from there the extent of the artwork.

If you do bare bones covers, make certain your contact information is on the cover. You can write it, print it, or use a sticker that won't come off. This applies to each piece of paper you send.

Can I fax my information?

Only if they ask you to fax it to them. Unsolicited faxing is frowned upon. Many media now have unlisted fax numbers because of the abuse to the system.

What are the guidelines for following up?

- If it's an out-of-town media outlet, send your materials by overnight, second, or third day carrier. That way you know exactly when they've received your package
- Count three to five days after the day it arrives and then call
- Don't ask, "Did you get my materials?" Instead say, "I've sent you materials on the latest improvement in roofing materials, and I'm calling to see if this interesting application is something your readership would find as fascinating as my clients do"
- Always have two or three more story angles to talk about in case the editors aren't interested in the approach you've presented in your letter
- If they reject all of your angles, ask if they see an angle that would interest their readership
- Always say thank you, even if you don't feel like it

NOTE: Here's a professional tip used by some of the best: Before you send your request letter and backup materials, call and pretend you already sent it. When they tell you they can't find it, describe the contents and what it would look like if you did send it. That gives you legitimate chat time. Offer to send it again ASAP. This time they'll be on the lookout for it. Then mark on the outside of the package in big red letters: REQUESTED MATERIALS! Call to follow up.

RESOURCES

- *You Can Hype Anything: Creative Tactics and Advice for Anyone With a Product, Business, or Talent to Promote* by Raleigh Pinskey (Citadel Press)

- *The Zen of Hype, An Insider's Guide to the Publicity Game* by Raleigh Pinskey; 1223 Wilshire Blvd., #502; Santa Monica, CA 90403; (310) 209-0990; *Raleighbk@ aol.com*. An eight-audiocassette publicity home study course

89

CALENDAR LISTINGS

If you list it they will come. . . .

Why are calendar listings a good marketing tool?
- Think of them as a type of direct-mail piece going directly to your target market, for free
- If the editors don't print your news release, or they don't interview you for a feature story before the event, at least you'll have your name listed in the week's calendar of events for everyone to see

What's an appropriate event for a listing?

Anything you are holding, giving, presenting, or offering falls under the heading of an event. From a gala to a support group in your living room.

Is there a listings or calendar editor?

Each newspaper is different. Check your paper over a period of time to see what it lists, or call the paper and ask for the details. Usually each section lists events pertaining to its subject content.

How far in advance should I send in my listing?

Each section usually has a name and address of where to send the information, and guidelines for the copy. It is here that you will also learn how far in advance you need to send it in.

A good rule of thumb to follow: Send the calendar listing in the day you sign the contract for the room or begin to plan the event. Even if it's several months out, the editors file it until the time comes to print it.

What are the guidelines for submitting a listing?
- Follow the instructions located in the column, and follow them exactly
- Don't leave anything out. Before you put it in the envelope, do a checklist
- If you're missing information it could mean your listing won't go in
- Usually, editors won't call you to get the information. They don't have time. Besides, they gave you the instructions. Some will, but don't count on it

If my newspaper doesn't give a specific list of things to include, what do I include?
- Who: name of the organization or person presenting the event
- What: the purpose of the event
- Where: complete address, including cross streets
- When: date and time
- How much: price of tickets, even if they're free
- Phone number: for information call, or, to RSVP call (always put your phone number at the bottom as program contact, in case those that call need more information)

RESOURCES

Books
- *You Can Hype Anything, Creative Tactics and Advice for Anyone With a Product, Business, or Talent to Promote* by Raleigh Pinskey (Citadel Press)
- *The Zen of Hype, An Insider's Guide to the Publicity*

Game by Raleigh Pinskey; 1223 Wilshire Blvd., #502; Santa Monica, CA 90403; (310) 209-0990; *raleighbk@aol.com; http://www.cmihub.com/t/Raleigh.htm/.* An eight-audiocassette publicity home study course

Check your local papers on Thursday and Friday for weekend listings. Also, check every day in the individual columns for targeted happenings.

90

CAMERA OPPORTUNITIES

"You ougtta be in pictures. . . ."

What is a camera opportunity?

A camera opportunity alerts the media that if and when they come to your event, you will have interesting, exciting, entertaining, amusing, unique, or rare opportunities to get great still and moving pictures.

Of course if you tell them this, you'd better deliver.

Some people still call this a photo opportunity, but with today's multiple technologies, the appropriate term is camera opportunity. A photo opportunity is for still cameras. We don't want to alienate the electronic media, now do we?

How do I make a camera opportunity successful?

- Local or national celebrities are always a camera calling card (see the chapter, ''Marketing with Celebrities'')
- Animals, especially dressed up for the occasion
- Children participating in the event
- Local participants, especially in costume
- Local celebrities or organizational participants actively involved in the event, i.e., speaking, cooking, serving, running, et cetera

- A parade, skit, or something out of the ordinary added to the event

How can I turn a business meeting into a camera opportunity?

Is there a speaker? Will you be giving an award? Can you add a touch of humor? Try it. If your local paper or TV station supports local activities, then you'll be *in the running*.

After I make the plans, then what should I do?

Write up the who, what, where, when, and why and send it to the photo editor and the news desk at the newspaper, and the assignment editor at the TV station.

How else can I get camera coverage?

- Call the photo desk of the newspaper and the newsroom of the TV station and ask if you can submit your own film
- Ask for specifications, what they'll accept and won't accept
- Ask about immediate deadlines, and how many days after the event before it's no longer good
- If you don't have photographers or a camera crew, ask if they have any recommendations

How can I extend the life of the camera opportunity?

Take a picture, or a freeze-frame of the TV coverage, and send it out to your current and potential client base. Use it as the artwork on a marketing piece or postcard campaign. Show them someone out there thinks you're special.

91

SEND YOUR NEWSLETTERS
TO THE MEDIA

Networking at its finest

What are the benefits of sending my newsletters to the media?

- You're a lawyer, and in one of your newsletters you wrote an article about prenuptial agreements. Donald and Ivana Trump are all over the news about their divorce, which includes a prenuptial agreement. It's a good bet that your local paper probably won't be able to interview the Trump lawyers, but they can talk to you about it
- You're a breast cancer survivor. For a friend's newsletter you wrote ten tips on how to treat a family member diagnosed with cancer. A famous person makes the news as having been diagnosed with breast cancer. They pull out your article and contact you. If you're not already speaking on the subject, or have written a book, this could be a springboard for you to help others and start a new career
- You own a catering company, and each issue of your newsletter has wonderful recipes for entertaining at home. You send it to your local paper, which doesn't have a resident food editor. After months of receiving and often publishing your recipes, the paper asks you to be its contributing food editor. This leads to a radio show and a TV show. The special sauce you created gets rave reviews from a supermarket owner who wants to bankroll production, and before you know it you're a household name nationwide
- I self-published a book of my motivational sayings that I use in my speeches and in my life. Each issue of my

newsletter contained several as "thoughts for the day." My local paper did an article on me and included the book and the thoughts for the day. A reader called and asked me if I would teach a class on how to write little books of personal sayings. It opened up a whole new market for me. Now I'm on the second edition. I sell these books at my seminars and retreats, and as premiums to businesses and organizations

Will the media throw away my newsletters if they're unsolicited?

Radio and TV news and talk shows, magazines and newspapers keep interesting information on file for future stories, bits of information and filler. Since you don't know or can't guess what is interesting to them, why not send it? You could, like the people I've mentioned, have your version of Andy Warhol's fifteen minutes of fame from including the media on your mailing list.

NOTE: There is an in-depth resource list at the end of the chapter, "Newsletters."

RESOURCES

- Ad-Lib Publications; 51 W. Adams; Fairfield, IA 52556; (800) 669-0773. Ad Lib offers media lists and all kinds of lists
- Bacon's Information, Inc.; 332 South Michigan Ave.; Chicago, IL 60604; (800) 621-0561 or (312) 922-2400
- Burelle's Information Services; 75 East Northfield Rd.; Livingston, NJ 07039; (800) 631-1160
- New Editions International, Inc.; Box 2578; Sedona, AZ 86339; (800) 777-4751. First Edition covers the new age media
- Gebbie Press, *All-In-One* Directory; Box 1000; New Paltz, NY 12561-0017; (914) 255-7560
- Media Distribution Services; 8592 Venice Blvd.; Los Angeles, CA 90034-2549; (800) MDS-3282. MDS will do all the stamping, stuffing, and list maintenance for you. It's a good deal if you want to do a mailing but want to

save your nerves and nails. I use the company all the time
- Publicity Blitz Media Directory-On-Disc; Bradley Communications; Box 1206; Lansdowne, PA 19050-8206 (800) 989-1400
- Oxbridge Communications; 150 Fifth Ave.; New York, NY 10011; (800) 955-0231; *http://www.mediafinders.com*
- Gale Research; 835 Penobscot Bldg.; Detroit, MI 48226; (800) 877-4253; *http://www.Gale.com/Gale.html*

92

HOST YOUR OWN RADIO SHOW

"There's no business like show business"

One network radio you have to be a big shot in the industry or have paid your dues for many years. But there is another way you can have your own show, and it's not pirate radio. Buy your own airtime. There are many stations on AM and FM that sell time to anyone who clears the FCC regulations.

How can I find out about this?
Get a list of your local radio stations from the yellow pages or your local government office. Or go to the library and ask for the *SRDS Radio Directory*.
Call each of the stations and ask if they sell airtime. Be certain they understand that you don't want to buy ad time.

Is it expensive?
Not as expensive as you think. Prices will vary depending on which market and which time slot you want to book.

How can I sustain a full hour or even a half hour of talking?

That's what guests are for.

How do I attract guests?

Promote others while promoting yourself. That's what makes this such a great marketing tool for you. Reach out into your community. Depending on your topic:

- Contact your chamber of commerce for a list of business and service people
- Ask your vendors
- Ask your doctor, dentist, psychologist
- Ask your children's teachers

What if I can't afford the airtime?

If you can't afford the airtime, get sponsors. You might even make some money selling your time.

How can I use the radio show to promote myself further?

- Use the opportunity to promote yourself as an after-dinner or keynote speaker
- Transcribe the entire show or its highlights and send out a newsletter to your data base and your guest's data base
- Use your celebrity status to be a toastmaster at charity events
- Transcribe your show into a newspaper or magazine column

Why is this a good marketing tool?

- It allows you to market yourself as an expert in every nook and cranny of your community
- If the station has good wattage and spills over into surrounding areas, it's an opportunity to spread your services as well
- It gives you an opportunity to introduce you and your services to many more people at one time
- Many stations will allow you to syndicate your show. This allows you to spread your services across the country if you so desire.

NOTE: Many stations have waiting lists. That's how meaningful it is.

RESOURCES

- SRDS; 1700 Higgins Rd., Des Plaines, IL 60018-5605: (800) 851-7737; *http://www.SRDS.com*
- NARTSH (National Association of Radio Talk Show Hosts); 134 Saint Bolph St., Boston, MA 02115; (617) 437-9757
- *Talkers* Magazine; Box 60781; Longmeadow, MA 01116-0781; (413) 567-3189. (*Talkers* is a talk show industry newspaper. It's very helpful for knowing the players and the formats
- Look in your yellow pages for your local stations

93

HOST YOUR OWN TV SHOW

As seen on TV!

Public access television affords you the opportunity to have your own TV show without any prior experience as a host or television production know-how.

How much will it cost to hire a crew and a studio?

That's the beauty of public access television. Because it's government owned and run, it is a service to the community. This means that all the services needed to create a show are *free* to the community. These include:

- The studio
- Cameras
- Camera operators
- Editing facilities
- Editing personnel

The only cost to you is the tape stock the show is taped on. That cost averages $30, but usually you can bring your own tape if you can get it cheaper.

How do I apply to host my own show?

Call the cable company that bills you for cable service. Tell them you're interested in having your own show on public access cable. They'll direct you to the proper phone number.

Although each county may have different rules, the basic requirement is that your topic and format have to meet FCC regulations.

How do I learn what to do?

My studio in Santa Monica, California, had me come for three one-hour classes, in which they showed me how to format and time my half-hour show, gave me makeup and clothing hints, and showed me basic camera posing.

What if I can't sustain a show?

You don't have to. You can have on as many guests as you want for a half hour. You can have them on individually or as a group. Once your script is approved, you're the boss.

How can I attract guests?

It's a great marketing tool. Ask your clients, vendors, associates, or noncompeting professionals to come over for a chat.

How is this a great marketing tool?

- You can promote what you do for half an hour
- You can give out your address and phone number
- You can ask people you've always wanted to meet to be a guest on your show
- You can use the fact that you have a TV show in your promotional materials

- You can spread your name and expertise in new markets with your guests
- You can use the opportunity to do a mailing
- You can transcribe the show for your newsletter
- You can use the audio portion for your newsletter
- You can play the tape in your waiting room or store
- You can use it to advance your career for a guest expert slot on network TV

Will the show air only in my area?
Usually, but what you can do is contact all the cable companies in the United States and submit your tape to their systems. This is called *bicycling your tape*, as if you were riding from place to place delivering a tape to each one.

Where can I get a list of all the cable companies?
Ask your local public access station for the list, or look in *Standard Rate and Data* Directory.

RESOURCES

SRDS; 1700 Higgins Rd.; Des Plaines, IL 60018-5605; (800) 851-7737; *http//www.SRDS.com*

94

BE A GUEST ON TV AND RADIO TALK SHOWS

*Fifteen minutes of fame can be yours,
over and over again*

How can I get on a talk show?

The bottom line is, if what you have to offer the show can satisfy its content needs, then you're in the running to be a guest. These show needs include:

- Filling an audience need
- Solving a problem
- Entertaining the audience
- Telling them something they didn't know
- Appealing to their target audience with appropriate subject matter

Why do these sound familiar?

They're the same needs you find throughout every chapter that has to do with promoting yourself, your product, or your service to any audience.

Is it true that the media have their own agenda and put that before what you want to talk about?

This is what Peter Meyer of The Meyer Group told me about being media friendly:

"The media care more about their own needs than they do about ours. This only means that they are as human as the rest of us. Remembering this, I followed the principles in my book *You Can Hype Anything: Creative Tactics and Advice for Anyone With a Product, Business or Talent to Promote* and con-

340

tacted CNN, focusing on its needs. CNN loved it, and passed me around inside the news groups until I got recommended to Lou Dobbs' team. Last February I had my first of two live spots with him. If I had not followed those principles, I would never have gotten live coverage.''

What are the show's content needs?

For example, Jeremy Cato is the host of a terrific talk radio automotive show. If you wrote a book on gardening, you would be wasting your time and money requesting a guest spot on his show. But a chiropractor could be a guest on an automotive show, offering information on the proper position people should take when changing a tire.

Nelson Davis produces a great TV show called "Making It," dedicated to helping the minority businessperson succeed. You won't find entertainers and fiction writers as guests on his show talking about their books, movies, or recordings, unless they are there to talk about success principles.

It is true that many of the talk shows are general in format and will accept all types of guests with all types of subject matter. But there are just as many that specialize in one topic. It's senseless to waste your time, effort, and money writing to the more than 2,000 shows. To quote an old marketing saying, *find your niche and fill it.*

How do I find out which talk shows take what subjects?
1. Watch or listen to the show. Several if you can. If you're going to an out-of-town show, ask them to send you a copy of a broadcast so you can study the host, the format, and the ambience
2. Buy directories that identify shows or rent lists specific to your needs. The resource lists at the end of this chapter and at the end of the book will give you that information

Is approaching radio talk shows different than TV talk shows?
The basic premise is the same. The major difference is to whom the request is addressed.

- For radio talk shows, whether it's the local or national level, there is usually only one producer or one talent booker who makes the decisions. In many cases the show's host wears all hats

- With national TV talk shows, there are usually several segment producers who concentrate on specific topic areas. As in radio, local TV shows might only have one person in charge of choosing the guests, and once again this might be the host

Is it important to know everyone's name at every show?

You could send your correspondence "Attention: Producer." But that's the same as when you get something marked "Resident." (Attention: Producer is the choice over incorrect names if you're mass mailing and haven't checked the list names for accuracy. Calling and getting the names right is the best way.)

I recommend checking the names, addresses, and show format before you send out the mailing. It helps your image and your cause when you call to follow up. Besides, when you call, it gives you a few moments to engage the person in conversation so you can discuss the best topic fit.

If the list has been cleaned (meaning mailed out and corrected) within the last month, chances are it's an okay list.

Will they call me when they get my letter or news release? Do I have to call them?

They have been known to call if your topic is compelling, weird, or trendy enough. But you should be prepared to call them and follow up at least one week after they've received your pitch letter.

What do I say?

Here's the follow-up pitch I'm currently using for *Babyscapes*, a two-CD package of musical lullabies for prenatal and postnatal mothers by electronic musician Mars Lasar.

"Hello, I'm following up on a release I sent last Monday on the product *Babyscapes* relaxation and stress reduction music for the pregnant and postpregnant mother and baby. I'm calling to see if you would be interested in having the composer come on the show and play the lullabies for your audience. He composed them for his wife and soon-to-be baby. We could also provide you with a behavioral psychologist who could talk about how this soothing music scientifically works.''

What are some do's and don'ts?
- Be prepared with a script
- Be brief
- Don't ramble
- Include in the statement that you are calling to be a guest and exactly what you have to offer the audience
- Be prepared to add an angle (such as bringing along the behavioral psychologist)

Here's the pitch for my client Guardian Angel, a magnetic engine additive.

"Hello, I'm calling to follow up on the Lynn St. James/ Guardian Angel car care product release I sent last Monday. Guardian Angel adds twelve hundred miles to your oil changes, twenty miles to a gallon of gas, lowers toxic emissions, and lets you drive without oil for miles. We're calling it Guardian Angel . . . vitamins for your engine. I'm interested in having Lynn St. James and Don Shriver come on your show to talk about how your audience can save money, prevent engine wear, get longer life from your engine, and increase your safety on the road with the new generation of engine additives like Guardian Angel. By the way, Don Shriver is the man who brought the world Slick 50.''

What if they say they haven't received the release?
Ask for their fax or e-mail number and send it off immediately.

What if they say no?
Ask them if it's the type of client or the topic focus. In either case, try and see if there is a common ground for audience benefit. If not, say thank you and move on.

If I get on the show, how can I get more marketing mileage out of it?
- Transcribe the tape for your newsletter
- Send the tape as a promotional piece to your data base

- Send a flier or broadcast fax to your data base before the show
- Send a notice to your local paper that you're going to be on and ask for a story on what you'll be discussing

NOTE: If you have a product to sell, have an 800 number. If you don't have a product to sell, offer a free report or a list or something, so you can add the listeners to your data base (see the chapters, "800 and 900 Numbers" and "Send Special Reports").

RESOURCES

For publishers of directories of trade and consumer publications see the "Million-Dollar Media Rolodex" in the back of the book.

95

TIPS, TRENDS, AND SURVEYS

The three marketing musketeers

Why are tips, trends, and surveys such great marketing tools?
- They make great subjects for postcard campaigns, door hangers, direct mail pieces
- They're a meaningful way to approach the media for attention on your product or service
- They show you off as an expert in your field
- They turn your hold button into an information center
- They enhance the information in your newsletter or a friend's newsletter

- Put them into a pamphlet and give them out as holiday cards or gifts
- Use the article, the tape of the radio show, or the video of the TV program for direct marketing and advertising opportunities

Can you give me an example of someone who has used these as a promotional tool?

Financial adviser Rick Byron told me, "Honking my own horn didn't get me any media attention. But when I started to give out advice in the form of tips and trends instead of me-directed kudos, the media not only printed what I had to say but they now call me for quotes for all kinds of feature and news stories they're doing around my subject. I take the articles and transcriptions and use them as a marketing tool. As a marketing tool it's increased my seminar attendance three-fold, and my consulting business exponentially."

Why do they make such great mailing pieces?
- They're informative
- They entertain
- They're brief
- They don't manipulate the reader
- They're catchy, light, and noninvasive

Why are the media so hot on tips, trends, and surveys as a way of doing a story?
- Journalists and segment producers don't have time to rummage through pages and pages just to find out what you want to tell them
- The information is presented in a brief, very to-the-point style, allowing for quick and easy absorption and quick decisions
- The information is useful, geared to teach, to help, to impart skills and attitudes rather than provide fluff or hype

What's the key to writing a great tip, trend, or survey?
The intent must be selfless, not selfish:

- Selfish: presenting information to enhance your own stature. Selfish copy evokes the editorial response: "If they want to toot their own horn, tell them to take out an ad!"

- Selfless: presenting information that educates, contributes, or elevates status, attitude, or skill, making it possible for the audience to act instead of react

What guidelines should I follow when compiling my information?

- The information should be interesting, newsworthy, timely, relevant, useful, informative, and educational
- It should catch the eye, the ear, the brain, the funny bone!
- It should make you want to say, "Wow, I didn't know that!"
- It should be information people care about, need to know, want to know, or should know

What are tips in this context?

Tips are practical information presented in as concise a way as possible. They're helpful, informative, and useful, especially if they're short, sweet, and to the point. For example:

- Three Simple Steps to Organizing Your Office
- Ten Ways to Be Romantic
- Five Things You Need to Know When Buying a Pet
- Five Things You Can Do to Avoid Headaches When Fasting
- Six Reasons to Put Soul Back in Your Business
- Four Important Steps Necessary to Raise Self-Esteem in the Workplace

What are some examples for specific businesses?

- If you're an accountant, educate businesses with "How to Save Your Payroll Thousands of Dollars a Year"
- If you're the owner of an executive temp service, show businesses "How to Put Money Back in Their Pocket by Utilizing Consultants Instead of Full-time Employees"
- If you have a swimming school for children, share "Five Ways to Get Children to Be Comfortable in the Water"
- If you're a printer, educate your audience with "What You Know Before Bringing Your Job to the Printer Can Save You Time and Money"
- If you teach people how to become computer literate, give them reasons "Why Having a Blank Mind Will Help You

Learn to Use a Computer Faster and More Efficiently''
- If you own a nursing home, give them "Four Important Questions to Ask When Selecting a Nursing Home as a Prospective Residence for Yourself or a Loved One''

What is a trend in this context?
- Trends are where the future is going to be, where the past has been, and what is happening now in business, economics, politics, education, fashion, architecture, automotive design, retail . . . you name it
- Trends map the attitude that make anything succeed, fail, or just plain be. Trends tell you what's hot and what's not
- Trend watchers report on ideas and actions on the verge, or calculate their impact after trends are gone
- Trendsetters are people who are the buying, thinking movement that the trend watchers watch and report on

How can I cash in on trends?
One of the best ways to get media placements is by spotting an emerging trend or fitting into an existing one. The media love anything that is coming, especially if they can get their hands on it before anyone else does. Since many of you are directly related to the buying public, you have a pulse on the nation's trends. For example, you can report on the trends in:

- Office supplies
- Equipment rentals
- Increases or cutbacks in office visits
- Office attire
- Use of consultants over hiring employees
- Number of dog-grooming appointments
- Switching from desserts to fruit
- Ordering iced tea instead of sodas, et cetera

What is a survey?
Here's my favorite "power of the survey" story. It's about a small, one-unit restaurant in a tiny Long Island, New York, tourist community that made all the way to the *Life Lines* section in *USA Today*. The restaurant surveyed its patrons by putting this question in with their check: "What would you order if it were your last day on earth?" The largest segment

reply was pizza, with hamburgers a close second and tuna melts coming in third.

Do I have to limit my surveys to my business?
Not at all. You can ask your data base anything. Favorite vacation spots, favorite toys, how many ties do you own.

Where's the best place to research surveys?
USA Today, in every section, presents surveys under the heading of *USA Snapshots*. Here are some topic examples:

- A look at statistics that shape the nation:
  An explosive Fourth (who attends, sets off, and watches fireworks)
  Driving to distraction (what drivers do while driving)
- A look at statistics that shape your finances:
  It pays to ask for a raise (percentage of who asked and who got)
  Tied to the job (percentage of who called in while on vacation)
- A look at statistics that shape our lives:
  Underwear creeping up (popular bedtime attire in the last ten years)
  There ought to be a law (percentage bike helmet wearers)
  Eat-out holidays
  Tummy upsetters (stress, spicy food, fatty food, no sleep . . .)

RESOURCES

- Read and study *USA Today* very closely every day for a week. It is filled with tips, trends, and surveys. Then keep reading it often
- Watch "CNN Headline News." Between segments it presents surveys under the heading *Factoids*
- Study article composition in your local newspapers and magazines
- Watch news broadcasts and listen to radio talk shows. Become aware how they use tips, trends, and surveys and how they credit the source

- Read trade journals and newsletters in and out of your field
- Read business magazines. They are big on using this writing style to convey information
- BE CREATIVE!

96

WRITE LETTERS TO THE EDITOR

Speak out and speak your piece

Can I write on any subject I choose?

Nicole Millman-Falk suggests this tip in her *MFC Messenger: Communication and Marketing Tips* newsletter: "Don't write on whatever topic suits your needs. Respond specifically to an article or news story that has appeared recently in the publications."

What are the guidelines for writing a letter to the editor?

Decency and clean language give you a better chance to make it into the preliminary decision round.

What's the marketing benefit of writing a letter to the editor?

People like heroes. People like to associate with heroes. Customers, clients, patients, patrons, vendors all respond in a positive way to others who do good in and for their community. If it's your name on that letter, responding to what you feel or something that is out of line, the people who support your business have one more reason to give you their loyalty.

Having your name seen is another imprint on the road to being a household word.

Does the newspaper or magazine edit the letters?

Some papers and magazines do, others don't. I suggested a client write a letter to the editor. The letter was edited, so I encouraged him to write another letter about the editing. That one didn't get in.

How is it determined which letters get in and which don't?

In all my twenty-plus years in this industry, I have yet to get a straight answer to this question, but I believe the decision is based on the merits of the letter itself, with a little editorial executive decision thrown in.

Is there a particular style I should use?

There is no official form, but I suggest you study the Letters to the Editor section over a period of time to see how those that made it into print are structured.

- Carefully look at how the letters are crafted
- See how the letters are worded
- Count how many words make up an average letter
- Evaluate the subject matter: Is it complimentary or opinionated?

What is the most acceptable structure?

Nicole Millman-Falk, CEO of Millman-Falk Communications, Inc., a public relations and newsletter publishing firm, offers these stellar suggestions on how to construct your letter so it has a better chance to end up in print:

1. In paragraph one: Identify the article you're commenting on
2. In paragraph two: Summarize the article, then explain why you agree or disagree with it. Add quotes, anecdotes, and other supporting information, particularly statistics from your organization
3. In paragraph Three: Succinctly summarize your main point

She also suggests the following:

- Keep your letter short
- Make sure the letter is neat
- Proofread it carefully before sending it out
- Include your full name and address, title, and work and home telephone numbers

How quickly should I send my letter before the subject matter is considered outdated?

- Dailies don't usually print letters more than a week old. Some won't take them over two days old
- Weeklies don't usually print a letter that has to do with a story more than two issues old
- Monthlies usually won't carry it over the first issue. The same with quarterlies

NOTE: Speak your piece. It's good for the mind, good for the soul, and good for business.

RESOURCES

Nicole Millman-Falk; *MFC Messenger: Communication and Marketing Tips* newsletter; Millman-Falk Communications, Inc.; 32 Franklin Pl.; Glen Rock, NJ 07452; (201) 652-1687. This is a PR and newsletter publishing firm specializing in, but not limited to, trade and professional membership associations and other not-for-profit organizations

97

OP-ED PAGES AND COMMENTARIES

Viewpoints make for consumer loyalty

What is an op-ed piece?

Op-ed stands for opposite editorial, and as you possibly can guess, an op-ed piece belongs in the newspaper or magazine, on the page opposite the editorial.

It's the opposing viewpoint or opinion to the editorial.

What is the purpose of an op-ed piece?

These pages offer the average everyday citizen an opportunity to tell the world exactly what they feel about issues that matter or should matter in their lives. As Marilyn Ross states in her *National Directory of Newspaper Op-Ed Pages:*

- They are a spectacular sounding board for legislative issues or to conduct public policy debates
- They are a powerful way to lobby Congress
- For many they represent free advertising
- For others they afford an opportunity to inform, persuade, satirize
- They typically offer a biting, funny, or touching dialogue with nontraditional voices

Why is this a good marketing tool?

- It's not just for nonprofits. It's for entrepreneurs, educators, authors, speakers, corporate communications departments, and anyone who wants to make a difference
- It's my impression that deep down inside everyone is a caretaker of society. They just might not know it until their hot buttons are pushed hard enough. So let's tell everyone about it; you never know who's being hassled

about what and wants to do something nonviolent about it
- This is a place where you can put your money where your mouth is
- As we discussed in "Write Letters to the Editor," your voice in pressing matters makes you a hero, and I don't know anyone who doesn't respect a hero
- Writing an essay for the op-ed page is another way to contribute to your community (see the chapter, "Community Involvement"). Shaping people's opinions is a powerful way to imprint
- Involving yourself in something like this is part of responsible business practices. It's the business of business ethics
- It's a good vehicle to get a book deal, speaking engagement, or job on the newspaper

What if my patrons don't see the paper that day?

One of the great things about being in print or on the air is the longevity of what we say. In the industry we say it has legs or it has shelf life, meaning it will be around for a long time. Take the piece, have it copied, and send it out to your data base.

Would I get paid for writing an op-ed piece?

Some newspapers pay, and others don't. The pay range is from nothing to a thousand dollars. On pricing, Marilyn Ross tells us:

- Hot topics may command more than run-of-the mill stuff
- In one case it depends on where your piece appears on the page
- Several editors reward you more generously after you make your first sale to them

How many words does an op-ed piece require?

For most newspapers, 700 words is the norm. But it can range anywhere from several hundred to several thousand. Call and ask the editor for the specifications.

How soon do I have to submit it?

Much like in the chapter "Write Letters to the Editor," if you're responding to a timely subject, it needs to be timely. You need to ask for your newspaper's guidelines. Call the main number; tell the operator what you want to know.

How can I find out the names of the newspapers who have op-ed pages?

The easiest way is to get the *National Directory of Newspaper Op-Ed Pages*. It's the only book of its kind. It covers:

- Contact information in the United States and Canada
- Pay scale
- Word length
- Copyright information
- Must-live-in area information
- Frequency of publication

The other suggestion is to rent lists from the media directories, and mass-mail your piece blind. Getting the book seems like the better suggestion of the two. I'm sure it's in the library.

What goes into writing this kind of piece?

I interviewed several op-ed editors, and this is the consensus:

- Be assertive
- Be passionate
- Be on target with your subject matter intent
- Give fresh ideas about the subject; don't rehash the news
- Add statistics; they make the cause or viewpoint more real
- Come from the offensive, not the defensive; be provocative
- Most of all, have the piece match the paper's views and informational style

How can I find out the paper's views and informational style?

Study your newspaper for several weeks. If it's a timely piece and you need to jump on it, the paper will sell you back issues. Or, you can trust in the laws of the universe and just go for it!

NOTE: Not all papers have op-ed pages. Most papers have a Commentary page. *USA Today* calls its page *Guest Columns*. Some call it Essays; others call it Voices. But every paper has a page where you can speak out for what you believe. I encourage you to do so. Then put it in your newsletter and a friend's newsletter. Make copies and mail to your data base. Tooting your own horn is not the issue here; the issue is the issue here. Also at issue here is how to make friends and influence people. Go for it. Promote yourself and prosper.

RESOURCES

National Directory of Newspaper Op-Ed Pages by Marilyn Ross; Communication Creativity; Box 909, Buena Vista, CO 81211; (719) 395-8659

Part VIII

TELESHOPPING

98

HOME SHOPPING PROGRAMS

Shop till you drop . . . in your armchair

What are the benefits of marketing this way?
- Instant visibility and name or brand recognition
- Opportunity to showcase your product to millions of viewers at once
- Undivided attention of a targeted buying public
- Immediate sales
- Creates leverage for distribution
- Great product credibility
- The fastest, cheapest way to launch a product
- Saves on the advertising and marketing budget
- Can use the status of "As Seen on QVC!" in promotional materials

What are the disadvantages?
- You have no control over the marketing
- You take a significant inventory risk if the product doesn't sell
- You can't regulate when or how often your product appears
- You can't plan for repetitive showings
- Units are generally placed on a consignment basis
- Unsold units are returned to you
- If your product scores big, you must fulfill the order *immediately*

What are the teleshopping networks looking for? What products attract their attention?
- Mass appeal
- Uniqueness

- Quality
- Exclusivity packaging
- Value pricing
- Items that make for good demonstrations
- Items that make for good conversation and entertainment value
- Items that are trendy, in the news, the latest rage

Can I approach them myself or do I need an agent?

Yes, you can approach them yourself. Each network has a different title for its buying department, so just tell the operator you have a product you want considered. The operator will either give you to the proper person or inform you on the proper submission procedure.

Do the networks take a percentage?

Yes, they do, but it varies from product to product. So you need to ask when you approach them.

Is it better to use a middle person?

- Con: Since the networks accept personal submissions, if you have the product they're looking for and it meets the sales profile, they'll take it. Brokers, reps, and agents take a percentage of the sales. Why give up a percentage if you can do it yourself?
- Pro: On the other hand, people who deal with the buyers on a frequent basis knows what will make it and what won't. They know how to package it and how not to package it. I think they're worth their fee

These experts can play a prominent role by helping you package your product for maximum acceptance. Some brokers will consult even though you are not using them for placement; others will only consult when that is part of the package.

What are my options if my product doesn't get accepted by the big shows?

Many local communities are getting on the bandwagon on your basic cable network with their own "advertorial" shows. There are two types of programming:

1. Those patterned after the Home Shopping Network format with a host and call-in number
2. Those in which you provide your preproduced on-air segment and pay a package fee for multiple airtime exposure

Why would I want to use these avenues instead of just advertising on cable?
Because they appeal to a captive audience that is targeted and preset to buy. Although local shows aren't as big or compelling as the national shows, merchants in the local market can sometimes come out better by being on local shows.

NOTE: "Teleshopping works best as a springboard to other marketing opportunities, rather than as the cornerstone of your marketing efforts," advises successful teleshopping agent Michael Lesser.

RESOURCES

Broker and Expert
- Michael Lesser; TV Direct; Box 4035; Warren, NJ 07059-0035; (908) 563-4451; fax (908) 563-4453
- For other brokers, look in or call *Response TV* and *Electronic Retailing* (see below)

Magazines
- *Response TV:* (800) 346-0085. This magazine covers the teleshopping industry, including how to get your products on the air. The publisher also puts out *Response TV's Industry Directory*
- *Electronic Retailing:* (800) 624-4196. This magazine provides information on teleshopping, direct response TV, and more

Networks
- Home Shopping Network: (813) 572-8585
- QVC: (610) 701-1000

Check with your local cable provider for local teleshopping programming

Industry Event
Home Shopping Buying Symposium, presented by Steve
Dworman's The Infomercial Marketing Report; 1153 Thurston
Circle; Los Angeles, CA 90049; (310) 472-5253

Part IX

IN-STORE PROMOTIONS

99

MAKING BUYING FUN

It's your personal in-store circus, so come one, come all. . . .

What are some ideas for promotions to spice up a very usual day?

- Give out free samples from a bakery; serve tea and coffee
- Create a "first annual" anything
- Create a "one time only"
- Go for a *Guinness Book of World Records* record
- Celebrate your birthday or anniversary
- Think seasonal in season
- Think seasonal out of season
- Celebrate newborn babies, newlyweds, home buyers
- Give a gift with purchase
- Give phone cards
- Have a free trial
- Hold a preview of seasonal or incoming merchandise
- Have an all-you-can-carry day
- Have a food campaign or an old clothing day
- Have a private letter sale
- Have an after-hours sale
- Do a truckload sale
- Develop a product-of-the-month club
- Conduct a raffle
- Utilize point-of-purchase displays

If you have a promotion you would like to share with me, I'll put it in the next book! It can be one you've done, or one you know about; please write: Raleigh Pinskey; 1223 Wilshire Blvd., #502; Santa Monica, CA 90403. Or call (310) 209-0990 or e-mail *Raleighbk@aol.com*; *http//www.cmihub.com/+/Raleigh.html*

Part X

THE INTERNET

100

MARKETING ON THE HIGHWAY
IN THE SKY

The wave of the now

I understand that most Internet marketing today is based on something called the Aladdin's lamp theory of Internet marketing. What is this?

Audri and Jim Lanford of NETrageous, Inc., offered this definition:

"It is when you make three wishes, rub the lamp, and then you expect them to instantly come true. For example, you have probably seen promotions claiming you don't need to know anything about the Internet, anything about computers, or even have a product or service, and yet you can make your fortune on the Internet. Although this sounds good, it just doesn't work!

"In fact, if you take this approach and you don't know what you're doing, marketing on the Internet is one of the fastest ways to lose a ton of money!"

How can I determine if I'll be successful marketing on the Internet, or if my products or services are even right for marketing on the Internet?

The Langfords offer these four simple questions to ask yourself to determine whether it's worth your time and energy to market on the Internet:

1. Do I have a high-quality product or service?
2. Am I open to new things?
3. Am I willing to learn about the Internet's culture and rules?

4. Am I willing to invest the resources to make my Internet plan successful?

If you answered yes to all four questions, marketing on the Internet can help you make a lot of money! (If not, don't waste your money.)

What are the benefits of marketing on the Internet?
From the Lanfords' special report "Benefits of Using the Internet to Promote Your Business":

1. **You'll make a lot of money by selling your products or services on the Internet.** There are two types of products you can effectively sell on the Internet:
   - Horizontal products, like diet products, which appeal to a very large portion of the population
   - Specialized niche products, which appeal to a specific market. Niche products work very well

   Are you concerned that your product is too specialized to be successful on the Internet? Well, you don't need to be concerned. One of our customers owns a ranch in Montana and does cattle breeding. He is planning to sell bull semen on the Internet! Yes, you read that right. And if that's not a very specialized niche market product, I don't know what is! Although agricultural and farming products are probably not the first kinds of products you'd think would work well on the Internet, we believe he'll sell a ton of it.

2. **You'll get leads very inexpensively.** The Internet can be a great source of very low-cost, high-quality leads. Teresita Pena Dabrieo is a successful independent technical consultant who built a multimillion dollar consulting business before she turned thirty. She recently started sharing her secrets with other technology consultants, and is marketing her advice entirely over the Internet.

   Teresita has collected qualified leads with phone numbers and demographic information for just twenty-one cents apiece! And Teresita converts 11% of the leads she gets on the Internet to paying customers! Not bad!

3. **You'll increase your credibility and shorten your sales**

cycle. These are two of the hidden benefits of using the Internet for your marketing. I'll illustrate the power of the Internet to accomplish both of these by using a great example from Beth Ellyn Rosenthal.

Beth Ellyn has a company called Meltdown International, which specializes in helping people lose weight using a process called TMA, or tissue mineral analysis. The headline of Beth Ellyn's Web site is "Learn How to Burn Fat Twenty-Four Hours a Day! Even While You Sleep!"

Beth Ellyn includes a vast amount of fascinating, readable, in-depth, scientific, and nutritional information on her Web site. For example, you can learn about such topics as:

- Is your biochemistry out of whack?
- How can too much calcium make you fat?
- Ways to prevent hair loss: how too much or too little copper can cause hair loss.

It's an impressive Web site. And it's producing results: Beth Ellyn's revenues increased 254% in 1995!

I asked her how she accomplished this growth. Her answer is very interesting. She said:

The only thing I've done differently this year is that I set up my Web site in March [1995]. The main thing my Web site did for me was to give me instant credibility. It gave me the opportunity to show people that I really know what I'm talking about. Until I had the site, people always asked where I got my MD. In fact, I lost up to sixty percent of my prospects because they didn't trust or believe me, even though I have an excellent background in biochemistry and work closely with a doctor. Since I've had the site, not one person has asked me about my credentials. There is so much information at my site, they are assured I know what I'm talking about.

Which she does! Beth Ellyn continued:
The site sells the TMAs for me. Before I put up the site, I spent about twenty-five minutes on average ex-

plaining the program. Now I rarely have to explain any-
thing. People already understand, because they have
visited the site. So now I can sell seventy-eight percent
more people because the site does all the selling for me.

Finally, here's some more interesting news: I'm now
receiving more leads from my marketing on the Internet
than I am through my traditional advertising. This is par-
ticularly remarkable, because my traditional advertising
costs me about three thousand dollars a month, which is
over sixty times what I spend on my Internet marketing
program! However, as good as these results are, this
didn't happen instantaneously—it's taken about ten
months for the awareness to build for this to happen.

Five Star Tip: Teach people something new and interesting at your Web site. This will differentiate you and
your company from your competition. Remember, provide useful information, not hype!

4. **You'll save money using e-mail to communicate with
   your customers, prospects, suppliers, employees, investors, et cetera.** Now, let's consider three important
   ways to save money.

   You can slash your fax charges, FedEx bills, and your
   long distance phone bills by using e-mail instead. For
   example, our company saved more than $5,000 in 1995
   just by using e-mail. And we've been saving a lot more
   in 1996 as more of our business partners, customers, suppliers, et cetera, get e-mail accounts.

   Here's why: Let's say you live in Kansas City and you
   use a local Internet service provider (ISP) to connect to
   the Internet. (An ISP is a company that rents connections
   to the Internet so you can access the Internet.) That
   means all of your phone calls that connect to the Internet
   are local calls (unless you really live in the boonies!).
   When you explore or "surf" the Internet, you'll be visiting Internet sites from around the country and around
   the world. And you'll be sending e-mail to people from
   around the world. However, all of this will be done via
   your local connection to the Internet. That means that
   whether you're visiting a Web site in Cairo, Tokyo, or

San Francisco, or sending e-mail to people in these cities, all you pay are your local phone charges (and the cost of your local Internet account)!

So it's virtually free to communicate with people from all over the world. That's one of the most exciting aspects of the Internet!

Let's take this one step further. Let's say you have 5,000 customers who have e-mail addresses. You can create a list of their e-mail addresses, which is very easy to do. Then, whenever you want to send them a sales letter or newsletter or other important information, you just basically push a button and your message goes to your entire mailing list almost instantaneously—and almost for free! It's about as easy to send your message to all 5,000 of your customers as it would be to send it to one of them.

And you can do it over and over again with just one or two mouse clicks. So, you can save a lot of time—as well as a small fortune in postage and printing costs.

Five Star Tip: Always have back-end products and services to offer your customers, and offer them monthly. With e-mail, you can do this for free!

Now, one very important caveat: Some of you may be thinking that you can send your sales message to prospects as well. And that's true. *But* it is essential that *you only send e-mail to people who want to receive information from you.*

In other words, *don't send "bulk e-mail."* This is called "spamming." It can ruin your Internet reputation *very* fast. It can also create a lot of other huge problems for you. You should avoid sending bulk e-mail like the plague!

We'll spend a few minutes explaining why this is so important. Let's start out by defining "bulk e-mail." Bulk e-mail is promoted as the electronic equivalent of direct mail, where you can send your electronic message to a large number of recipients via e-mail on the Internet.

Proponents of bulk e-mail say there are huge advantages to using it for your marketing. They point out that the costs of bulk e-mail are almost trivial compared to the costs of sending out direct mail. And they say it is much faster than other forms of marketing and advertising: Recipients get your message almost instantly, rather than having to wait days, weeks, or months. Some claim the response rate can be higher than other forms of advertising. They often promise that bulk e-mail "assures a hundred percent readership." And finally, they point out that it is "environmentally friendly," since no paper is used.

And there are many people who will tell you that sending out bulk e-mail is the road to riches. After all, they claim that since the cost of sending out your e-mail is virtually zero, you can reach hundreds of thousands—or millions—of potential prospects for free. And since some of these prospects will be interested in your offer, you can make millions of dollars by sending out this bulk e-mail.

No way!

Let's look at just a few of the reasons why:

- Many people on the Internet hate getting unsolicited e-mail. They feel very strongly about this. They believe unsolicited e-mail violates "Netiquette," the rules for being a good Internet citizen. Enraging and completely turning off a significant proportion of your prospects is not a good marketing strategy!

- Bulk e-mail just plain doesn't work. There are countless examples of companies that have sent out bulk e-mail, and not only did they not get the results they hoped for, they also ruined their Internet reputations for future Internet promotions

- You put your own e-mail account and Web site at risk. Some of these people who become enraged will do more than simply not buy your products. If they are polite, they may just e-mail your Internet service provider (ISP) and ask that your account be closed. One complaint won't cause an ISP to close your account—several hundred probably will. Or they may request that your Web pages be removed from access to the Internet.

If they are not polite, they may "flame" you, which means they send nasty or derisive e-mail. It's like someone stuffing your mailbox with a lot of junk.

Quite obviously, there are much better ways to achieve the results you are seeking.

Now, back to the good news. . . .

5. **You'll save money printing catalogs, manuals, schedules, directories, or other large documents you publish.** Again, let's look at an example. Broderbund, the software company, can create its on-line product catalog for one-fifth of the cost of just designing its print catalog!

And that doesn't include all the money it saves on printing! You can anticipate similar savings. What's more, you won't waste money on obsolete catalogs when prices or products change. No more waste as out-of-date catalogs go into the Dumpster.

Instead, you can just edit changes on-line within minutes. You can make changes any time you want, twenty-four hours a day, and your customers always get the latest information. Don't you wish you could do that with your printed catalogs after they've left the printer?

6. **You'll save money on customer service and improve customer satisfaction.** By having your information available to your customers on your Web site, your information is available twenty-four hours a day, seven days a week. So whenever customers have questions or are having problems, they can go to your Web site for the solution—they don't have to wait until normal business hours.

For example, Synopsis has used the Internet for their own product, called SOLV-IT! According to the company, they were able to have a full-time team of five people in place of twenty-eight engineers, saving the company $875,000 in one quarter, or $3.5 million per year.

And these cost savings were not even their primary goal for their Internet site: Their major reason for doing this is they wanted to increase their level of customer satisfaction by providing almost instantaneous service for many customers!

One more thing: Many businesses are now directing their prospects to their Web sites in their sales literature. For example, you could write: "Do you have more questions that you'd like answered? Check our Web site for frequently asked questions (FAQs). Then, if your questions still aren't answered, please call our offices at (800) 555-5555 or send us an e-mail at *questions@your-company.com*."

7. **You'll become a leader and gain a competitive advantage.** Fortunately, we're still at the very early parts of the Internet explosion. But now is the time for savvy entrepreneurs to start using the Internet. By getting in now, you can reap the profits from this exploding phenomenon and gain a huge competitive advantage. But this opportunity to be a leader and reap these competitive advantages won't last much longer!

In conclusion, marketing on the Internet offers businesses with high-quality products and services tremendous opportunities to save—and make—serious money!

We've provided just a few examples of the kinds of advantages companies are experiencing today by using the Internet. And, as you can see, making money on the Internet is not just something that may happen in the future. It's something that is happening today! And you can gain these seven powerful advantages of using the Internet to "shamelessly" promote your products and services—starting today!

What are the guidelines for marketing on the Internet?

These "Guidelines for Marketing Smart on the Web" are offered by copywriter Carl Galletti:

1. **Register your Web page(s) with the various search engines.** The only way people will find out about your site and visit is if they can find it. The best way to find anything on the World Wide Web is to use the search engines. Visit the site: *http://www.search.com* and you will get access to *all* the search engines on the Net. These search engines are like electronic directories. They make it possible for anyone to enter a few words to locate Web pages that contain relevant information.

2. **Link your Web page(s) to other similar or supportive Web pages.** Find other Web sites that attract the kind of prospects that might be interested in your products or

services. Then offer to "swap links" with them. This means they put a link to your page on their site, and you do the same for them.

When users visit their site, they will also find out about yours and, if interested, come visit. The users most likely to be interested in your products will show up.

Some sites charge for putting a link or links in their pages. You must evaluate the economy of this. If they have a large number of "hits" (i.e., visits by users), you are likely to get a lot of action. But beware; none of these "hits" figures are yet auditable. So the figure you are being handed could be a lot of hot air.

Instead, go by results, especially if you have to pay— and especially if you have to pay a lot. Make the arrangement contingent on results—*your* results. If you are generating sales and the figures make sense, continue the relationship. Otherwise, drop it and try elsewhere.

3. **Use graphics sparingly.** It still takes awhile to load graphics. Some browsers don't display until after everything is done loading. If you have lots of graphics that take a long time to load, you are going to lose your audience. And consequently your sales.

Instead, put the graphics at the *end* of the experience.

For example, if you want to show a picture of the product, let it be a clickable option that the user can click on or ignore. That way, you don't force your audience to wait for the graphics unless they want to and feel a need to see them.

4. **Make your graphics useful and relevant.** Having your prospects wait sixty seconds for the graphics to be downloaded, only to find that it adds nothing to the experience ... well, this will certainly *not* endear them to you or your product.

5. **Good marketing principles still apply.** Just because the Internet is a different medium than print, radio, or TV doesn't mean that workable marketing techniques have been suspended. The same basic principles that work off the Net often work just the same on the Net.

You *may* have to make adjustments in the implementation, but don't abandon the techniques that have been proven to work.

For example, we know from print advertising that reverse copy (white letters on a black background) doesn't work nearly as well as black on white. The words are harder to read, and you lose readers. The same goes for confusing backgrounds. And yet everyone is going wild putting intricate backgrounds on their pages. Sure, users can usually turn off the background, but most won't. And if you let them decide whether your words will be readable or not, you are likely to end up with a lot fewer sales than you would have had otherwise.

I prefer black type on a plain white background. It won't win any awards, but I bet it generates a lot more sales.

What are some other tips on crafting an effective campaign?

These are from business consultants Peter Meyer, who consults on and with management, and Teresita Pena Dabrieo, who consults with consultants. They want you to remember that "effective sales results come from effective tools. Use these well to get a great return on your investment of time and money."

1. **Tailor your USP.** Make sure that your universal selling proposition (USP) is both very short and totally focused on the effect that your client will get from working with you. Resist the temptation to talk about yourself, your company, and your product

2. **Give value away.** Internet prospects are likely to be used to looking at value before image. The best way to create an image of value is to deliver it. Consider providing a free report that shows how to resolve a critical problem. Do not be afraid to give away your secrets

3. **Make sure you have the right systems.** Internet prospects expect much faster turnaround than traditional prospects. Make sure you can respond quickly to volumes, and that you have a system to keep in touch with your customers and near customers

4. **Put effect ahead of technology.** Just because the latest technology is available to you does not mean that it is available to your clients. Keep far enough behind the

technology curve that you are with your customers. Remember that content is more important than being cool
5. **Become real.** People buy from people, especially over the Net. Make a real effort to be seen as a person in addition to a company

What is in store for the future of Internet marketing?

These "Six Crystal Ball Gems for the Future of Internet Marketing" come from a lecture by fran pomerantz, president of the pomerantz group, whose company offers *solutions for new media business:*

1. Although HTML and other tools are enabling the playing field to be equaled so that non-programmers can input on the Web, programmers of the world will be more important in the future as the technology develops further
2. The Internet will be programmable for your specific entertainment, study, and news gathering formats. "Smart Agents" will go out onto the Web and retrieve the information that you want to see and have it ready for you when you tell it to
3. Commerce will be an everyday occurrence on the Internet
4. Virtual worlds will be commonplace. When buying a new house you will "walk through" the house, "see" the schools, and visit the local bookstore and restaurants
5. Travel arrangements will be made by viewing a city and deciding on a hotel by the conditions you enter. Then you will "see" the room assigned to you, conference rooms, and all other amenities necessary for your stay
6. Original entertainment will be viewed on the Internet; however, the size of the screen will resemble your TV. You will be a character following a story, and because of the choices you make the story will unfold differently for you than your neighbor. On-line multiplayer games will unite the world. Teams made up of players around the world will compete with one another. This medium will go a long way to eradicate gender differences and prejudices, and unite, stimulate, and draw us closer together

RESOURCES

Experts

- Audri and Jim Lanford: NETrageous, Inc.; 225 Cross-roads Blvd., #403; Carmel, CA 93923; (408) 624-6700; fax (408)626-6416; *success@netrageous.com*, *http://www.netrageous.com*. The Lanfords also publish a free electronic newsletter, *Internet ScamBusters!* Visit and subscribe at *http://www.scambusters.com*
- Teresita Pena Dabrieo; Success Partnership Network; 1217 Broadway St., Pella, IA 50219; (800) 943-0012; *teresita@dabrieo.com; http://www.dabrieo.com*
- Carl Galletti; One Paddock Dr.; Lawrenceville, NJ 08648; (609) 896-0245; fax (609) 896-2653, *carl@edit.com*. Galletti offers copywriting seminars and courses, and the Internet site Writer's Web
- Peter Meyer; The Meyer Group; 883 Cadillac Dr.; Scotts Valley, CA 95066; (408) 439-9607
- fran pomerantz; the pomerantz group, *solutions for new media business*; 625 Montana Ave., 2nd Fl.; Santa Monica, CA 90403; (310) 319-6100; fax (310) 319-6103; *franp476@aol.com*
- Beth Ellyn Rosenthal; (214) 390-0323; page (214)/795-8117; *bethellyn@intex.net; http://www.intex.net/meltdown/*

Audiocassette

- *Everything You Wanted to Know About the Internet But Were Afraid to Ask!* by Mike Rounds and Connie Yambert; Rounds Miller & Associates; 6318 Ridgepath Ct.; Palos Verdes, CA 90275, (310) 544-9502; fax (310) 544-1822; *Rounds@Zoom.com; Rounds1@aol.com*

Books

- *Fishin' With a Net, How to Do Business on the Internet* by Mike Rounds; Rounds Miller & Associates, 6318 Ridgepath Ct.; Rancho Palos Verdes, CA 90275; (310) 544-9502; fax (310) 544-1822; *Rounds@Zoom.com; Rounds1@aol.com*

- *Guerrilla Marketing, On Line* by Jay Conrad Levinson (Houghton Mifflin)
- Check the computer magazines for the most recent, approved selections
- Ask your local bookstore for the latest best-seller
- Check with computer course teachers at your local adult education facility for the books they use or recommend

Magazines

- *Wired*; 544 Second St., San Francisco, CA 94107; (415) 904-0660; fax (415) 904-0669
- *Home Office Computing*; 555 Broadway; New York, NY 10012; (800) 288-7812. For information or questions: (800) 678-0118

Part XI

KEYS TO SUCCESS

101

A SUCCESS SYSTEM
TO UNLOCK THE DOOR

The keys to the kingdom and beyond

1. Believe in yourself
2. Believe in success
3. Believe that you can and deserve to be successful
4. If you don't believe in yourself, in success, or that you can be successful, invest in yourself and find out why you don't believe
5. Appreciate yourself. If you don't appreciate yourself, you won't fully succeed at making your clients feel appreciated
6. Honor each life experience, both positive and negative, that has brought you to this point in your development. See these as positive stepping-stones that have brought you this far
7. List your strong points. Put them in order of which works best for you
8. List what you have been told are your weak points and see if they are really strong points in disguise
9. Develop a proper appreciation of both your strengths and weaknesses
10. Ask yourself what it is *you* really want from yourself. List your expectations
11. Ask yourself what it is your family wants from you. What are the expectations they are imposing on you
12. Ask yourself which expectations are reality and which are ego driven. Study them well, make peace with both, then choose which work best for you

13. Create two goal sets. A long-range overview goal and immediate, possible, achievable goals
14. Be flexible with your goals. Don't suffer if they are not working for you. Reevaluate your methods, then adjust them to be more reasonable and go from there
15. Don't have others do work without first understanding how it should be done
16. Don't be afraid or ashamed to ask for guidance. Seek out the wisdom and guidance of others who have walked the same road
17. Love and respect everyone you come in contact with, because, like you, they are all children of the universe. But know that you don't have to like everyone just because they are all children of the universe
18. Think carefully as to how you want to be treated, then treat everyone with the same intent
19. Give money-back guarantees because you believe in them, not just because you know it's good business
20. Take time to understand your market. To really understand your market
21. Give back to the community that supports you
22. Take calculated risks
23. Promote yourself, promote your business, promote your values
24. Use the LUCK system ... *Learn* *Under* *Conscious* *Knowledge*

RALEIGH PINSKEY'S MILLION-DOLLAR MEDIA ROLODEX

http://www.promoteyourself.com

American Jewish Press Association: 1828 L Street, NW, Suite 402, Washington, DC 20026; (202) 785-2282; *http://www.ajpa.org*

American Passage Media Services: 215 W. Harrison Street, Seattle, WA 98119; (800) 473-6474; *http://www.americanpassage.com* (college newspapers for advertising)

Bacon's Information Inc.: 332 South Michigan Avenue, Chicago, IL 60604; (312) 922-2400, (800) 621-0561; *http://www.baconsinfo.com* (multidirectory publisher—includes editorial calendar, clipping service, media releases, broadcast fax)

Book Marketing Update: John Kremer, Open Horizons Publishing Co., Box 205, Fairfield, IA 52556-0205; (800) 796-6130; *http://www.bookmarket.com* (newsletter print, radio, and TV interview leads for marketing books to the media)

Bradley Communications: Box 1206, Lansdowne, PA 19050; (800) 989-1400; *http://www.rtir.com* (publishes *Publicity Blitz, Radio-TV Interview Report* and *Book Marketing Update*)

Broadcast Interview Source: 2233 Wisconsin Avenue, NW,

#406, Washington, DC 20007-4104; (202) 333-4904, 1-800-YEARBOOK; *http://www.yearbooknews.com* (experts directory, media lists)

Burrelle's Information Services: 75 East Northfield Road, Livingston, NJ 07039; (800) 631-1160; *http://www.burrelles.com* (multidirectory publisher)

Business Wire: 1990 S. Bundy, Los Angeles, CA 90025; (310) 820-9473; *http://www.businesswire.com* (newswire for media releases and photos)

Catholic Press Association: 3555 Veterans Highway, Unit 0, Ronkonkoma, NY 11779; *http://www.catholicpress.org/ index.html* (*Catholic Press* Directory)

Communication Creativity: Box 909, Buena Vista, CO 81211; (800) 331-8355; *http://www.about-books.com* (*National Directory of Newspaper Op-Ed Pages*)

Contacts: 500 Executive Boulevard, Ossining, NY 10562; (914) 923-9400 (newsletter on what media is looking for what stories, personnel changes)

Direct Mail Association: 1120 Avenue of the Americas, New York, NY 10036; (212) 768-7277; *http://www.the-dma.org*

Foreign Press Center: 898 National Press Building, 529 14th Street, NW, Washington, DC 20045; *http:www.fpcusia.gov*

Gale Research: 835 Penobscot Building, Detroit, MI 48226; (800) 877-4253; *http://www.gale.com* (multidirectory publisher, *Associations* Directory, InfoTrac research database)

Gebbie Press: Box 1000, New Paltz, NY 12561-0017; (914) 255-7560 (*All-In-One* Directory); *http://www.gebbie.com*

Infocom Group: 2115 Fourth Street, Berkeley, CA 94710; (800) 959-1059; *http://www.infocomgroup.com* (*Western Media Contacts, Lifestyles Media Relations Report* includes what media is looking for what stories, personnel changes)

Luce Clipping Service: 420 Lexington Avenue, New York, NY 10017; (800) 628-0376; http://www.lucepress.com (tracks placement of your media releases)

Media Distribution Services: 307 W. 36th Street, New York, NY 10018; (800) MDS-3282; http://www.mdsconnect.com (fulfillment house for media releases, photos and products)

Metro Publicity Service: 33 West 34th Street, New York, NY 10001; (212) 947-5100, (800) 223-1600; http://www. metrocreativegraphs.com (columns, feature packages)

National Council for Research on Women: 11 Hanover Square, 20th Floor, New York, NY 10005, (212) 785-7335; http://www.ncrw.org (directory of women's media and reports on women and girls)

National Forensic Center: 17 Temple Terrace, Lawrenceville, NJ 08648; (800) 526-5177, (609) 883-0550; http:// www.expertindex.com (National Forensic Services Directory for expert witnesses)

NewsEdge: 84 Blanchard Road, Burlington, MA 01803; (800) 414-1000; http://www.newsedge.com (customized filtered business news)

New Editions International, Inc.: Box 2578, Sedona, AZ 86339; (520) 282-9574, (800) 777-4751; http://www. newagemarketing.com (New Age Marketing—lists, resources, media)

News USA Inc.: 8300 Boone Boulevard, Suite 810, Vienna, VA 22182; (800) 355-9500, (703) 827-5800; http:// www.newsusa.com (broadcast fax, web pages, news features)

Newsletter Clearing House: 44 West Market Street, Rhinebeck, NY 12572; (800) 572-3451, (914) 876-2081; http:// www.newsletter-clearinghse.com

Newsletter Publishers Association: 1401 Wilson Boulevard, Suite 207, Arlington, VA 22209; (800) 356-9302, (703) 527-2333; http:www.newsletters.org

North American Precis Syndicate Inc: Chrysler Building, 59th Floor, 405 Lexington Avenue, New York, NY 10174; (800) 222-5551, (212) 867-9000; *http://www.napsnet.com*

Oxbridge Communications: 150 Fifth Avenue New York, NY 10011; (800) 955-0231; *http://www.mediafinders.com* (multidirectory publisher)

Para Publishing: Box 8206, Santa Barbara, CA 93118-8206; (805) 968-7277; *http://www.parapublishing.com* (all you want/need to known on self publishing)

Partyline: 35 Sutton Place, New York, NY 10022; (212) 755-3487; *http://www.partylinepublishing.com* (newsletter on what media is looking for what stories, and personnel changes)

PR Newswire: 1515 Broadway, New York, NY 10036; (212) 596-1540, (800) 832-5522; *http://www.prnewwire.com* (newswire for media releases and photos)

Public Relations Society of America (PRSA), 33 Irving Place, New York, NY 10003; (212) 995-2230; *http://www.prsa.com*

Radio-TV Interview Report, Bradley Communications: Box 1206, Lansdowne, PA 19050; (800) 989-1400; *http://www.rtir.com* (newsletter that your picture and media release in front of radio and TV hosts, also has media lists on disc)

Reed Elsevir New Providence: 121 Chanlon Road. New Providence, NJ 07974; (800) 521-8110; *http://www.reedref.com* (multidirectory publisher)

Special Libraries Association: 1700 18th Street, NW, Washington, DC 20009; (202) 234-4700; *http://www.sla.org*; fax-on-demand (888) 411-2856 (directory of special libraries)

SRDS: 1700 Higgins Road, Des Plaines, IL 60018; (800) 851-7737; *http://www.srds.com* (multidirectory publisher)

Only Television and Radio Resources
Guest Finders: LORMAX Communications, Box 40304, Raleigh, NC 27629-0304; (919) 878-9108; *http://www. guestfinders.com* (online service for listing guests)

Talkers Magazine: Talkers Inc., Box 60781, Longmeadow, MA 01116-0781; (413) 567-3189; *http://www.talkers.com/* (inside information about talk shows and their hosts, has tour availability listings)

Talk Show Hosts: 566 Commonwealth Avenue, Suite 601, Boston, MA 02215; (617) 437-9757; *http://www. talkshowhosts.com*

Television News and Talk Show Video Tracking Services
Video Monitoring Service: 330 W. 42nd Street, New York, NY 10036; (212) 736-2010, (800) 867-2002; *http:// www.vidmon.com*

Internet Media Release and Broadcast Fax Distribution centers
- *http://www.baconsinfo.com*
- *http://www.bourque.org*
- *http://www.burrelles.com*
- *http://www.businesswire.com*
- *http://www.imediafax.com*
- *http://www.internetwire.com*
- *http://www.newsbureau.com*
- *http://www.prnewwire.com*
- *http://www.xpresspress.com*

PERMISSIONS

The Chamber of Commerce—An Organization Worth Joining, reprinted by permission of Brian Dyches, president, Retail Resource Group.

Focusing on Referrals, reprinted by permission of Sally Wright, CEO, MarkeTeam.

10 Steps to Gaining a Better Understanding for Marketing in a Diverse Market, reprinted by permission of Lynne Choy Uyeda, president, Lynne Choy Uyeda & Associates Advertising/Public Relations.

27 Powerful Points to Keep in Mind When Writing Copy for Your Ads, Sales and Direct Response Letters, and "Guidelines for Marketing Smart on the Web," © 1996, reprinted by permission of Carl Galletti.

Copyrighting That'll Help Your Promotions Deliver © 1996, reprinted by permission of Erin Thomas Palmeter, The Palmeter Group.

"How Do I Get My Products Considered by Mail Order Catalogues?" from *Mechanics of Mail Order* © 1992 and 6 Tips to Be Aware of in Direct Mail © 1992, reprinted by permission of Mike Rounds and Nancy Miller, Rounds-Miller Associates.

"What You Need to Know to Make a Bumper Sticker ©," "What Makes a Good Bumper Sticker©," and the list of custom bumper stickers are reprinted by permission of Erin Rado, The Goddess Shoppe.

"What You Really Need to Look for in a Production Company and Production Tips and Product Enhancements," reprinted by permission of Janita Cooper, Master Duplicating Corporation.

Ten Reasons Why Your Company Needs Promotional Products! reprinted by permission of Jay Kristal, president, Crystal Kreations.

"Tips on Crafting an Effective Internet Marketing Campaign" from *Effective Sales Results Come from Effective Tools*, reprinted by permission of Peter Meyer, The Meyer Group and Teresita Pena Dabrio of Success Partnership Network.

"6 Crystal Ball Gems for the Future of Internet Marketing," reprinted by permission of fran pomerantz, the pomerantz group.

10 Tips to Becoming a Good Speaker, reprinted by permission of Marjorie Brody, president, Brody Communications, LTD, and author of *Power Presentations* (John Wiley).

RALEIGH PINSKEY is CEO of the Raleigh Group, a Los Angeles-based international, multi-faceted visibility marketing and public relations company founded in 1979, that specializes in making entrepreneurs, small businesses, and entertainers visible and prosperous.

Visibility consulting clients include men's and women's apparel and accessory stores, shoe stores, pet stores, doctors, lawyers, travel bureaus, restaurants, grocery stores, non-profit organizations, generator manufacturers, engine additive developers, fancy fortune cookie bakers, architects, and the original singing telegram company. She's also worked with musicians such as Sting, Paul McCartney and Wings, David Bowie, Blondie, KISS and Herbie Mann, as well as fitness guru Callen Pinkney's Callenetics, *Chicken Soup for the Soul* authors Jack Canfield and Mark Victor Hansen, and The Bronx Zoo's A Great Snake Named Jake.

She is the author of the internationally successful *You Can Hype Anything: Creative Tactics and Advice for Anyone With a Product, Business, or Talent to Promote* (Citadel Press); *Talk Your Way Onto Talk Shows*; *The Zen of Hype: An Insider's Guide to the Publicity Game*, an eight-cassette public relations home study course; *The Musician's Guide to the Zen of Hype*, four cassettes and a twenty-one-page booklet with media releases; and *Soul Candy: Sayings that Nourish the Body, Mind and Spirit* (all available from RRP Publishing).

An internationally known professional lecturer, Raleigh speaks on the topic "Promote & Prosper: Visibility Marketing Secrets That Grow Your Business." She's taught at UCLA's Extension School of Journalism and Public Relations and is a member of the National Speakers Association.

Raleigh walks her talk. She's a frequent guest on radio and TV and contributes to consumer magazines and business journals. She's the visibility marketing columnist for *International Business Woman* magazine, host of a weekly radio show, a guest expert for *Entrepreneur* Magazine's World Wide Web Online marketing programming, and a guest host for the America OnLine Lunch programming.

You can contact Raleigh at *http://www.promoteyourself.com* or (310) 209-0990; fax (310) 209-0890.